THE COLOUR OF ENGLISH JUSTICE

Dedicated to my parents

The Colour of English Justice

A Multivariate Analysis

BONNY MHLANGA
Centre for Criminology and Criminal Justice
Department of Social Policy, Hull University

Avebury

Aldershot • Brookfield USA • Hong Kong • Singapore • Sydney

Published by
Avebury
Ashgate Publishing Limited
Gower House
Croft Road
Aldershot
Hants GU11 3HR
England

Ashgate Publishing Company
Old Post Road
Brookfield
Vermont 05036
USA

British Library Cataloguing in Publication Data
Mhlanga, Bonny
The colour of English justice : a multivariate analysis. -
(Avebury series in philosophy)
1.Sentences (Criminal procedure) - England - London - Brent
2.Discrimination in criminal justice administration -
England - London - Brent
I.Title
364.6'0942185

Library of Congress Catalog Card Number: 96-79369

ISBN 1 85972 495 7

Printed and bound by Athenaeum Press, Ltd.,
Gateshead, Tyne & Wear.

Contents

Figures and tables

Statutes

The Acts listed below are the principal statutes in the network of offending and its processing (for young offenders), together with those which introduced changes in the network during the period of this research.

Child Care Act 1980
Children and Young Persons Act 1933
Children and Young Persons Act 1969
Criminal Attempts Act 1981
Criminal Damage Act 1971
Criminal Justice Act 1982
Criminal Justice Act 1991
Criminal Law Act 1967
Misuse of Drugs Act 1971
Offences Against the Person Act 1861
Police Act 1964
Police and Criminal Evidence Act 1984
Powers of Criminal Courts Act 1973
Prevention of Crime Act 1953
Prison Act 1952
Public Order Act 1986
Road Traffic Act 1972
Theft Act 1968
Theft Act 1978

Abbreviations

ABITS	Area-based intermediate treatment social workers
Absdis	Absolute discharge
ACO	Attendance centre order
BOTKP	Bound over to keep the peace
CASDIS	Cases dismissed
CHE	Community home with education on the premises
CJA '82	Criminal Justice Act 1982
CO	Care order
Comp	Compensation
Condis	Conditional discharge
CRC	Community Relations Council
CRE	Council for Racial Equality
CSO	Community service order
Ct App	Court appearance
Ctn	Caution
CYPA '69	Children and Young Persons Act 1969
DC	Detention centre
Defd	Defined
DVars	Dependent variables
GLC	Greater London Council
GLIM	Generalised Linear Interactive Modelling
HSG	Handling stolen goods
Indict	Indictable
IT	Intermediate treatment
IVars	Independent variables
MAP	Multi-Agency Panel
Mult	Multiple

NACRO	National Association for the Care and Resettlement of Offenders
NCW & P	New Commonwealth and Pakistan
NDHS	National Dwelling and Household Survey
NFA	No further action
Non-cust	Non-custodial (sentences)
NOSIR	No Social Inquiry Report
Nospec	No specific (recommendation)
OPCS	Office of Population and Census Surveys
Pdec	Police decisions
Poss	Possession
Prob	Probation
PROP	Preservation of Rights of Prisoners
Remcar	Remand in care of Local Authority
Remcus	Remand in custody
Resco	Residential care order
Resida	Residential area
SAR	Supervised activities requirement
SEG	Socio-economic group
SES	Socio-economic status
SIR	Social inquiry report
SIRAG	Social Inquiry Report agency
SIRR	Social Inquiry Report recommendation
SO	Supervision order
SOIT	Supervision order with intermediate treatment
SPSS-X	Statistical Package for Social Sciences - version X
Sum	Summary (offences)
S/W	Social work
TIC	(Offence) taken into consideration at the same hearing
UC/EC	Underclass/Earning class
UK	United Kingdom
USA	United States of America
YC	Youth custody
YTS	Youth Training Schemes

Preface

The continuing gap between the percentages of black and white people entering the criminal justice system (particularly prisons), observed both in North America and in England and Wales, raises an old, but still very important question of whether the over-representation is the result of proportionately more black than white people committing offences or offences of a particular kind, or whether it is the result of racial bias in the administration of criminal justice. The data provided in this book shows that there were racial differences in the treatment of young offenders at each stage of the criminal justice process. However, that differential treament could not be explained by significant racial differences in involvement in criminality.

The study involved a multivariate analysis of all male referrals and their outcomes during a five year period from the inception of the Criminal Justice Act 1982, in the London Borough of Brent, which comprises the largest numbers of ethnic minorities in the United Kingdom. The study found that it was not possible to attribute outcomes in the local youth justice system on the basis of significantly more young people from one of the three racial groups of defendants being associated, for example, with committing certain types of offences when compared to the other two groups. In other words, there was no significant interaction found between race and each of the control variables of interest, such as the type of primary offence, the type of offence taken into consideration at the same hearing as the primary offences, the total number of offences dealt with at the same hearing and the number of arrests or court appearances in any model predicting court outcomes.

However, evidence is provided which suggests that black young persons were significantly more likely than white young persons to have been acquitted in the courts because of insufficient evidence from the police rather than to have received police diversionary measures, notwithstanding the influence of the control variables of interest considered in combination with each other. A similar result was found in respect of custodial sentences, where black young persons were again significantly more likely to have received custodial sentences compared to their white counterparts, the latter proving significantly more likely to have had no further action taken against them by the police or to have been cautioned. There were differences between the probabilities of acquittals and of custodial sentences between black and Asian young persons in favour of black young persons, but these were not significant. Likewise, the difference in the probabilities between Asian and white young persons in the custodial sentences analysis was not significant, although it was in favour of Asian young persons.

Given the concern shared by administrators of the criminal justice system and organisations campaigning on criminal justice and race issues, in connection with the treatment of ethnic minorities in the criminal justice system in recent years, it is hoped that the research reported in this book has a contribution to make to our understanding of ethnicity and offending and of the influence of race in the administration of criminal justice.

As usual with research projects of this kind, I owe a great debt of thanks to Geoff Elford, my manager in the London Borough of Brent, for his support and influence which made it possible for me to obtain permission to undertake the study and for access to official data to be granted . Since this book stems from my PhD thesis, I am especially grateful to many of the staff in the Department of Sociology at the University of Surrey for their valuable assistance, advice and support. My many thanks go in particular to Dr Jane Fielding for her expert assistance with computing problems, to Dr Robert Crouchley for his help with GLIM and to Agnes McGill for answering my numerous enquiries with good humour. Most of all, I am indebted to my supervisor, Professor Nigel Fielding, for his encouragement through the years it took me to complete this analytical journey, and for passing on to me his own enthusiasm for social and criminological research. Finally, this book is dedicated to my parents who helped me to persevere in the challenges of scholarly research.

1 Introduction

The research problem and aims of the study

The general research problem examined in this study constituted testing a differential outcome hypothesis on the basis of race, in the treatment of young offenders by a local youth criminal justice system of the London Borough of Brent, following the inception of the Criminal Justice Act 1982: that differences in sentencing outcomes are associated with the racial background of the defendant, notwithstanding local policies designed to:

> develop sensitive...programmes, to address imbalances in sentencing policy [between 'welfare' and 'legalistic' measures]...in relation to black youth and the court system.   (Committee Report 40/82).

Since the purported difference in the sentencing of white and non-white offenders may be due to various 'legitimate' explanations, such as one group committing more serious offences, this study set out to analyse data on age, socio-economic status, area of domicile, type of offence(s) allegedly committed, recidivism, sentencing practices of particular courts, Social Inquiry Report (SIR) recommendations (including type, whether they were specific or not and absence of SIRs), appeals against original sentences and local and judicial policies, in order to determine the extent to which the difference is explicable in terms of these other variables. The independent and dependent variables analysed are shown in the hypothesis model in Figure A1.3 in Appendix 1 (p. 152). A glossary of the abbreviated variable names is also shown on pages xiv and xv.

Accordingly, the aim of the study was specifically to examine the probability for defendants of being prosecuted by the police and of receiving a particular disposal in court as against the probability of being diverted from court through a no further

1

action (NFA) or a caution from the police, either independently or through a local multi-agency panel (MAP) and race controlling for the influence of the other independent factors considered in combination with each other. It should be born in mind that cautioning young offenders as a method of diverting them from a court appearance began to gain some momentum from the mid-1960's culminating in the publication of Home Office White Papers (1965, 1968 and 1980), a consultative document on cautioning (1984) and Circular (14/1985). For instance, the consultative document states that:

> it is recognised both in theory and in practice that delay in the entry of a young person into the formal criminal justice system as represented by the institution of criminal proceedings may help to prevent his[her] entry into that system altogether. The Secretary of State commends the policy adopted by Chief Officers that the prosecution of juveniles is not a step to be taken without the fullest consideration of whether the public interest may be better served by a disposal which falls short of prosecution. (Home Office 1984).

Earlier, a White Paper *Young Offenders* (Home Office et al. 1980) had suggested that:

> All the available evidence [and later, Farrington and Bennett 1981; NACRO 1988] suggests that juvenile offenders who can be diverted from the criminal justice system at an early stage in their offending are less likely to reoffend than those who became involved in judicial proceedings. (para. 38).

As diversion from court appearances was an explicit local youth justice policy, in many ways this study is an evaluation of whether or not black young people living in the Metropolitan Police District of Brent, received equal treatment with respect to that policy when compared to their white and Asian counterparts; and given the background that cautioning practices had been shown to vary between police forces in England and Wales (Rutter and Giller 1983; Mellish 1984; Moxon et al. 1985). Moreover, Parker, Casburn and Turnbull (1981), Barrow, Derbyshire and Jordan (1983) and Tipler (1986) concluded in their respect studies that cautioning was underused and according to Tipler:

> There is some evidence that while cautioning overall is being underused, this underuse is more pronounced against black and ethnic minority young people. (p. 5).

One reason for the anomaly in the use of cautions between black and white defendants suggested by Tipler, may be the criteria that the police use for cautioning that might be 'inadvertently' be working to the disadvantage of black and other ethnic minority young offenders. Mellish (1984) suggests that:

2

The one common policy which all forces operate is that three criteria have to be satisfied before a caution can be issued: a) the evidence is sufficient to support a prosecution in normal circumstances b) the juvenile admits the offence c) the parent or guardian agrees to a caution being administered.

(MPD, A7 Branch Document, Community Relations Branch).

It could be that, as a higher proportion of black defendants than white tend to plead 'Not Guilty' (prefering to be prosecuted and tried, in the hope of being acquitted) they do get prosecuted, but in turn, they do receive a higher rate of acquittals than whites in the courts (Vennard 1982; Walker 1988). This study also attempted to test this hypothesis.

Overview

Since the early 1980s, there has been growing interest in the position of ethnic minority groups in relation to the criminal justice system in Britain, as it has often been alleged over a considerable number of years, in America and Britain, that ethnic minorities do not receive equivalent treatment to their white counterparts in criminal justice. Moreover, in recent years much attention has been focussed on the role of the police as 'gatekeepers' to the criminal justice system and the interface between them and black youth. Although causal connections between black people and their unequal treatment are difficult to make, there is considerable documented evidence (for example, Smith and Gray 1983; Reiner 1985; Norris 1987; Graef 1989; Cashmore et al. 1990) claiming the existence of hostile, stereotypical and prejudiced attitudes towards black persons on the part of the street level police officers, which may have some effect on the numbers of blacks appearing in official crime statistics.

However, NACRO (1988) suggests that evidence of racial bias in court dispositions from research studies is contradictory. For instance, McConville and Baldwin's (1982) study into 'The influence of race on sentencing in England', Crow and Cove's (1984) study which attempted to assess the relationship between ethnic group and court disposals in nine courts (four were youth courts) in London and the Midlands, Moxon's (1988) study into *Sentencing Practice in the Crown Courts* and Brown and Hullin's (1992) 'A study of sentencing in the Leeds magistrates' courts: the treatment of ethnic minority and white offenders', are examples of some research studies conducted in the United Kingdom, which found no evidence of direct racial bias in sentencing. Although these studies came to the same conclusion, they have some limitations and are open to criticism as pointed out by Mair (1986). Mair argued that McConville and Baldwin only looked at sentencing in the Crown Court, and so did Moxon, thereby ignoring the Magistrates' Courts where the vast majority of sentencing decisions are made. For example, 2 million sentences were passed in magistrates' courts in 1983, as opposed to only 83,000 in

3

the Crown Courts (H.M.S.O. 1986: 3).

The drawbacks on the research reported by Crow and Cove include their sample which was very small. Out of a total of 668 cases collected, 536 were white. Likewise, Moxon's sample size consisted of 88% whites and only 8% blacks and 5% Asians. Brown and Hullin's sample was 91% white, while blacks and Asians accounted for only 6% and 3% respectively. Brown and Hullin, in fact, provide their data with a caveat that the methodology used in their study 'was not a perfect one', as their information was supplied by the court clerks who were generally busy to provide fuller data.

Contrary to the findings of the above studies, there has also been some research in the United Kingdom which found links between ethnic minorities and unequal treatment at the hands of the criminal justice system, such as the works of Stevens and Willis (1979), Fludger (1981), Landau (1981), Kelly (1982), Landau and Nathan (1983), Home Office (1983a, 1986, 1989, 1991 and 1992), Pitts (1984), Tipler (1986), Genders and Player (1989), Hudson (1989), Voakes and Fowler (1989), Walker (1986, 1987a and b, 1988, 1989 and et al. 1989), Skogan (1990), Broad (1991), NACRO (1991), Hood (1992), Maden et al. (1992) and Norris et al. (1992).

Of the previous Home Office research, the Stephens and Willis (1979) study on race, crime and arrests was significant in showing that black people were more likely to be arrested than would be expected on the basis of their numbers in the population; and that the incidence of crime in an area is not related to the proportion of people belonging to non-white ethnic groups. This was backed by a further Home Office Statistical Bulletin report (the 1983a 'Crime statistics for the metropolitan police district analysed by ethnic group'), as well as Skogan's (1990) *The Police and Public in England and Wales*, both of which showed that those arrested and convicted in London included a disproportionately large number of black persons, particularly for offences of robbery. Likewise, Norris et al. (1992) in a recent study into the influence of race on being stopped by the police in London and Surrey, concluded that:

> Our data confirm that blacks (and especially young blacks) are more likely to be stopped by the police than whites, although they are, on average, stopped for the same types of offences. It would appear that blacks are liable to more speculative grounds for being stopped than whites. (p. 207).

Landau (1981) and with Nathan (1983) also came to the same conclusion in his study of young offenders and the police in London and argued that some selection takes place in the way black young offenders are dealt with. Similarly, Walker et al (1989) found that blacks were over-represented in arrest rates in Leeds.

The other Home Office evidence relates to the disproportionate numbers of black people in prisons. Thus, with regard to custodial sentences, Fludger (1981), Kelly (1982), PROP (1983), Pitts (1984), Home Office (1986, 1989, 1991, 1992, 1994

4

and 1995), Walker (1986, 1988 and 1989), Voakes and Fowler (1989), Broad (1991), Brown and Hullin (1992), Hood (1992) and Maden et al. (1992) found that black young and adult offenders were over-represented amongst the custodial population. PROP (1983) had earlier revealed figures which indicated that black people constituted 17% of the overall prison population and that on young offenders wings, this percentage rose to 35%, even though ethnic minorities make up only about 5% of the UK population (1981 and 1991 Census data). Since youth custody came into being as a result of the Criminal Justice Act 1982 replacing Borstal training, another study of establishments in London and the South East by Guest (1984) found the same process at work and suggested that:

> the most striking feature to arise from this research is the disproportionately large population of black Afro-Caribbean youths in the youth custody system.
> (pp. 160-1).

In another study conducted in the London Borough of Hackney, Tipler (1986) also found race-specific dispositional differences in that local youth criminal justice system, albeit his results did not reach statistical significance.

An interesting aspect of criminal justice and ethnic minorities in Britain is the overwhelming discrepancy both in numbers and sentencing outcomes between the Asians and the African-Caribbeans. Stevens and Willis (1979), Berry (1984) and Martin (1985) found in their respective surveys that Asians were consistently under represented in arrests and on Probation Service caseloads (e.g. 2%, compared with their percentage in the population in Croydon of 7.3%), whereas African-Caribbean people were over-represented (18% of Probation caseloads compared with only 4.7% of their population in Croydon). In the Nottinghamshire study by Berry (1984), Asians represented only 1.9% of the 1,217 cases coming before the court during the monitoring period. The prevalent notion about the Asian community in Britain is that Asians are generally law-abiding people (Batta et al. 1975) and that their crime rates are substantially lower than white rates, except for a slight excess of assaults in all age groups over 15 (Stevens and Willis 1979). Likewise, Asian sample sizes in some recent studies by Voakes and Fowler (1989), Hood (1992), Moxon (1988), Tipler (1986), Crow and Cove (1984), this study, Brown and Hullin (1992), Walker et al. (1989) and Walker (1989) were 11%, 8%, 5%, 4%, 4%, 4%, 3%, 3% and 2% respectively. However, Mair (1986) in a pilot study of 'Ethnic minorities, probation and the magistrates' courts', and Rutter and Giller (1983) in their extensive review of the literature on *Juvenile Delinquency, Trends and Perspectives*, suggest that next to nothing is known in criminological research as to why crime rates should be lower in Asian youths and higher in black youths. This suggests that empirical research is needed to address this.

Until recently, little research had been carried out on criminal justice and black people in the United Kingdom and according to Crow (1987) their situation reflects not only the way that black people are dealt with by different criminal justice

5

agencies, but also their position in society at large. Crow's point is also reinforced by Reiner (1985) and Solomos (1988). Reiner concludes:

> the disproportionate black arrest rate is the product of black deprivation, police stereotyping and the process by which each of these factors amplifies each other. (Reiner 1985: 132).

Looking at the picture in the London Borough of Brent, which has a combined Asian and African-Caribbean youth population of, approximately 46% of the total Asian, black and white youth population (1981 Census data), it seems that attention should be paid to the patterns, rates and the institutional processing of delinquency in ethnic minority groups. This is so, as Rutter and Giller argue:

> if only because such groups constitute a substantial proportion of the child and adolescent population in many of the urban centres in UK and USA..., an understanding of the characteristics, origins and treatment modalities of delinquency in any of its constituent parts, seems essential in order to determine any differences from those of the population as a whole, if effective services are to be developed for the total population.
> (Rutter and Giller 1983: 148).

Hence, in a multi-racial society, there is a need not only to guarantee fairness and equality of justice, but also to demonstrate convincingly to all sections of the community that that is done (Faulkner 1988).

This study was therefore interested in the problem of the relationship between race and differential outcomes in the youth criminal justice system in Brent (specifically the bivariate probability of court sentences as against police diversionary measures), and to control for the impact of the other independent variables mentioned on page one. As the majority of previous studies have provided us with findings based on bivariate analyses of their data, a multivariate approach to analysing data as employed by this study was important in that it was useful in isolating the race effect on outcomes, either of itself or interactively. Moreover, data analysed in this way (that is, in relation to age, social class and the various legal and non-legal variables thought of in sociological and criminological research as likely contributors to criminality) means that valid conclusions about black people's different offender rates and over-representation in the criminal justice system could be drawn (also see Walker 1987a). However, it is also acknowledged in criminological research that even if all possible factors were incorporated, the statistical evidence alone cannot prove or disprove the existence of discrimination or fairness (e.g., Walker 1987a; Hudson 1989; FitzGerald 1991), unless supported by data of a qualitative nature. In this regard, the researcher was a participant observer of the local criminal justice system, as a youth justice practitioner. This was very helpful not only in terms of obtaining access to official data, but also in gaining

6

insights into the problem under investigation 'in its natural social setting', so as to understand the quantitative data. In this regard, it is hoped that the findings from this study will contribute to the debate on race and the criminal justice system, as well as towards the making of policy and practice recommendations both locally and elsewhere.

The following chapters in this book fall naturally into the different themes stemming from the research material:

First, in chapter two, there is an outline of the major analytic themes and theoretical issues in criminal justice with specific reference to the 'welfare' and 'justice' approaches to youth justice policy, as well as a discussion of theories relating to the class/crime and the race/crime inter-relationship. The chapter helps us to understand the perspectives adopted by the various criminal justice agencies in their administration of criminal justice vis-a-vis crime causation, punishment and/or treatment of young offenders, in particular.

Chapter three provides a description of the political-economy and demographic profile of the London borough of Brent, in which the research was undertaken. The location was significant in that the borough comprises the largest proportion of ethnic minorities in the United Kingdom (1981 and 1991 Census data), thus greatly increasing the ethnic minority sample size as opposed to previous studies. The borough also exhibits the many 'disadvantage' indices known in some sociological and criminological research literature to affect offending behaviour. That relationship is tested in this study with respect to police and court decision making. The policies operated by the local criminal justice agancies are also discussed in chapter three and provide the framework within which justice was being administered to young people in Brent.

The research methods and measures used in the study are discussed in chapter four. Apart from detailing the measures of the independent and dependent variables, the chapter defends the adoption of a multivariate approach to the study of race and criminal justice using GLIM statistical software. This enabled four paired dependent variables (police decisions versus each of the four categories of court decisions) to be created. By using this method, it was possible to assess the probability of being prosecuted and of being sentenced in the courts as against the probability of being diverted from a court appearance altogether, in line with local policy.

Chapters five through eight are the results chapters of the bivariate probability of acquittals, court non-custodial sentences, social work and probation sentences and custodial sentences as against police diversionary measures and the influencing factors.

The conclusion in chapter nine pulls together the different findings and refutes the 'differential involvement' in criminality hypothesis for explaining the differences found by race in relation to outcomes in the criminal justice system.

2 Conceptual framework and theoretical issues in youth criminal justice: A review

Introduction

A youth criminal justice system can be influenced by either 'welfare' or 'legalistic/justice' considerations, when processing defendants (see Bean 1976). One of the most unsatisfactory features of youth justice as pointed out by Freeman (1983) is that in reality there is very little 'justice'. He suggests that neither pre trial procedures nor court processes themselves observe the sort of elementary natural justice requirements that are taken for granted in a court dealing with adult offenders. The problem is partly the product of a confusion of purposes between social welfare objectives or assessments of needs and social control or justice objectives. As ideal types, these orientations call for different patterns of response and different organisational structures, as discussed below. There is, however, a wealth of evidence which suggests that these standpoints are riddled with inconsistencies, as what is in the best interests of the child may conflict with what is in the best interests of the community (Morris and Giller 1978). For example, since institutional processing of young offenders is the raison d'etre of three major actors, namely, the police ('gatekeepers' to the system), the courts (the sentencers) and social workers and probation officers (information providers in mitigation), the problem of inconsistency and disparity in the system becomes magnified when expectations, with respect to effective responses to youth crime and justice, are in direct conflict (see Morris et al 1980, Geach and Szwed 1983, Morris and Giller 1983). Moreover, Hoghughi (1983) points out that social workers' and probation officers' acts of 'omission and commission' in dealing with young offenders:

> are as much aspects of injustice as are the vagaries of the court.
>
> (Hoghughi 1983: 288).

The welfare response

A welfare orientation to the processing of young offenders is inspired, inter alia, by *strain* (Merton 1938, 1957; Cohen 1956; Cloward and Ohlin 1960; Johnson 1979), *subculture* (Mays 1957, 1972; Akers 1964, 1973; Downes 1966, 1978; Willmott 1966; Sutherland and Cressy 1974) and *labelling* (Becker 1963; Lemert 1972; Giggs and Erickson 1975) theories. The relevance of each to this project will be examined in turn.

Strain explanation

Strain explanations of law-breaking by young people are founded on Durkheim's concept of anomie (Merton 1938, 1957). Its basic premise is that delinquent behaviour is the result of socially induced pressures and, in particular, that it results from the 'strain' caused by the gap, or anomic disjuncture, between the culturally induced aspirations/goals and realistic expectations or the means available for the achievement of those goals (Rutter and Giller 1983). Johnson (1979) states that although the individual internalises society's goals, s/he would use illegitimate ways in order to obtain them, after realising that legitimate avenues to success are blocked. He concludes:

> The frustrated, deprived or strained individual breaks society's rules to obtain the commodities that society has convinced him/her are important to obtain.
> (Johnson 1979: 2).

It is clear according to Rutter and Giller (1983) that anomie is a class-based theory which assumes that most delinquent behaviour is concentrated in the lower social classes. Young people in the lower social strata experience frustrations from the lack of opportunity to participate in the rewards of economic success (Merton 1957) or, according to Cohen (1956), from the lack of ability to acquire social status and prestige. In relating strain theory to the specific case of ethnic minority offending, some writers (e.g., Lea and Young 1984) have argued that:

> of all the groups on the receiving end of social deprivation - black, Asian and white - blacks most acutely experience the combination of social deprivation and lack of political power, within the established framework, to change their situation as a group. We argued that this combination of economic and political marginalization lay behind the high crime rate within and around the black community, which affected a minority of the community and only sporadically. Crime was a negative manifestation of this discontent, whereas the uprisings of 1981 [in Britain] were an extremely positive response to deprivation.
> (p. 112).

9

However, the research literature suggests that evidence on the problem of the association between social class and criminal behaviour is inconsistent and often weak, as discussed below. For example, Hirschi (1969) and Elliott and Voss (1974) contend that high aspirations in working class [and black] youths have not been found to be related to delinquency. Furthermore, most of its critics (for example, Rutter and Giller 1983) say that strain theory fails to account for middle class delinquency; and that the original notion of strain has not been empirically supported (Matza 1964, Downes 1966, Hirschi 1969).

Subcultural explanation

The assumption by the theories of anomie that delinquency is concentrated in lower-class groups is also shared by the subcultural approaches, albeit the latter postulate neither strains nor frustrations. The subcultural approach rather suggests that the delinquent is socialised into law-breaking in order to gain acceptance or to live up to the expectations of his/her deviant peer group. The proposition is that deviant behaviour results from conformity to a separate set of accepted norms and values. Delinquency is seen simply as 'normal' behaviour for the particular subculture and hence it is learned in the same way as any form of social behaviour (Mays, 1954, 1972; Downes, 1966; Willmott, 1966). For example, some contributors (Lea and Young, 1984) to this debate suggest that African-Caribbean youth have developed a culture of discontent resulting precisely from the visibility of deprivation, a visibility highlighted by the very process of integration into British standards and expectations of life. Furthermore, this purported black youth 'street subculture' which is distinctive from the older generation of African Caribbeans, has been thought of as epitomised by the establishment of black neighbourhoods, which:

> opened up for some, the possibility of surviving by alternative means, by a process of hustling involving activities such as gambling, undeclared part-time work, ganja selling, shoplifting, street crime, housebreaking and distributing stolen goods. Sections of the white working class have long chosen to survive through similar strategies. (Friend and Metcalf 1981: 156).

Friend and Metcalf (1981) go on explicitly to identify the crimes of young people as a direct challenge to capitalism, with black youth being in the forefront of such a struggle.

The 'normal subculture' approach thus views most cases of delinquency as terminating after adolescence and that many delinquents, especially minor first-time offenders, show no general disturbance of behaviour, emotions or relationships, as shown by consistent evidence to this effect (Rutter and Giller 1983). Mellish (1984) for example, argues that:

up to 69% of the offences involving [young people] dealt with, in the MPD in 1982, were for minor crime or non-criminal. (p.3).

Miller, President of the National Centre on Institutions and Alternatives, Washington DC., in a speech in 1985 on recent developments in the United States of America on decarceration, also suggested that 45% of people in adult prisons in USA in 1968 were youth justice alumni, but that that figure decreased to 19% in 1985. Murray and Cox (1979) and Rutherford (1986) make similar observations in their respective essays which posit youth misbehaviour as transient, with a focus on the role of 'maturation' and the 'regression' artifacts in delinquency. Murray and Cox (1979), for instance, state that delinquents, including that tiny residue of chronic offenders, are expected to commit less crime after intervention simply because they have grown older. In 'regression', any evidence of change is seen as a function of the laws of probability which assume that there is a 'natural' or 'mean' rate of crime among young people which remains relatively constant throughout their careers. Murray and Cox, in their maturation and regression hypotheses, thus suggest that arrests seem to increase with age throughout the pre-intervention and intervention periods and decrease slightly with age in the post-intervention period, as illustrated by their study on *Beyond Probation: Juvenile Corrections and the Chronic Delinquent*, in Chicago. Moreover, Wolfgang (1972) and West (1982) coined the term 'spontaneous remission' to describe young people's distance from crime overtime.

Deviation in both strain and subculture theories is thus viewed as the product of certain inter-personal or social conditions; and as mentioned above, the strict subcultural prediction would be that the underclass (Johnson 1979) hold values more compatible with delinquency and, therefore, exhibit more delinquency (although this warrants further empirical research).

Labelling explanation

Becker (1963) describes the influence of labelling in deviancy by suggesting that:

> one of the most crucial steps in the process of building a stable pattern of deviant behaviour is likely to be experience of being caught and publicly labelled as a deviant..., being caught and branded as a deviant has important consequencies for one's further social participation and self-image. (p. 31).

One's further participation or 'secondary deviance' (Gibbs and Erickson, 1975; Plummer, 1979) is viewed in labelling theory as:

> a special class of socially defined responses which people make to problems created by the societal reactions to their deviancy. (Lemert 1972).

11

In connection with ethnic minority offending, the proposition here is that the increased rate of black crime and police predisposition to associate black people with crime become part of a vicious circle which criminologists have termed 'deviancy amplification'. The police begin to focus upon black youths as likely criminals, and this results in a rise in the crime statistics for blacks (Lea and Young 1984). Similarly, Sim (1982) suggests that:

> The key to understanding the disproportionate number of black people in the official criminal statistics could be found in the practices of the Met both bureaucratically and on the streets.... By concentrating both manpower and resources in areas such as Brixton, the police were likely to pick up more black people, especially the black youth who spent much of their time on the streets. This group then found their way into criminal statistics, thus leading to an even greater police and media concentration on the activities of black people. This in turn, led again to more of them being picked up. (p. 59).

Furthermore, empirical evidence and some research (Bahr, 1979) supporting the labelling theory point out that a Court appearance did make it more likely that a boy/girl would maintain anti-social attitudes and increase his/her delinquent activities. On the other hand, Gold and Williams (1969), Foster et al (1972), Ageton and Elliott (1974) view this 'secondary deviation' as perhaps the knowledge of being considered delinquent by others, which in fact 'produces' lower occupational or educational expectations and a more delinquent value orientation that lead to even greater delinquent activity.

Thus, labelling is both an effect and then a cause of further delinquent behaviour (Johnson 1979). But as stated by Wellford (1975), Bahr (1979) and Plummer (1979), the theory is applicable only to certain types of delinquency, as it probably plays little role in the most persistent forms of recidivism, and people vary in how they respond to labelling. They also suggest that labels need not be permanent and irreversible.

The above mentioned theoretical perspectives to deviancy place the welfare model as viewing the offender as a victim of circumstances, social, economic, psychological and biological, which are the crucial determinants to his/her law breaking, and which have to be taken into account in any formal processing of delinquent youth. The aim would be to provide him/her with the resources to overcome these adverse circumstances.

The justice response

Control theory

The opposite perspective to the welfare view, the justice response to crime and its treatment, views the delinquent as a conscious law-breaker who endangers the community. Social control is traditionally achieved within a criminal justice framework, so that decisions reflect fairness and equality. The justice model, then, is understood in terms of control theory, which is concerned with factors that prevent deviance rather than motivations or provocations to causes of delinquency (Nye 1958; Briar and Piliavin 1965; Polk and Halferty 1966; Hirschi 1969; Hewitt 1970). In social control theory, there is the assumption that 'everyone' has a predisposition to commit delinquent acts and the issue is how people learn 'not' to offend and why people violate the rules in which they believe (Hirschi 1969). It is argued that although there are direct social controls (as through external restriction and punishments), indirect and internalised controls based on affectional identification with parents are the most crucial (Nye 1958). According to Hirschi (1969) delinquent acts result when an individual's bond to society is weak or broken. The key elements in that bond are provided by 'attachment' to other people, 'commitment' to an organised society, 'involvement' in conventional activities and 'belief' in a common value system. When compared with explanations centred on strain or subcultures, the control perspective emphasises irrational and situational aspects of deviant acts (Johnson 1979), and a calculational component in both conformity and deviation (Hirschi 1969).

The justice model thus stresses the need for society to be protected from the 'conscious' delinquent, through formal institutional procedures. In doing so, the model does not, however, approve special treatment on the basis of disadvantage. For instance, the first principle of the Minnesota sentencing guidelines (the scheme which comes nearest to a pure 'deserts' model) is that:

> Sentencing should be neutral with respect to the race, gender, social or economic status of convicted felons.
>
> (Minnesota Sentencing Guidelines Commission, 1980: 1).

Similarly, the Washington sentencing code, as well as most commissions, specifically excludes sex, race or colour, creed or religion, and social or economic class from being considered in sentencing (Griswold 1983). Thus, Hudson (1987) has stated that:

> One of the ... arguments for deserts-based sentencing is that it would mean punishing people only for acts they had actually committed, rather than penal systems being used to repress or isolate members of groups who are seen by governments as posing some sort of present or potential threat to the social order. In particular, it is urged that deserts systems would stop people being incarcerated because they were black, or because they were unemployed.
>
> (p. 94).

However, Fielding and Fielding (1991) have argued that:

To listen to many police officers one would assume that law enforcement is fairly cut-and-dried, merely the consistent application of unambiguous statutes. But law enforcement, let alone order maintenance, is not epitomised by the fixed penalty ticket. Discretion, not fixed, is the universal of police practice.

(p. 39).

Furthermore, at the level of formal mandate, Fielding and Fielding go on to suggest that:

commonsensically, one knows that procedures based on notions of equitable fairness are not always followed to the letter. In so far as the policing of ethnic minorities is concerned, the notion that the police should be especially careful in their dealings with ethnic minorities,....smacks of favouritism to the police, especially if it is linked to ideas of positive discrimination and a more tolerant exercise of discretion. From the police perspective, black citizens pose special problems of law enforcement and exhibit several negative traits. They spurn peers who join the police force, are sullen and uncooperative, and liable to use accusations of victimisation as a bargaining lever where an offence is suspected.... The principle that personal attributes should be irrelevant is disarmingly put in the police view that all offenders are equal when it comes to guilt.

(p. 46).

The relationship between social class and crime and race and crime will be examined in turn.

Social class and criminality

The implication from both strain and subculture theories suggested in the literature is that the frequency, seriousness and even the basic patterns or types of delinquent behaviour should vary by social class position. Control theorists, on the other hand, commonly make no assumption about the relative strength of social controls or bonds in different classes and hence make no class-related claims.

Thus, there has long been a widespread assumption that juvenile delinquency and adult crime are both prevalent among the lower social classes. Moreover, this presumed strong association between delinquency or crime and some of the traditional variables, such as, sex, race, social class, area of domicile, socio economic status, et cetera, constitutes the basis for most of the leading sociological theories of crime as evidenced by some pioneer research, for example, Shaw and Mckay (1942). Hirschi (1969) pointed out in his review of the empirical evidence on this point that most research data contradict these sociological assumptions. For example, Tittle et al (1978), in their re-examination of social class findings from a wide variety (mainly American) of self-report and official delinquency

14

studies, concluded that the data:

> show only a slight negative association between class and criminality..., and that numerous theories developed on the assumption of class differences appear to be based on false premises. It is now time, therefore, to shift away from class-based theories to those emphasising more generic processes.
>
> (Tittle 1978: 643-56).

Most of the evidence used to support predictions of class differences is drawn from official statistics (that is, police records, courts, social and law enforcement agencies). But differences of opinion exist in sociological literature between those who argue in favour of the accuracy of official statistics with respect to class and those who argue that the statistics are artificially inflated as a result of official bias and that they are riddled with error (Merton 1957; Box 1986). When early self-report studies (for example, Tittle and Villemez 1977) failed to show class differences in the propensity to delinquency, this was regarded as proof that class differences in official measures were the result of bias in the criminal justice system itself (Braithwaite 1981).

Contrary to the above view, Cressey (1964), supporting the use of official statistics in criminological research, suggested that:

> Despite all the limitations, the criminal statistics give information which is important to our understanding of crime and delinquency and to hypothesis and theories about them. Similarities and differences in crime rates for certain categories of persons are so consistent that it can be reasonably concluded that a gross relationship between the category and crime exists in fact....The statistics on ordinary crime so consistently show an over-representation of lower class persons that it is reasonable to assume that there is a real difference between the behaviour of social classes, so far as criminality is concerned.
>
> (p. 50).

Kitsuse and Cicourel (1963) also argued in favour of the usefulness of official statistics as sociologically relevant data, by stating that:

> In modern societies, where bureaucratically organised agencies are increasingly invested with social control functions, the activities of such agencies are centrally important 'sources and contexts' which generate, as well as, maintain definitions of deviance and produce populations of deviants. Thus, rates of deviance constructed by the use of statistics routinely issued by these agencies are social facts 'par excellence'. (pp. 131-9).

Murray and Cox (1979) underline this argument by presuming that major offences such as robbery, assault and burglary that make up the records of the offenders, as was the case in their study in Chicago, are somewhat more likely to be apprehended than lesser offences and likely to lead to official documentation when they are apprehended.

The disparity between official statistics and self-report data (the latter reports a weaker social class association), has been accentuated because the two do not necessarily tap the same domain of behaviour (Rutter and Giller 1983). As both Hindelang et al (1979) and Elliott and Ageton (1980) note in their reviews of this topic, many self-report questionnaires are largely made up of quite trivial behaviours, which would be unlikely to result in prosecution in most cases. Hindelang (1978) adds that a) many self-report studies have drawn samples from school populations with the likely consequence that findings relating to the lower class and the Black group, are likely to have been biased as a result of their higher drop-out rate, b) some are based on very small numbers, c) many have a substantial non-response rate likely to introduce bias, and d) delinquents and delinquency-prone groups are consistently less likely than non-delinquents to complete self-report questionnaires (see also Hirschi 1969: 45-6).

A word of warning is offered by Box (1986) in relation to this debate. Box, in his survey of the literature on the class/crime relationship problem, concluded that caution should be exercised in attributing delinquency as located at the bottom of the stratification system purely on the basis of official statistics. In that survey, consisting of 40 studies bearing on the issue of self-reported delinquency and social class, he reveals that 16 report lower class adolescents as more delinquent than their middle class peers, and 24 discover no such relationship. As these studies varied so much in methodological sophistication, representativeness of samples and measurement of the two major variables - class and delinquency - Box eliminated some as:

being too technically impoverished or simply irrelevant to count.
(Box 1986: 76).

Thus, out of the 16 which appear to support a negative class-delinquency relationship, he cites only three studies (Walberg Yeh and Paton 1974; Johnstone 1978; Cernkonvich, 1978b):

which do provide evidence consistent with the view that lower class children are more involved in delinquency...,'serious' delinquency is negatively related to social class. (Box 1986: 78-9).

Of the 24 studies which discovered no class-delinquency association, after elimination of the others for reasons mentioned above, Box listed 13 studies (Arnold 1965; Christie et al 1965; Gold 1966, 1970; Hirschi 1969; Bachman et al 1970; Jaakkola 1970; Williams and Gold 1972; West and Farrington 1973; Berger and Simon 1974; Elliott and Voss 1974; Gold and Reimer 1974; Braithwaite 1979;

16

Johnston 1979) and concluded that:

> the vast majority....of research....have been unable to produce evidence supporting a greater involvement in delinquency of lower-class adolescents.
>
> (Box 1986: 78-9).

Although the debate is endless, Hindelang, Hirschi and Weiss (1979), Murray and Cox (1979) and Rutter and Giller (1983) suggest that, if official and self-report delinquency are to be compared, it is necessary to use self-report data which refer to somewhat more serious offences and that:

> when this is done, much of the discrepancy between them disappears.
>
> (Rutter and Giller 1983: 135).

As the majority of the studies mentioned above are quintessentially American, the picture in Britain is summarised by Rutter and Giller (1983) thus:

> on either set of data (official and self-report) there seems to be 'some' social class correlation in Britain, in contrast to what has been claimed to be a negligible one, in the present-day United States.... As to the extent to which this is a real difference..., no entirely satisfactory answer is possible on the basis of the available data. On the other hand, at least some of the data do suggest that the social class-delinquency association may be slightly greater in Britain. There are no strong grounds for supposing that this 'should' be the case..., certainly the social milieu is not the same in the two countries.
>
> (pp. 134-5).

British data showing some association between social class variables and delinquency are provided by the British National Survey (Wadsworth 1979), the Aberdeen survey (May 1975), the inner-London study of young people attending schools (Rutter et al 1979; Ouston 1983) and on a socially more restricted sample, the West and Farrington (1973) longitudinal study of London boys. Earlier studies (for example, Mannheim et al. 1957; Morris 1957) tended to show rather stronger social class associations, while Little and Ntsekhe (1959), West and Farrington (1973) and Farrington (1979) found a social class distribution which was not greatly different from that of the general population.

Both British (Wadsworth 1979) and American (Elliott and Ageton 1980) studies, using official delinquency and self-report data respectively, shared similar conclusions with respect to social class differentials when seriousness of offences was taken into account, that is, findings of no difference in relation to very minor offences, as opposed to serious offences against property or persons, the latter showing some association with class.

The logic of class differences entrenched in delinquency literature and the endless debate surrounding social class definitional problems is characterised by the way class is usually conceptualised and with the variety of ways in which class is measured. In his review of the literature, Braithwaite (1981) suggests that, although social class has been defined in a variety of ways in the literature on the class-crime relationship, these various definitions have almost always been 'operationalised' in the same way. In the case of young people, the operationalisation of social class is almost always based on their parent's occupations or educational attainments. Other socio-economic status (SES) indices include the social class of an area, most frequently operationalised as the percentage of the adult male population of the area who are in lower-class occupations, the percentage on welfare or unemployed or below the poverty line and occupying sub-standard housing or some combination of these. This would imply that ethnic minority youth would be 'operationalised' as lower social class, as a disproportionate number of adult African-Carribeans, in particular, experience a combination of the above mentioned disadvantages in British society (see Chapter three for a breakdown of socio-economic status by race in Brent).

Moreover, unemployment and inadequate housing have been frequently associated with the black population (Crow 1987), as well as the lower social classes. In the United Kingdom, even before the rise in mass unemployment in recent years, unemployment among black people has been higher and they have generally found employment in lower status, low income sectors of the labour market (Smith 1981; Department of Employment 1984; Barber 1985). Difficulties in discerning direct links between unemployment and delinquency have remained for some time (Wootton 1959; Field 1990), but some relationship exists between unemployment and treatment received in the criminal justice system (Howard League 1987). The Howard League states that:

> increasing custody rates among young people, are in part, a consequence of the reluctance of Courts to use fines on unemployed people, and 'higher tariff' disposals which lead on progressively to more severe sentencing are part of escalation of penalties into which custody rates are now locked.
>
> (Howard League 1987: 9).

Assigning young people a class position in order to study the class distribution of delinquency is not without complications, as evidenced by the debate between Tittle et al (1978) and Stark (1979). Stark's central point is simply that the proper data for ascertaining the social class of teenagers is not the social class of their families, but rather their positions in a high school status hierarchy. With social class thus measured, he argues, the class/criminality relationship is empirically supported. The reply by Tittle et al to Stark is dismissive of this argument by stating that:

> We dispute, however, the use of teenage status as a measure of social class..., because high school status systems are too transitory and varied from school to

school, to embody things implied by theories about social class and criminality. (Tittle et al 1979: 668-70).

Richard's (1979) contribution to this debate suggests that class is seen as a continuum that can be quantified along dimensions such as education, occupation and income. He states that:

> Upper, middle and lower classes are identified by rather arbitrary high, medium and low cut-off points along this composite range. (Richards 1979: 5).

Young people, Richards argues, are seldom fully active members of the work force and, therefore, do not participate directly in production. Their role is mediated by institutions such as family or school, and thus do not occupy clear class positions themselves. It is, nevertheless, acknowledged that SES models focussing on lifestyle considerations or educational characteristics of their parents (usually their father) make it easier to skirt the issue (Richards 1979). He concludes:

> Just as adolescents are classless, so they possess no socio-economic status of their own. (p. 6).

Although a direct relationship between unemployment and delinquency has not been shown to exist as stated above, a few studies (Hirschi 1969; West and Farrington 1973: Farrington 1979) did show a stronger association when measures of poverty, family income or unemployment or reliance on welfare were used, as opposed to measures of parents' SES, which revealed a generally weaker association with delinquency in these studies. Hirschi, for example, found that boys whose fathers had been unemployed and on welfare had a rate of recidivism twice that in the rest of the population, using self-report data from a Californian high school sample. Similarly, Braithwaite (1981) found that the income gap between the poor and the average income earner was shown to be a significant predictor of crime rates, while proportion of the population below the poverty line was not. He had used a number of inequality indices to predict average crime rates on Uniform Crime Report Indices for 1967 to 1973, in 193 USA cities. Earlier, Berger and Simon (1974) and Johnson (1979) had failed to show that an underclass/earning class (UC/EC) conceptualisation supported a great causal influence in generating delinquency. The data used by Johnson to test this UC/EC model was based on a self-administered anonymous questionnaire to 734 high school sophomores, but only 58 respondents were categorised as underclass.

Given the problems of articulating class in delinquency; and in the light of the foregoing discussion, the next question is whether, in fact, there are social class biases in the detection or processing of young offenders and/or in police or judicial practice. In connection with this, Chambliss (1969) asserts that:

19

persons are arrested, tried and sentenced who can offer the fewest rewards for non-enforcement of the laws and who can be processed without creating any undue strain for the organisations which comprise the legal system.... The lower class person is a) more likely to be scrutinised and, therefore, to be observed in any violation of the law, b) more likely to be arrested if discovered under suspicious circumstances, c) more likely to spend the time between arrest and trial in jail, d) more likely to come to trial, e) more likely to be found guilty, and f) if found guilty, more likely to receive harsh punishment than his middle or upper class counterpart. (p. 85).

A number of studies (Hardt and Bodine 1965; Belson 1968; Bennett 1979), inter alia, support the above contention. Bennett, for instance, found in a London study that compared with working class youths, middle class offenders were slightly more likely to be cautioned rather than sent to Court. Boys in the top social group who admitted to a lot of stealing were much less likely to have been caught by the police in the Belson study, while an earlier study by Hardt and Bodine suggested that there was a distinct tendency for the lower class boy to be more likely to be picked up by the police and sent to the youth court. Hirschi's (1969) 'official reaction hypothesis' for explaining differential official rates sounds persuasive, when he suggests that the police do patrol more heavily in lower class areas, as well as, black areas and that:

the police do think that blacks are unusually likely to commit acts; the police are no more enlightened in their attitudes toward blacks than are others of comparable education and background; and finally blacks are more likely to report 'non-delinquent' offences involving interaction with and requiring definition by officials other than the police. (pp. 78-9).

This leads us directly to the relationship of ethnicity and crime.

Race and criminality

Patterns of beliefs concerning the social distribution of delinquency by race and class are similar (Box 1986). Box argues that just as self-report data on delinquency reveal that official statistics distort and exaggerate the lower class contribution to delinquency, they show a similar deficiency when the contribution of racially oppressed minorities is examined. Research evidence (Hirschi 1969; Quinney 1970; Taylor et al. 1974; Hindelang 1978) has tended to show negligible differences between rates of black and white youth involvement in delinquency. Others (Chambliss and Nagasawa 1969; Gould 1969; Gold 1970; Forslund 1975) discovered no significant correlation between race and self-reported delinquency. These findings of no significant association between race and crime led some commentantors to conclude that the race differences in arrests are likely to have arisen through police and court processing biases of one kind or another and have little or no basis in actual behaviour (Hirschi 1969; Quinney 1970; Taylor et al. 1974; Hindelang 1978).

But studies which have utilised official crime statistics (Williams and Gold 1972; Wolfgang et al 1972; Berger and Simon 1974; Jenson and Eve 1976; Kelly 1977; Elliott and Ageton 1980) found that crime rates among blacks in the USA have consistently been well above those for whites. For example, the *US National Youth Survey* carried out by Elliott and Ageton (1980) found offence-specific differences by race. Designed to meet the criticisms of self-report data, Elliott and Ageton's sample consisted of 1,726 youths, of whom 259 were black. The self report instrument allowed separate analyses according to the seriousness of offence and type of offence. Their results indicated a total self-reported delinquency rate that was greater in blacks than whites, in particular, with respect to serious offences against the person (mean score of 79 v 46). Differences remained even after controlling for social class differences between blacks and whites, in that study. Hindelang et al (1979) had earlier pointed out that the ratio of black to white arrest rates for more serious property offences exceeds that for less serious crimes (3.14 v 1.71); and that for violent crimes is several times that for property offences (9.08 v 3.14). Wolfgang et al (1972) found very much the same thing, in their longitudinal study of local samples, when serious offences, especially those involving violence, were applied in the analysis.

Victimisation data shown in official statistics also seem to indicate black/white differences in crime rates (Hindelang 1978; Hindelang et al. 1979). Victimisation data, however, have problems, not the least of which is the uncertainty about the validity of the victim reports (Rutter and Giller 1983).

However, having reviewed the literature on the race/crime problem, Rutter and Giller (1983) concluded that:

> the strong probability is that there is a real difference between Blacks and Whites in the USA in crimes involving violence against the person..., at least with minor crimes involving theft, the official statistics probably exaggerate the extent of black/white differences.... and that the findings in USA, suggesting black/white differences is not just a function of social class variations.   (p. 155).

Factors, such as possible biases in police and/or judicial processing or assessments, may also act to the disadvantage of blacks (Chambliss and Nagasawa 1969; Black and Reiss 1970; Sullivan and Seigel 1972; Piliavin and Briar 1974; Cicourel 1976; Landau 1981; Reiner 1985; Tipler 1986; Norris et al. 1992).

Until recently, there has been much less empirical data available in the United Kingdom regarding the position of ethnic minorities in the criminal justice system. Earlier, some writers (Frith 1978; Hall et al. 1978; Pryce 1979; Brake 1980) had, however, suggested that second and third generation African-Caribbean youth had developed a distinctive subculture, which may facilitate the development of a deviant life-style. Examples of this deviancy expressed in their most extreme form are said to be their (the African-Caribbean youth) 'colonizing' of certain streets or neighbourhoods, with distinctive roles and styles which emphasise black pride, with crime as part of the value system. Seen in this light, the role of the police is said to be one not only of enforcing the law, but also of confronting a culture that they do not understand (Dodd 1978). Predictably this was followed by accusations that the police discriminated against black people (Cain 1973; Moore1975; Institute of Race Relations 1979). Hall et al (1978) extended this analysis by suggesting that black crime and its policing signify fundamental class schisms. However, how far there are distinctive African-Caribbean youth subcultures and the implications for delinquent activities and their control, is a matter for empirical research, so far not yet undertaken.

The disputed links between low social status and crime, and race and crime, remain a matter of controversy. Evidence of any association from the research literature is a modest one and applies mainly at the extremes of the social scale. The association is also said to be due in part to social class differentials in detection and prosecution; and that, in so far as it applies to real differences in delinquent activities, the relationship is largely confined to the more serious delinquencies (see Chapter One). Rutter and Giller (1983) suggest that the class/crime association may be a consequence of the problems that accompany low status, rather than low status per se. Doubts about the true facts regarding delinquent behaviour in ethnic minorities in Britain also remain, as extrapolations about the situation in Britain cannot be made on the basis of the American experience. The literature emphasises that there are likely to be subcultural factors which need to be taken into account, in coming to an understanding of possible changes in patterns of delinquent activities among black teenagers and in patterns of black community/police relations in Britain. The tendency in community/police relations has been to pursue more proactive policing, in contrast to the demand for more reactive policing (see Kinsey 1985; Young 1986). Furthermore, Fielding (1987) suggests that:

> The likelihood of reactive policing meeting crime, major or not, is doubtful. The case for public involvement must be plainly predicated on increased 'proactive' contact.... If one is to stimulate closer police/community cooperation, their (the Police) role definition must value the negotiational skills critical in eliciting reliable local knowledge. (pp. 68-9).

This leads us to a brief look at the principal elements of the welfare and justice approaches which underpin both local and judicial policy with respect to youth crime.

Policy implications of theories of crime and its treatment

The welfare approach

The principal elements of the welfare approach summarised from the Black Report (1979), which shape both local and judicial policy, are that:

1. Delinquent, dependent and neglected young people are all products of an adverse environment which, at its worst, is characterised by multiple deprivation.
2. All young people in trouble can be effectively dealt with through a single uniform process designed to identify and meet their needs.
3. Prevention of neglect and alleviation of disadvantage will lead to the prevention of crime.

The policy implications for the above model, like strain theory, is then primarily to seek to correct inequalities of opportunities through reformist means and to promote institutional provision of welfare (Downes 1978). Thus:

> an extention of welfare programmes for dealing with young law-breakers would prevent the worst effects of criminalisation.   (Collison 1981: 165).

The justice approach

The principal elements of the justice model, again summarised from the Black Report, are:

1. Most crime is a matter of opportunity and rational choice.
2. In so far as a person is responsible for his/her actions, s/he should be held accountable.
3. The sole justification for punishment should be commision of a specifically defined offence.
4. Punishment is a valid response to criminal behaviour as an expression of society's disapproval and as an individual and general deterrant.
5. There should be proportionality between the seriousness of the crime and the penalty.

The implication for policy then, for the justice model, incorporates the above elements and aims to foster attachment to conventional institutions by much the same means as strain theory, but with less emphasis on the priority of re-distributing resources in favour of low-income groups (Downes 1978).

23

Legislation and judicial policy

The policy implications of these models to youth criminal justice are embodied in the provisions of the legislative framework through which young persons received institutional intervention, that is, the Criminal Justice Act 1982 (CJA '82), which replaced the Children and Young Persons Act 1969 (CYPA '69) in May 1983.

Firstly, the philosophy behind the CYPA '69, was to further a benign approach toward offenders and make provision for all deprived young children up to the age of 14, to provide identical treatment to the erstwhile delinquents, with emphasis increasingly laid upon prevention, early diagnosis of difficulty and widely-based community and casework care (otherwise known as intermediate treatment).

The aim of the CYPA '69 was to increase the flexibility of 'authorities' dealing with young people in three basic ways:

1. To reduce the likelihood of a child appearing in Court at all,
2. To lessen the inevitable stigma attached to criminal proceedings, and
3. To encourage the development of a wide range of diversionary measures for children at 'risk', who may not necessarily be offenders.

The CYPA '69, therefore, linked delinquency and deprivation as having the same causes and held that these causes could be ameliorated by social work intervention. Thus, delinquency required an individualised response to the personal and social situation of the young person concerned. This approach, however, has had to compete with the alternative of operating a straight-forward tariff which linked re-offending with an increasing set of disposals. This latter approach reflected the position advocated by components of the justice model. Secondly, the CJA '82, has been seen as a compromise between competing notions of welfare (the recognition of the association between poverty in all its forms and crime) and justice ('law and order' considerations). Thus, the CJA '82 considerably lengthened the tariff of disposals. For example, s.20 lays great emphasis upon the development of community alternatives for young offenders who might otherwise receive a custodial sentence, while at the same time, Ss.1-7 increased the range of custodial disposals. Four principles seem to be clearly articulated as underpinning the policy:

1. Diversion from Court. The concept of diversion has certainly been the subject of re-assessment since the publication of the White Paper *Young Offenders* (Home Office et al. 1980) leading to the legislation in the CJA '82 (Giller 1986). In *Young Offenders* it was stated that:

> All the available evidence suggests that juvenile offenders who can be diverted from the criminal justice system at an early stage in their offending are less likely to re-offend than those who become involved

in judicial proceedings.   (para. 38).

In view of the marked inconsistencies in the use of formal cautions between Police Forces in England and Wales in the 1970s (Ditchfield 1976; Laycock and Tarling 1984), the Government constituted a consultative review group shortly after the publication of the 1980 White Paper, to consider the criteria which ought to obtain for cautioning, if it were to achieve real consistent diversion (for young people and adults alike). That review group published a consultative document in June 1984 (Home Office 1984) and in February 1985, a Home Office circular (14/1985), which provided a new set of guidelines for the development of diversion for all offender groups. The circular attempted to achieve three major developments, that is, a greater use of diversion from Court for a wide range of offenders (both formal and informal), the expansion of diversion by multiple use of non-Court decisions, and greater inter Force consistency in the way the police apply the criteria for diversion (see Tutt and Giller 1984a).

2.   For those who eventually enter the youth court, the policy embodied in the CJA '82 unequivocally states that the adversarial nature of the proceedings is the most appropriate method whereby to adjudicate and sentence the case, as clearly illustrated in Ss.3 and 24 of the Act, under which the young person has enhanced rights to legal representation when faced by removal from the community into care and custody (Giller 1986).

3.   The use of determinate sentencing in the light of the, hitherto, growing criticism of the inequity of indeterminacy, especially in relation to young people (crystallised in the use of the care order for offending). The decline of the rehabilitative ethic made the concept of indeterminacy increasingly outmoded (Giller 1986). The new sentences introduced by the CJA '82, therefore, were all determinate.

4.   Proportionality in sentencing young people is one of the main tenets of the 1982 Act, that the sentences imposed by the youth court should be proportionate to the offence that brings the young person into court. For example, s.1(4) of the Act says that magistrates may only impose a custodial sentence if appropriate because of the seriousness of the offence or because of the need for the protection of the public. Proportionality thus reinforces a gradation of intervention (of which custody is the ultimate) related to offence-oriented issues.

It is important to note, however, that while the above principles underpinning the current policy context deal with young offenders, they are also those which underpin both the young adult and the adult sentencing system. With regard to this, Giller (1986) states that:

> the amalgamation of the young offender group into the policy discourse on young offenders facilitates the caricature of the typical delinquent to be the predatory actor who acts with callous calculation with the intention of achieving maximum gain for himself [and/or herself], while demonstrating a reckless indifference to others. (p. 165).

The Criminal Justice Act 1982 acknowledges the competing ideologies of welfare and justice, by on the one hand, emphasising the importance of the Social Inquiry Report (SIR), while on the other, increasing the safeguard for young people in court (on legal representation and by increasing the number of community alternatives, as mentioned above). S.2(2) of the Act states that the Court shall obtain a SIR before passing a custodial sentence, unless it is of the opinion (s.2[3]) that it is unnecessary to do so. S.2(6) also says that the Court shall state in open Court the reason for its opinion that it was unnecessary to obtain such a report. Previous to the CJA '82, the CYPA '69 (s.9[1] and [2]), had made it the duty of the local authority to provide such information relating to a young person's home circumstances, school record, health and character as would appear likely to assist the Court, or other information that the Court requests. Moreover, the Magistrates Courts (CYP) Rules 1970, Rule 10(1), where a young person is found guilty of an offence after a guilty plea or not, allow the Court to consider a written report from a probation officer, social worker, or a registered practitioner, without being read aloud. The overall purpose of a SIR is to provide an assessment of the social situation of the young person, the nature of the offence and the offending pattern, a discussion of the dispositional options open to magistrates and finally, a recommendation about the most appropriate disposal.

However, Burney's (1985) study of nearly 300 offenders aged 14 to 20 years old sentenced to custody in twelve Petty Sessional Divisions in the South-East of England in the first half of 1984 clearly shows that:

> in the majority of cases Courts break the law by failing to follow the statutory sentencing formula or failing to record it. (p. 288).

Similarly, Reynold's (1985) study of the custodial sentencing of young offenders in Northamptonshire in 1984, found not only the statutory criteria mis-applied, but also:

> the extended sentencing powers given to juvenile Courts by the CJA '82, combined with magistrates' interpretations of the wording of the Act, are allowing custodial orders to be made .... earlier in the delinquent career and much lower down the tariff than was the case before the Act. (p. 297).

26

Moreover, when reports are being produced, report writers are moving to a style of reporting which is more 'offences focussed', concentrating on issues such as the offender's culpability, the context of the offending behaviour and ways in which community-based programmes may address the issues of offending (Denman 1982; Morris and Giller 1983; Tutt and Giller 1984b; Raynor 1985). This has meant that, within the past few years, there has been a significant switch away from the welfare model, because of its 'over-reaction' and therefore, 'inappropriate response', towards 'minimum intervention' and 'justice' issues being seen as paramount (Nellis 1985; NACRO 1988). As Hoghughi (1983) has pointed out, both welfare and justice are varieties of social control, albeit aimed at different targets. The problem this posits is that:

> The individual young person appearing before a court cannot be chopped up into his[her] public protection/justice and his[her] welfare bits.   (p. 180).

With the advent of the independent Crown Prosecution Service, in July 1986, it will be interesting to see if the service operates as an additional sifting or diversionary mechanism, or whether particular rules or practices are developed for youth court referrals or whether generic principles of prosecution referral will be developed (Giller 1986). This problem also awaits research.

Summary

The discussion in this chapter has attempted to offer a snapshot picture of the dilemmas in approaching the problem of youth crime and its control, considering the fact that of the over three million offences reported every year in Britain, about half are committed by young people under the age of 17 (Hoghughi 1983). This dilemma reflects the widespread competition between the major theoretical orientations in sociological research on deviancy, consequently leading to the development of a diversity of causal images. One group of theorists stress psychological causations, while others sociological ones. Some eclecticism might be called for, by way of regarding all the theories as having unexplored strengths, as well as evident weaknesses (Downes 1978; Johnson 1979) and that the way forward would be to pick and choose in the light of the quality, as well as the quantity of relevant evidence.

The present state of the art suggests that perspectives held by people about the way in which problem youth should be handled cannot be divorced from their political beliefs and/or moral values (Adams et al. 1981). The *Right*, for example, tend to lean more closely to a classical approach to crime, by emphasising the authority of legal institutions, while not entirely rejecting a 'welfare' element. The *Left*, at the other end of the spectrum, are influenced by positivist theories concerning young people's delinquency and personality in general. Hence, they criticise the current youth court system as oppressive to the nation's most vulnerable youth.

Finally, while the validity of official, self-report and other data sources as estimates of lower-class and ethnic minority involvement in crime has been questioned (e.g. McNeely and Pope 1978; Box 1986), such data are likely to shape public perception and underscore various criminal justice policy decisions. Furthermore, McNeely and Pope (1981) state that an accumulating body of research suggests that the ecology of criminal justice decision-making or relevant organisational characteristics may have a direct impact on outcomes, especially for non-white offenders. Differences in sentencing outcomes may also be due in part to the overall problem of inconsistency and disparity in the criminal justice system as a whole (Ashworth 1986; Samuels 1986).

3   The London metropolitan police district of Brent

Introduction

Previous studies mentioned in literature reviews which have attempted to examine the association between the 'disadvantage' variables (e.g., race, sex, lower socio economic status, unemployment, et cetera, which have formed part of the sociological theories on deviancy) and criminality have in some cases utilised small and inappropriate samples (see, e.g., Hindelang 1978). Brent, which has the highest proportion of the ethnic minority population in the UK (1981 and 1991 Census data), was for purposes of this study, an ideal location for research and the testing of differential outcome hypotheses in the institutional processing of young offenders on the basis of race, while simultaneously examining the impact of the other 'disadvantage' indices prevalent in Brent. The significance of this was that the greatly increased ethnic minority sample size assisted in giving the study in Brent a much more objective basis for making generalisable conclusions about the problem under investigation. The purpose of this chapter then is to profile the context in which the local criminal justice system operated.

Demographic profile

The London borough of Brent was formed under the Local Government Act 1963, as a result of which the Greater London Council and the 32 London boroughs were created. Describing the conditions of life for the population of Brent is to tell in broad terms the tale of two boroughs. Brent, even more markedly today, reflects the marriage at the time of London government re-organisation in 1965 of two boroughs, Wembley and Willesden. The borough is bisected horizontally by the

North Circular Road. Wembley in the North is 'Metroland', prosperous and pro Tory, with its affluence reflecting the comparison of South-East England to the rest of the country; and Willesden in the South is deprived and pro-Labour with an abundance of the social ills associated with inner-city areas (Brent Cross-Cultural Review 1984). Platt (1985) describes the borough as shaped like a triangular wedge driven towards the heart of London; and on a map of social problems:

> it would resemble a section sliced from an infirm and ageing tree - sound and healthy on the outside, but with a canker spreading from the centre. The rot stops by and large at the North Circular Road - the most obvious physical expression of the old Wembley/Willesden boundary, though this actually followed the river Brent, a little to the North. Here, the inner and outer cities collide. (p. 446).

Placed within the London context, the 1981 Census provides an opportunity to compare social, economic and living conditions in Brent with other London Boroughs (see Table 3.1).

Table 3.1
Brent's demographic and living conditions compared with the rest of London

Indicator	Brent's position in London
Population from ethnic minorities	1st
Households with 3+ children	3rd
Households living at over 1 person per room	3rd
Households living in furnished rented accommodation	6th
Households that are one parent families	7th
Population under 5 years old	8th
Households that share basic amenities	8th
Population unemployed	11th
Population loss (1971-81)	15th
Households that are pensioners living alone	27th
Population over 75 years old	31st

Source: 1981 Census Data for London

Although Brent is classified as an Outer London Borough by the Government and the now defunct Greater London Council for statistical purposes, an analysis of the results of the 1981 Census reveals the borough (even with its affluent segment) as the eighth poorest local authority in England, in terms of various indices of disadvantage, namely unemployment, social welfare, overcrowding, sharing amenities, lone parents, homelessness, discrimination, ethnic origin, population change, et cetera. Three of the eight most deprived wards in London are in Brent (Brent Cross-Council Review 1984).

Population structure

Brent's population as a whole has steadily declined from 311,000 in 1951 to 251,238 in 1981 (1981 Census Data). The population loss between 1971 and 1981 was anticipated in various population projections (OPCS) and it has been seen to slow down in recent years, so that the future population level was estimated to remain stable at around its 1981 level. The Census reports Brent's population loss as very close to the Greater London average, but notes that the decline in Wembley of 4.5% is similar to the Outer London average, whilst the Willesden decline of 15.4% is close to the Inner London average.

The decline in population in Brent, nonetheless, coincided with the growth of an increasingly disadvantaged and deprived ethnic minority community. In the past thirty years or so, the proportion of black and Asian communities has risen from 29.3% in 1971 to 33.5% in 1981 (GLC Report 1984). The GLC Report attributes this growth to a response to the demand for labour of local industry in the 1950s and 1960s. In many ways this large black and Asian community provides one of the great strengths of the Borough in terms of, for example, its cultural diversity. In response to this, previous Brent Labour Councils acknowledged the demands for changes in some of the Council services, not least Social Services, Education and Housing, in order to reflect this ethnic mix.

According to the 1981 Census figures, Brent has a higher New Commonwealth and Pakistan (NCW & P) population, numerically and proportionately, than any other Borough in the Greater London Area, if not the UK as a whole. Over 83,023 people (or 33.5% of Brent's population in 1981) were of NCW & P origin. This compares with 14.5% in Greater London as a whole, 19.4% in Inner London and 11.8% in Outer London and about 5% nationally. In addition, Brent also has large Irish and Jewish populations with their own particular needs (see Table 3.2 overleaf, for Brent's ethnic origin estimations).

Initially, statistical difficulties arose in estimating the number of black and Asian ethnic minorities in the Borough because the 1981 Census did not include a question on racial origin. The indicator used was the number of persons living in households headed by someone born in the New Commonwealth. Ethnic minority figures are thus generally recognised as an underestimate of the position at that time and the figures could be larger than indicated. For instance, as the communities from the NCW & P become better established, birthplace figures lose their accuracy

31

as a measure of the size of the ethnic origin. Despite the limitations, however, these statistics are the only comprehensive figures available of the ethnic structure of the total population and the OPCS suggest that they are the most accurate for the areas with a large ethnic minority population such as Brent.

Table 3.2
Ethnic origin estimation for Brent

Ethnic group	N	%
UK	114,562	46.2
NCW & P*	83,023	33.5
Eire	28,141	11.3
Rest of the World	22,366	9.0
Total	248,092	100.0

* = New Commonwealth - West Indies, India, Bangladesh, East Africa, Cyprus, Hong Kong and Singapore.

Source: 1981 Census Data

Information on the respective profiles of Brent's Asian, black and white populations by age group prepared by Brent's Development Department utilising the 1981 Census data suggests that there has been a mean difference of only about 9% between the combined Asian and black youth population who comprised 46% of the total youth population in Brent and the white youth population who accounted for 55% of that population. This was significant in reducing methodological problems in relation to this study, in that there were sufficiently large numbers from the groups on which to make more objective generalisations from the findings as opposed to studies which have drawn and analysed data from very small samples of people from ethnic minorities, as stated before.

Political economy

With regard to economic factors, the GLC West London Report (1984), Durkin (1985) and Walker (1985) placed Brent's economic demise within the context of the expansion and later decline of the London economy as a whole, pre and post the two World Wars. They suggest that, after the international economic recession of the 1920s and 30s, most of the economic growth took place on the greenfield sites

32

in North West London (Brent area) giving rise to its economy developing as a centre of manufacturing industry such as in engineering, aircraft, automobiles, buses and the other myriad products of the engineering industry, as well as a strong food and drink industry. That period also witnessed workers in other parts of the country escaping from depressed areas left devastated by the decline of previous generations of economic development (mines, steel, shipbuilding, textiles) to find work in this area (GLC Report 1984). In terms of its position in the World Market:

> Brent was in the 1930s on the greenfield fringes of the largest city in the World. London, with its production growing at 13% was the core of the booming Midlands and the South-East, where output and, therefore, markets were growing.   (GLC West London Report 1984: 4).

Other favourable circumstances such as the abandonment of the UK's free trade policy (following the 1929-32 crisis) were cited by Walker (1985) to have played a part in encouraging foreign firms to build factories on the UK market, like American multi-national companies.

The economic boom was, however, short-lived as the period following World War Two began to show a decline in the scope of economic activity mentioned above. There had been powerful forces suggested by Durkin (1985) which stood behind the process of economic decline in Brent, one of which was the decision by the giant multi-national corporations (with world-wide subsidiaries) to discontinue production in that area and their failure to replace the 1930s, 40s and 50s machines which had become obsolete. The decline was, therefore, presented in this context coupled with other contributory factors like the UK's economy growing more slowly than those of mainland Europe and Japan, which Durkin (1985) argues had in the 1950s placed the firms producing on mainland UK (especially after the EEC was set up in 1957) at a big disadvantage on the European Market (since they had to pay shipping costs and were excluded from the EEC Customs Union). This then meant that West London ceased to be an attractive location for international capital as these firms searched for markets elsewhere. Thus, both periods, one of rapid growth and one of decline, represent the local effects of the re-structuring of industrial production at an international scale in response to a period of sustained economic crisis throughout the World Economy (GLC West London Report 1984).

The Brent Cross-Council Review Report (1985) points out that since the early 1980s the recession and general decline in manufacturing industry have resulted in a 'rationalisation' of economic activity in the Borough, with many firms, particularly in the manufacturing sector, closing down or moving out as mentioned above. The Review also explains that, although there has been some re-development activity on the industrial estates, such as retail warehousing, the services sector and public sector investment by a local authority through, for example, the Greater London Enterprise Board:

there is no indication as yet that other modern manufacturing activity is being attracted to the Borough, and it must be assumed that other locations in the South-East of England provide more attractive working and living conditions for the declining manufacturing sector.   (Brent Cross-Council Review 1985).

In fact Walker (1985) suggests that the last 20+ years have seen a 40% cut in industrial jobs in the UK. In Brent, the decline has been steeper still (41% in the decade 1971-81 alone) coupled with a decline in the number of Brent's residents who work in manufacturing industry, as opposed to the number of manufacturing jobs in the Borough itself. Walker (1985) states that:

roughly 50% of residents work outside Brent and roughly 50% of those who work in Brent live outside the Borough.   (p. 5).

Economic activity

In statist_cal and percentage terms, West London was presented by the GLC West London Report (1984) as less disadvantaged during the 1960s, with a significantly lower rate of male and female unemployment, a lower rate of job loss, a slower rate of firm closure and a lower incidence of associated social deprivation on nearly all indicators of disadvantage compared with London's inner city areas, such as Hackney and Tower Hamlets. The report points out, however, that the picture of a more buoyant local economy, as opposed to the rest of the Greater London Area, changed dramatically during the second half of the 1970s and especially during the past 10 years or so. It showed the years between 1979 and 1984 as a period during which West London out-stripped inner city rates of decline and then claimed, on various indicators of personal suffering and deprivation, higher percentage rates than some inner city Boroughs which received partnership status under the Inner Urban Areas Act 1978. This fact was sustained by Brent's experience of being specified as a designated district under the above Act, for Programme Authority Status in 1984/85. The GLC West London Report (1984) concludes by stating that for areas such as Brent and Ealing, their social and economic position in relation to inner city areas is worsening at an ever increasing pace.

Unemployment

The Brent Employment Bulletin (1982/83) points out that unemployment in Brent was fluctuating during the early and late 1970s, closely shadowing the national economy, but that since April 1979, the situation changed drammatically to a point where in 1982, the rate had risen by 240%. This rate of increase is higher than for both the Outer Boroughs and the Inner ones (see Table 3.3).

34

Table 3.3
Brent's unemployment and the rest of London (1979-82)

	N. 79	N. 82	% Increase
London Borough of Brent	4,633	15,746	+240
Outer London	64,651	192,725	+198
Inner London	61,879	189,054	+206
Greater London Total	126,530	381,779	+202

Source: Manpower Services Commission Monthly Information Notice (London Regional Manpower Intelligence Unit)

The unemployment total is based upon Benefit Office returns and, therefore, does not include those who are not eligible for unemployment benefit, for example, certain married women seeking work or young people on temporary unemployment schemes such as Youth Training Schemes.

On the other hand, figures prepared by the Job Centres and Career Offices showed a pattern of disproportionately high unemployment amongst ethnic minority groups, with their statistics increasing faster than the national average (Brent Employment Bulletin, 1982/83). Black unemployment in relation to the total amount of unemployment in the borough indicated that, whereas the Willesden Office had the largest number of ethnic minority unemployed, the Wembley Office had the highest proportion (43%), in spite of the affluence of the area. The National Dwelling and Household Survey (NDHS - 1977) revealed a much higher incidence of under-registration among ethnic minorities and it can be assumed that the figures may be much higher. The plight of unemployed black people was further highlighted by a Manpower Services Commission Report (1982/83), *Ethnic Minority Unemployed in the London Boroughs*, which showed the position in Brent compared with other similar London Boroughs, as first in overall ethnic minority unemployment and third for those aged 16 - 19 of this group within Greater London, in 1981, as illustrated in Table 3.4 overleaf. It should be noted that this age of data is most relevant to the court data collection period.

Youth employment, unemployment and under-employment

As with other statistics, youth unemployment after October 1982 was based on those registering at Benefit Offices and did not include those only registering at the Career Offices (Brent Employment Bulletin, Spring 1984). The trend in overall youth unemployment for the 16 - 19 year olds in Brent showed a continuing upward trend since 1978, with peaks and troughs reflecting the October school leaving bulge each year. The statistics also revealed that there was an increase in the number of those youth who had been unemployed for more than 12 months.

Table 3.4
Brent's ethnic minority unemployment and the rest of London

Absolute number of ethnic minority unemployment in Greater London (May 1981)	*Absolute number of ethnic minority unemployment aged 16-19 in Greater London (Feb 81)*
BRENT	Lambeth
Ealing	Haringey
Lambeth	BRENT
Newham	Hackney
Wandsworth	Ealing
Hackney	Southwark
Tower Hamlets	Wandsworth
Islington	Lewisham
Southwark	Islington
Lewisham	Tower Hamlets
Haringey	Hammersmith
Hounslow	Kensington

Source: MSC Report, *Ethnic Minority Unemployment in London*

Increases in the duration of youth unemployment occured in spite of the Government's Special Measures for youth employment which temporarily took people off the Unemployment Register (Brent Employment Bulletin 1984). Since September 1983, the Youth Training Scheme (YTS) had been the main government training scheme for 16 and 17 year old school leavers, divided into two types, Mode A and Mode B1 and B2. Mode A is employer-based and Mode B1 are the Training Workshops, Community Projects and Information Technology Centres. Mode B2 are College-based. Brent just had Mode A and Mode B1 schemes (see Table 3.5). An interesting feature shown by the statistics in Table 3.5 is that by Spring 1984, there were three times more places available in Mode A than those occupied, compared with Mode B places which were nearly filled (78.1%), but representing under one third of the available employer-based places.

Although ethnic figures were no longer available from the Benefit Offices from the mid-80s, an analysis of the statistics supplied by the Willesden Job Centre (April 1979 to April 1982) indicated that 40% of those registered as unemployed were black minorities; 33% in Wembley and 31% in Willesden were the 19-24 age group. This led Brent Council (1983) to conclude that, if one is young and black

36

in Brent, one is four times more likely to be unemployed. On a national scale, 16.2% of economically active black youth aged 16-20 were unemployed compared with 8.1% of the total male population unemployed in that age group (1971 Census). Studies (OPCS and the CRE 1978) demonstrated this anomaly further by suggesting that ethnic minority young people frequently are more dependent than their white peers on the statutory services when seeking work. Two further studies by the Community Relations Councils (CRCs) and the Council for Racial Equality (CRE) in 1978, in the Midlands, have shown similar patterns for young Asians. In terms of YTS, few young blacks were given places on Mode A employer-based courses and more likely to be on Mode B schemes which involved placements with community organisations and less likely to result in permanent jobs (CRE, October 1984; the Guardian, 23/10/84).

Table 3.5
Youth Training Schemes in Brent (1983)

	N Available	N Occupied
Mode A	1,059	377
Mode B	301	235
Total	1,360	612

Source: Careers Service/ Brent Employment Bulletin, Spring, 1984

Frith (1984) mentions that the Youth Opportunities and Youth Training Schemes were designed at least in part to keep young people occupied, to meet the fear that 'idle' youth are mischievous youth (but disputes the existence of statistical evidence to support this). As already discussed in Chapter Two, difficulties in discerning the consistent links between unemployment and delinquency/crime still exist (Wootton 1959; Howard League 1987). On the one hand, Rutter and Giller (1983) argued for the relevance of unemployment as a part of a delinquent life-style by citing Bachman et al. (1978), a longitudinal study of some 2,000 adolescent boys in American schools which found that unemployment and delinquency inter-correlated in 74% of the participants studied over an eight year period. However, they suggested that, although the Backman et al study had shown that:

> employment and unemployment may constitute influences on young people's behaviour which serve to protect from or predispose towards delinquency.., further investigation in this area was necessary. (Rutter and Giller 1983: 232).

On the other hand, Field (1990) in a recent study on *Crime and Consumption* has argued that unemployment is a 'lagging' indicator of crime rates relative to prosperity and that the key thing is to look at the relationship of crime to disposable income. That research study found that during periods when personal consumption is growing relatively rapidly, property crime tends to grow relatively slowly or even fall. During periods when personal consumption is growing more slowly (or even falling), property crime seems to grow more rapidly. Field suggests that:

> The relationship of consumption to property crime is an order of magnitude stronger than that of unemployment, and once the effect of consumption is taken into account, the unemployment rate adds nothing to the explanation of fluctuations in property crime growth. Although unemployment and consumption are both indicators of the state of the economy, consumption is a coincident indicator, whereas unemployment is a lagging indicator. Property crime, like consumption, appears to be a coincident indicator of the state of the economy. This means that in practice, as the economy - say - starts to emerge from a low point in the economic cycle, personal consumption will start to grow faster, and property crime to grow more slowly before unemployment starts to fall. (Field 1990: 8).

He also contends that the above finding is of wide applicability, in that the association between property crime and personal consumption has held throughout the 20th century in England and Wales, and that a similar association can be demonstrated in other industrialised countries. Field's conclusion is that:

> On the theoretical side, the finding demonstrates clearly that economic factors can have an important bearing on crime. While the nature of these factors requires further analysis, it suggests that attempts to reduce the level of crime could usefully address the economic circumstances of those perceived to be at risk of criminal involvement. (pp. 8-9).

Those exposed to such a risk are considered in sociological literature to be lower social classes and black youth, in particular.

Socio-economic groups (SEGs)

In describing and comparing the socio-economic status of Brent's residents, the NDHS (1977) used the following SEG classifications derived from the OPCS Registrar General's Classification of Occupations 1960 and 1970, that is,

38

SEG 1,2,3,4   Professional/Managerial
    5,6   Junior/Intermediate Non-Manual
    7,10,15   Personal Service/Semi-Skilled Manual
    8,9   Skilled Manual
    11,16,17   Unskilled Manual
    12,14   Self-Employed

For an illustration of the position of SEGs by ethnic origin in Brent, see Table 3.6. Both Table 3.6 and information from the NDHS (1977) suggest that Brent's black community is in a relatively worse economic position than the rest of the population. Since the NDHS was published in 1977, there have been significant changes in economic activity and ethnic minority population growth, so that the breakdown of the figures in Table 3.6 is likely to have changed by now.

Table 3.6
Socio-economic groups (SEGs) and ethnic origin (by head of household) in Brent

SEG	Asian N	%	Black N	%	White N	%	Other N	%	Total N	%
1,2,3,4	1,636	9.6	365	2.2	13,433	78.9	1,586	9.3	17,020	100
5,6	1,583	7.3	1,171	5.4	17,514	81.1	1,337	6.2	21,605	100
7,10,15	1,599	12.0	2,073	15.6	8,795	66.1	843	6.3	13,310	100
8,9	1,900	9.1	2,920	13.9	15,191	72.5	938	4.5	20,949	100
11,16,17	509	8.4	1,154	19.1	4,148	68.6	237	3.9	6,048	100
12,14	464	9.0	328	6.4	3,952	76.9	397	7.7	5,141	100
Total	7,691	9.1	8,011	9.5	63,033	75.0	5,338	6.4	84,073	100*

* = This figure omits all the economically active who are not household heads.

Source: NDHS 1977

However, the economic position of the black population is unlikely to alter, as the Greater London Enterprise Board (1984) points out. It suggests that the distribution of black workers across manufacturing industry in London is fairly wide, but is accompanied by a concentration in the personal service, manual unskilled and semi skilled jobs as evidenced by information in Table 3.6 in Brent's case, and also by Rutter and Madge (1976). In addition, black people are under represented in white collar occupations, especially professional and employer/manager occupations.

The Greater London Enterprise Board (1984) also indicates that Asian workers show a similar pattern of concentration in semi and unskilled jobs, particularly in the North West London manufacturing belt. However, it differentiates between black and Asian workers in white-collar occupations by citing the Asian group as having a greater proportion of its members in the employer/manager category than has the white population in some London boroughs. One factor which tends to conceal Asian employment problems is their particularly high proportion of self employed, salesmen, small shop and factory ownership, with considerable entrepreneurial success (Tayler 1976). For instance, the Runnymede Trust report (1983) concluded that blacks had a 6% çç share in self-employment compared to 9% of the Asians in Brent, even in spite of the GLC's initiatives (e.g. the Greater London Enterprise Board) to provide investment funds to ethnic minority business, on equal terms. Constraints and discrimination on access to finance and capital were observed by the report as influencing the position of the black minority group.

Housing

Brent's housing problems are among the worst in the country and can be described as both acute and chronic (Brent Cross-Council Review 1984). The National Dwelling and Housing Survey (D.O.E. 1978) found that Brent had the largest number of concealed households and the largest crude shortage of dwellings in London (one of only 7 Boroughs nationally still showing such a shortage). Brent Council's estimates at the time of the 1981 Census put the shortfall at 7,000 dwellings (the second highest deficit in London) and a waiting list of approximately 16,000 of local residents (Brent Cross-Council Review 1985). The Census also showed that Brent had 7,745 or 8.7% of households living at over one person per room (the third highest proportion in the country) and 6,761 or 7.6% not in self contained accommodation. This general shortage of accommodation exacerbated difficulties of gaining access to adequate housing faced by households on low incomes, particularly from a large proportion of homeless families of black ethnic minority origin seeking accommodation from the Council (Brent Cross-Council Review 1984). The overall shortage of accommodation in the Borough was, therefore, seen by the Review report as underlying the overwhelming demand for public sector housing at a time of continuing decline of the private rented sector and the high cost of house purchase. In fact, the Greater London House Condition Survey (1979) showed that about 25,000 dwellings or 28% of Brent's stock (the private sector constituting 85% of these) were unsatisfactory in terms of their unfitness, lack of amenities or serious disrepair. Thus, homelessness continued to be the single most pressing housing problem facing Brent. The Brent Cross-Council Review (1985) reported that in April 1984, 888 households were in temporary accommodation, 561 of these in bed and breakfast hotels. In June 1985, these numbers rose to 1,073 and 675 respectively. The then Labour controlled Brent Council acknowledged that most of the homeless families were rehoused on the Borough's large high-density council estates, such as Chalkhill situated in Wembley, and the rest, Gladstone Park, Kilburn, Stonebridge, Brentfield, St.Raphael's Way and Church End located in Willesden.

Policy makers and practitioners agree generally that there are three major and inter related areas of concern relevant to housing and minority groups, namely housing conditions, for which there is evidence (Smith 1976) to suggest that they are worse for the black population as a whole than for the white population; racial discrimination (Smith et al 1975; GLC, March 1976) which affects minority groups both in the private and public sectors; and concentration. In Brent, the population of New Commonwealth residents is highly localised. Much of the discussion on the concentration of black immigrants (Rex and Moore 1967; Cullingworth 1969) has assumed that ethnic residential concentrations are involuntary in the sense that immigrants are prevented from exercising choice by the existence of institutional and social barriers. However, what is beyond dispute is that areas of black settlement and their housing conditions are amongst the most deprived (CRE, May 1977). An analysis of residential statistics by Brent Council (July, 1983) reveals that most Asians and white professional owner-occupiers reside in Wembley and that most blacks and working class whites live in Willesden, with young single person households living in furnished accommodation and sharing basic amenities living in the Kilburn area (which has an above average proportion of Eire born residents). Thus, the Council, through its equal opportunities policies and the introduction of ethnic record keeping, seemed to recognise the significance of developing a viable housing policy which aimed at improving housing conditions (funds permitting) in areas of concentration and the furtherance of individual choice in housing by removing barriers to mobility (Brent Cross-Council Review 1984).

Political structure

Brent has been viewed in Council reports (1984 and 1985) as having for many years been a very politicised Borough, in which policies and the delivery of services inevitably took on a political dimension. Local government in the Borough has thus see-sawed in its political composition, adversely affecting sustained and coherent policy-making (Beckford Report 1985). From May 1982 until December 1983, the Labour group on the Council maintained a tenuous hold on political power by virtue of the Mayor's casting vote. Since then and until May 1986, no one group held an overall majority and the Liberal group held the balance, with members of the Conservative group holding the posts of Committee Chairs. No formal coalition existed between any of the three groups. The situation of a 'hung' Council was believed by some to be a built-in suppressor to the more extreme policies that either of the two main political groups might have pursued. Others took the view that the inherent political instability was not conducive to sound policy-making, particularly in the area of Social Services (e.g., in the formulation of a viable local youth and criminal justice policy). The Beckford Report (1985) suggests that:

Whatever the merits of these opposing arguments, there is little doubt that the political complexion of Brent induces a climate in which every issue is hotly debated, each side seizing the opportunity to score a political point. Predictably, given that climate, no one can tell at any time precisely what the outcome of any issue will be. (p. 179).

However, the Labour group gained an overall majority vote during the Local Government elections in May 1986, an outcome favoured by proponents of the latter argument. The Council has thus had two black leaders since then (the first being the first black woman leader of a local authority in the country), as well as having more ethnic minority councillors. This meant that 'political' proposals to combat ethnic minority problems were to be given a 'serious' consideration for implementation (Brent Cross-Council Review 1984).

Local criminal justice policies

Given the argument that the various indices of deprivation are related to rates of offending and, arguably, result in a hardened style of policing (as discussed in chapter two), Brent's modus operandi in relation to young offenders or those at 'risk' of offending was underpinned by labelling theory. Its policy was:

a)   to identify labelled youngsters,
b)   to prevent secondary deviation,
c)   to extend intermediate treatment (IT) provision,
d)   to foster inter-agency co-operation in promoting diversionary measures for those at 'risk' of custody, and to reduce Court processing,
e)   to prevent care and custody,
f)   that all Social Inquiry Reports (SIRs) would contain an explicit recommendation, that is, there would be no custodial recommendation in SIRs; and that all community options were to be explored and stated in the report. It was the report author's duty to say what community-based facilities were available, as the author was not in a position to second guess what magistrates would decide. Secondly, there were to be no recommendations for s.7(7) CYPA '69 care orders. The same procedure applied where a charge and control condition was being considered under s.22 CJA '82, s.20(a) CYPA '69. Thirdly, there were no pre-trial SIRs where guilt was admitted, except where the Court had requested one or where the young person was already subject to a supervision order or care order. Fourthly, SIRs were not prepared where there was a 'Not Guilty' plea entered, and
g)   to look at black youth and the youth Court system in terms of developing:

42

> sensitive training programmes..., in addressing the imbalance in
> sentencing policy, in the light of growing evidence that a
> disproportionate number of black young offenders receive custodial
> sentences and are in residential care.   (Committee Report 40/82).

Overall, Brent adopted a community care policy in its services to the community. A direct consequence of that strategy was a move towards deinstitutionalisation and community provision in the areas of fostering services and IT facilities for deprived and delinquent children. It is worth noting that nearly all of Brent's IT resources were taken up by those youngsters involved in primary deviance and those processed by the Courts. The concept of deinstitutionalisation has accelerated rapidly both in the USA and UK, although critics say that this has occurred in the absence of community after-care facilities and substantiation of the advantages for clients of community care (Wolpert and Wolpert 1976; Scull 1983).

As far as IT is concerned, the 1970s saw a substantial growth in community-based diversionary projects under its name, for children and young people who are seen as problematic or 'in trouble'. Essentially a pragmatic product of the CYPA '69 (Evans 1982), it was clear in the legislation governing IT and the value systems for its practice, that the message in the 1968 White Paper *Children in Trouble* (which laid much of the groundwork for the CYPA '69) placed intermediate treatment at the forefront of community initiatives for those young offenders who would in all probability have received a residential or custodial sentence, by dealing with them locally. In their assessment of case studies in IT, Adams et al (1981), nonetheless, concluded that the 1969 Act, apart from providing a legal and administrative framework for IT to occur, did little to help local authorities define models of care and treatment. This created confusion of purpose amongst local authorities to the extent that the IT concept, originally intended as a resource for youth courts, proved flexible to the point where it slips between the fingers of definition (Thorpe 1980). This discretion, combined with the non-implementation of certain sections of the 1969 Act, created discrepancies in practice, in particular, its assumptions about delinquency causation (Adams et al 1981).

Mention was made in Chapter Two about the switch, over the past decade, from the welfare approach in dealing with delinquency, which originally underpinned IT, towards the justice approach which has taken place against a 'law and order' backlash. One result of this backlash was the introduction of the Criminal Justice Act 1982, which completely altered the legislative context in which IT is developed. An example of this is the 'fixing' of intermediate treatment (even the tougher versions of it, which it dubbed 'supervised activities') firmly in the lower and middle regions of the tariff, and giving it, in formal terms, the legal status of 'adjunct to custody', which in practice it had already acquired (Nellis 1985). Nellis also suggests that while IT as an overall social policy (a national network of community-based alternatives to residential care and custody, which was to alter the map of child care) has had its difficulties, at the level of practice there have undoubtedly been some successful schemes and projects which in particular places and at particular times have, in acceptable ways, reduced the use of custody to an absolute minimum, and in others have conducted a steady war of attrition against punitive sentencing.

In pursuance of their IT policy, Brent fostered a 'continuum of care' philosophy, which placed the resources available under IT, not just within the framework of child care services, but also alongside other institutions in the community, such as the family, education and youth clubs, as stated by Roberts (IT Co-ordinator for Brent, 1982-86). The 'continuum of care' model, which could take place on four different levels (see Figure A1.1 in Appendix 1, p. 150), had as its starting premise the idea that IT should essentially be for known delinquents, but that resources should also be made available for those children and young people who are at 'risk' of a court appearance or a delinquent 'career'. Referring to Figure A1.1, the first level was a highly intensive programme offering full day care vocational training and remedial education for persistent offenders, who were at serious risk of residential and/or custodial care, as well as being used as part of a phased return for some youngsters already in Youth Custody, Detention Centre or Community Home with Education on the premises (CHEs). The second level was a high intensity programme designed also for persistent offenders in danger of residential and/or custodial care, but who were either at school or work. Thirdly, there was a medium intensity level geared towards less delinquent youth who, nevertheless, were known to the police and had appeared in court, and where the risk of further offending was likely to be in future. At the other end of this spectrum was a low intensity resource for the occasional offender. However, Brent's IT manager stated that:

in spite of this elaborate model, Brent recognised the reality of scarce resources and the difficulties inherent in making 'choices' and 'target' groups for IT.

Table 3.7 overleaf illustrates the levels of IT expenditure in Brent, since its inception in April 1980 up to 1987, the relevant period for the study. It can be seen from Table 3.7 that expenditure on intermediate treatment in Brent was rising each year up until the end of fiscal year 1986/87 and since then IT has been running on a reduced budget (see the 86/87 figure).

Apart from social workers (field), other key people in the local youth justice system responsible for the implementation of Brent's stated policy objectives were the Area-based intermediate treatment social workers (ABITS) and the local Multi Agency Panel (MAP) which consisted of the police, social workers, probation and education representatives, both established in January 1985. The function of the ABITS was to spearhead the implementation of policy objectives (a) to (g) mentioned above, through a negotiation process with others involved in processing young offenders, in particular with the Police (see a diagrammatic representation of this negotiating process Figure A1.2 in Appendix 1, p. 151). Brent, nonetheless, acknowledged that negotiating on behalf of young offenders along the lines suggested in the model in Figure A1.2, can be problematic and does not always succeed, since the idea that anomalies in sentencing patterns can be removed by adopting a straight-forward tariff of disposals linked to the number of times a young person has offended, although attractive, is simplistic. Clearly other variables are taken into account, as mentioned in Chapters One and Two, such as race, type of offence, circumstances of the offence, recidivism, sentencer's attitudes towards punishment, deterrence, rehabilitation etc., which will shape the perception of the 'tariff' and the appropriate use of each disposal. Blakemore (1984) has, however, argued that social workers, teachers and youth workers could contribute towards lessening the potentially adverse labelling effects of a court appearance by influencing magistrates against a custodial sentence or recommending low tariff sentences. Thus, the concept of the diversion of offenders from more serious societal reactions is relevant at all stages of a delinquent 'career' (Blakemore 1984).

Table 3.7
Brent's Intermediate Treatment (IT) budgets

F Y	*Actual Expenditure (£'s)*
80/81	95,532
81/82	118,600
82/83	259,888
83/84	686,172
84/85	916,480
85/86	1,021,135
86/87	1,000,100

Source: Revenue (Actual and Estimates) for both
Forbes House and Morgan Lodge IT Units.

Multi-agency panels (MAPs)

Multi-agency panels were encouraged by the CJA '82 in an effort designed to promote diversionary programmes for young people at risk of further offending. The need for a multi-agency approach to the problem of youth crime and its control was first introduced under s.5 CYPA '69, which made consultation between police and social services a statutory requirement before a decision is taken to prosecute a child or young person. This section of the Act, however, was never implemented. The impetus behind inter-agency cooperation appears to have been the Home Office Circular 211/1978, the *Ditchley Park* Circular (Pratt 1985), followed by the 1979

IT conference in Sheffield whose general theme was inter-agency cooperation (DHSS 1980). This idea was further endorsed by the Parliamentary All-Party Penal Affairs Group (1983) which examined a wide range of approaches to the prevention of youth crime.

The focus for the MAPs is on increasing the proportion and number of young offenders receiving cautions and secondly, to link cautioning with schemes of restitution or mediation, or offering the offender voluntary involvement in a programme of supervision or a community-based service supervised by a social worker/ABIT or by a volunteer adult recruited specifically to work with juvenile offenders.

Consultation has, nevertheless, been patchy and extremes exist between different Police Force areas and even in the same area (Mellish 1984). It is also known that police policy on cautioning varies widely and that it is being used as an explicit diversionary measure in several areas (Laycock and Tarling 1984). Part of the reason for these inconsistencies in the consultation process may be the fact that the final decision to either caution or to refer to the Crown Prosecution Service, as is now the case, remains with the police at senior officer level. To some social workers and probation officers, the process may 'just be another public relations exercise', as commented by one ABIT worker, or according to Fielding:

> In practical terms, inter-agency cooperation means getting probation officers, social workers and health visitors, to increase the flow of information to police. Yet crime prevention aims clearly can conflict with statutory (and implicit) obligations to clients. (Fielding 1986: 186).

Empirical data, however, is lacking in UK on the organisational characteristics of MAPs, which show any class or race specific outcomes in their processing of youth crime referrals. However, there are some studies carried out in the USA which do (Pope 1978; Holland and Johnson 1979; Meyers and Hagan 1979). Pope (1978), for example, in his examination of post-arrest police dispositions to release burglary arrestees, found that such decisions were influenced by extra-legal factors, race included, when legal factors were absent. Holland and Johnson (1979), on the other hand, found ethnic differences in sentence recommendations depending upon whether the decision-maker was a clinician or a caseworker. Whites were shown in that study to receive relatively lenient case dispositions compared to Mexican American and black offenders, based upon the recommendation of caseworkers. The effect of report recommendations on sentencing decisions generally is also echoed by some UK studies by Hine, McWilliams and Pease (1978) and Shapland (1986). Moreover, Meyers and Hagan (1979) and Landau (1981), when examining prosecutors' decisions to prosecute a case, found racial effects favouring whites, when strength of the evidence was held constant.

Summary

The aim of this research study was to investigate the functioning of a local youth criminal justice system in order to discover the position of ethnic minority youth in relation to the police, MAPs, courts, social workers and probation officers, in the light of the stated theoretical perspectives and the research hypothesis. Given the demographic, sociological, economic and political complexities of the borough, Brent has so far avoided a major 'disorder' or 'riot' such as those experienced in Brixton (1981 and 1985), Toxteth (1981) and Handsworth and Tottenham (1985), despite it being designated as a 'riot risk' area by the Metropolitan Police. Brent's Race Relations Unit attributed this as partly being due to:

> the Black community's high degree of politicisation combined with moves towards an 'aggressive' approach to the Borough's Equal Opportunities Policy in all areas of Council services.   (New Society, 27th September 1985).

A further factor for this could have been the regular consultations between local community groups and the police encouraged under s.106 of the Police and Criminal Evidence Act 1984, which provides that:

> arrangements shall be made in each Police area for obtaining the views of people in that area about matters concerning the policing of the area and for obtaining their cooperation with the Police in preventing crime in the area.
> (H.M.S.O. 1984: 99).

However, in order to meet the Council's 1988/89 £17m budget deficit, both the Brent Police and Community Consultative Committee and the IT budget were phased out in August 1988, on the grounds that they were a discretionary service. In terms of IT, this undermined the provisions of s.20 CJA '82 (s.12 CYPA '69) which relate to the statutory supervision of young offenders. Undoubtedly the cuts would have some impact on police/community relations in tackling crime, its policing and its 'treatment' in Brent.

4   Methods and measures

Sampling procedure

Most local youth criminal justice studies collect and analyse data on all cases, in preferance to representative samples, due to complex methodological problems, such as the risk of incorrectly estimating the true population value from the sample value. Accordingly, data for this project was collected on all male defendants (10 - 17) residing in Brent who were arrested between May 1983 and July 1986, and the research involved an analysis of the flow of referrals and outcomes of 1,682 cases of defendants in the local youth criminal justice system during that period. The cut-off points of the data collection are the dates when the Criminal Justice Act 1982 (CJA '82) and the independent prosecution service (CPS) came into being, respectively. The independent and dependent variables analysed are shown in Figures A1.3 and A1.4 in Appendix 1, pages 152 and 153, respectively.

Measures of the independent variables

Race

Race was categorised into three ethnic groups, that is, Asian (people originating from the Indian subcontinent), Black (African-Caribbeans and Africans) and White (UK origin and Eire), each representing 73 (4.3%), 719 (42.7%) and 842 (50.1%) cases respectively. Forty eight (2.9%) cases had information on race missing. These were excluded from the analysis. The racial identities of the defendants were obtained from the identification codes used by the police, that is codes 1 - 7, with code 1 representing White European, 2 Dark European (Mediterranean), 3 African Caribbean, 4 Asian or Indian, 5 Chinese and 6 and 7 for others and those not known. This information was, however, matched with information obtained from Court Sections of the Department of Social Services and their Area Offices and IT Centres and the Probation Service.

Age

As the law makes a distinction in terms of sentencing options by age group, this was classified into three groups, that is, between children (10 - 13 year olds who are not eligible for custodial sentencing) and accounting for 24.8% of cases; young persons (14 - 16, eligible for detention centres (DC) from 14, and following the CJA'82, to Youth Custody (YC) from the age of 15) and accounting for 70.6% of cases; and young adults (over 17 year olds) accounting for 4.6% of cases. However, in the multivariate analysis explained below, age at the hearing was collapsed to just two categories, that is, the under 14s and the over 14s (the custodial candidates). This enabled comparisons in treatment between children and young persons to be made in order to determine any differences between them.

Socio-economic status (SES)

The socio-economic status of a young defendant was determined by that of his parent (see Braithwaite 1981), that is, his father's and in his absence, that of his mother's. The 1980 Registrar General's Classification of Occupations was used to classify SES based on socio-economic groups (SEGs) which were collapsed to eight categories as shown in Table 4.1 overleaf. It can be seen from Table 4.1 that the majority of young defendants dealt with by the police and the courts were those coming from families with unemployed parents (38.1% of cases), followed by those whose parents were personal service workers (13.6% of cases), semi-skilled manual and unskilled manual workers (12.3% of cases) and self-employed:non professional (7.3% of cases). It should be noted that 17.5% of cases had information on SES missing. Those cases were also excluded from the analysis. Two other variables, residential area and type of housing, were included in the analysis as indices of socio-economic status (see Richards 1979; Braithwaite 1981). Residential area consisted of the two main geographical areas which together compose the borough of Brent, that is Wembley (29.5% of cases) which is situated north of the borough, affluent and pro-Tory, and Willesden (70.5% of cases) which is situated south of the borough, socially deprived and pro-Labour. Type of housing was measured in terms of Council Estates (53% of cases) and housing in the private sector (47% of cases), in order to compare the effect of living on council estates on outcomes as against residence elsewhere.

Table 4. 1

Categories of socio-economic status or SEGs for the study in percentages

employer:large and small	0.3
self-employed:professional/employee:professional	1.8
non-manual:intermediate/non-manual:junior	3.4
personal service worker	13.6
manual:foreman/skilled manual	5.7
semi-skilled manual/unskilled manual	12.3
self-employed:non-professional	7.3
unemployed	38.1
Missing data	17.5
Total	100.0

N = 1,387

Offences

Up to four offences were dealt with at the same hearing. In the analysis they are treated as primary offences (TYPE1), with a sample of 1,682 cases and TICs (up to three offences that were taken into consideration at the same hearing as the primary offences). Hence, TICs are the second, third and fourth offences dealt with at the same hearing representing 507, 199 and 102 cases respectively. The total sample size of all offences was 2,490. There were eight offence categories that were used in the analysis to describe the type of both the primary offences and the TICs. It should be noted that, although the combination of offences is unconventional, there is no single right method of offence classification. The combinations were as follows:

a)   Theft and handling stolen goods, contrary to s.1(1) Theft Act 1968 and s.22 Theft Act 1968 respectively and consisting of 790 cases or 31.7% of the total sample. The majority of theft offences involved shoplifting, and it made sense to combine theft with handling stolen goods. As s.22 of the Theft Act 1968 states:

'(1) A person handles stolen goods if ((otherwise) than in the course of the stealing)) knowing or believing them to be stolen goods he[she] dishonestly receives the goods, or dishonestly undertakes or assists in their retention, removal, disposal or realisation by or for the benefit of another person, or if he[she] arranges to do so.'

50

b)   Taking conveyances, that is, unlawful taking of motor vehicles without the owner's consent or lawful authority (TDA) and/or allowing oneself to be carried in or on it, contrary to s.12 Theft Act 1968; vehicle interference, contrary to s.9(3) Theft Act 1968; driving without insurance or licence or whilst disqualified or under age, contrary to the provisions of the Road Traffic Act 1972. Offences involving motor vehicles numbered 417 or 16.7% of the total sample. Given the current concern about problems of 'joyriding' by youngsters, it was useful to combine the above offences relating to motor vehicles, as oftentimes the youngsters who get apprehended, say for a TDA offence, would in most cases also be charged with driving whilst under age, with no insurance and, for a few recidivists, whilst disqualified. Furthermore, youngsters involved with TDA may do so in company with other youngsters (accomplices who get charged with being allowed to be carried in a stolen vehicle).

c)   Property offences, that is, burglary and aggravated burglary, contrary to s.9 Theft Act 1968; destroying or damaging property of another, contrary to s.1(4) of the Criminal Damage Act 1971. Property related offences amounted to 574 or 23.1% of the total sample. Burglary and criminal damage are combined in this classification since some of the young people who were charged with burglary were also charged with criminal damage to property. Section 9 of the Theft Act 1968 provides that:

> '(1) A person is guilty of burglary if-
> a) he[she] enters any building or part of a building as a trespasser and with intent to commit any such offence as is mentioned in subsection (2) below;
> (2) The offences referred to in subsection (1)(a) above are offences of stealing in the building or part of a building in question, ...; and of doing unlawful damage to the building or anything therein.'

Violent offences included assaults occasioning actual or bodily harm, aggravated assaults and malicious wounding, contrary to s.18 and 20 of the Offences Against the Person Act 1861; robbery and aggravated robbery, contrary to s.8 Theft Act 1968; carrying offensive weapons, contrary to s.1 of the Prevention of Crime Act 1953 as amended by the Public Order Act 1986. Violence related offences were 271 or 10.9% of the sample size. The offences grouped in this category would be offences against the person. It is conceivable that during the course of being robbed one can be wounded or suffer grievous bodily harm, if the perpetrator uses force on any person. It was also logical to include the carrying of offensive weapons in this category, since 'offensive weapon' is defined by s.1(4) of the Prevention of Crime Act 1953, as amended by the Public Order Act

1986, to mean:

> 'any article made or adapted for use for causing injury to the person, or intended by the person having it with him[her] for such use by him[her] or by some other person.'

d)   Police defined offences, that is, going equipped for theft or possession of articles for housebreaking et cetera, contrary to s.25(1) and (2) of the Theft Act 1968; criminal attempt, contrary to s.1(1) of the Criminal Attempts Act 1981. These offences amounted to 128 or 5% of the total sample. Generally, attempts are classified under the heading of the crime itself, for example attempted burglary would be in the same category as burglary, but in certain cases it is shown separately (Criminal Statistics for England and Wales 1990). However, since the police still define whether what they have seen amounts to an attempt to commit a crime, it was logical to group 'criminal attempts' with 'going equipped'. The provision of s.25(1) & (2) of the Theft Act 1968 (pertaining to 'going equipped') is expressed to be directed against acts preparatory to i) burglary contrary to s.9, and ii) theft contrary to s.1, whilst s.1(1) of the Criminal Attempts Act 1981 provides that:

> 'If with intent to commit an offence to which this section applies, a person does an act which is more than merely preparatory to the commission of the offence, he[she] is guilty of attempting to commit the offence'.

Thus, the essence of combining 'attempts' with 'going equipped' under police defined offences is that the police do interpret acts as acts preparatory to burglary and theft, as well as defining them (the acts) as more than merely preparatory to the commission of the offence.

e)   Offences against the police, that is, assaulting or obstructing police in the execution of their duty, contrary to s.51(1) and (3) of the Police Act 1964; using threatening, abusive or insulting words or behaviour, contrary to the repealed s.5 of the Public Order Act 1936 now s.4 of the Public Order Act 1986. They numbered 80 or 3.2% of the total sample classified as offences against the police.

f)   Possessing drugs, mainly cannabis, contrary to s.5(2) of the Misuse of Drugs Act 1971, which consisted of 37 offences or 1.5% of the total sample.

g)   Other summary and indictable offences, that is, fraud, contrary to s.2 Theft

Act 1978; deception, contrary to s.15(4) Theft Act 1978; arson; being drunk and disorderly, contrary to s.6(5) and (6) of the Public Order Act 1986; throwing missiles, contrary to s.1(4), as amended by the Public Order Act 1986; and breaches of the conditions of a current sentence, for example, the conditions of an attendance centre order, or a community service order, or a supervision order, or a probation order (see the measures of the dependent variables explained below). This group of offences amounted to 193 or 7.8% of the sample size.

The total number of offences dealt with at the same hearing

The total number of offences heard at the same hearing (NOH) was included in the analysis in order to determine the independent effect of this variable on outcomes rather than just the type of TICs, that is, the influence of one offence compared to a total of two, three or four offences dealt with at the same hearing. The total number of offences dealt with at the same hearing were each represented by 1,175 (69.9%), 308 (18.3%), 98 (5.8%) and 101 (6%) cases respectively.

Recidivism

Recidivism or the number of the arrests or court appearances (NOCA) was measured in this study on the basis of more than one arrest and/or court appearance and ranged from one to fourteen. There was only one case with a record of twenty one arrests and/or court appearances during the period of the study and it should be treated as exceptional. In the analysis the number of arrests and/or court appearances (NOCA) was collapsed to just nine, that is, one through to nine or more, each representing 27.3%, 22.1%, 15.2%, 10.8%, 7.1%, 5.4%, 3.8%, 2.8% and 5.5% of cases, respectively. Research literature (for example, Bazak 1981) suggests that the existence of the probability of recidivism, if based on prolonged offending behaviour in the past or on the severity of the present offence, may in fact result in a stricter sentence, according to Hassin:

... in order to ensure the peace and welfare of the community.

(Hassin 1986).

Courts

Courts were grouped into three categories in the analysis, that is, local youth courts (Acton, Harrow, Hendon and Willesden now Brent) which processed 56.5% of cases, external youth courts (courts in other Petty Sessional Areas dealing with Brent young people arrested for committing offences outside the borough) which dealt with 10.3% of cases and Crown courts who dealt with 1.5% of cases.

Social inquiry reports (SIRs)

The influence of SIRs was measured in terms of

a)   what social workers and probation officers recommend in court, that is, either court non-custodial recommendations, as represented by 14.4% of cases, or court social work and probation recommendations, made on 11.1% of cases or a custodial recommendation, made on only .2% of cases, and the extent to which these recommendations are upheld,

b)   the effect of non-specific recommendations, that is, reports which make pleas for leniency or where the author declares themselves unable to make a recommendation, consisting of 5.4% of cases,

c)   the relationship between cases without SIRs and custodial sentences which accounted for 1.2% of cases,

d)   the agency providing the SIR, that is, between the social services department who provided 479 reports on 28.5% of cases and the probation service who provided 44 reports on 2.6% of cases. Accordingly, 523 Social Inquiry Reports in all were presented in courts during the period of the study and accounted for 31.1% of cases.

Appeals

The influence of appeals against a custodial sentence in youth courts was measured in terms of whether an appeal was made to the Crown courts and if so, whether or not it was successful. There were 26 (22.4%) out of 116 cases which resulted in appeals against custodial disposals. Fourteen of them, 53.8% launched a successful appeal while 10 (38.5%) cases were unsuccessful. Two (7.7%) cases withdrew their appeals at the hearing and they were excluded from the analysis.

Local and judicial policies

Lastly, the researcher was interested in determining the impact of welfare objectives, such as diversion and those discussed in chapter three, or of judicial ones, as discussed in chapter two, using the results obtained in the bivariate and multivariate analyses discussed below.

Measures of the dependent variables

The dependent (outcome) variables were constructed on the basis of the 'tariff' of sentencing in the youth justice system as illustrated in Figure A1.3. However, the concept of a tariff in sentencing young offenders does not appear to be rigidly applied by the courts, as stated by Tarling et al. (1985). The findings of their study showed that the concept of a tariff applied only in a limited way to the younger (10 - 13) age group, with discharges being the most common disposal for all types of offence and, for the rest, an almost even distribution between 'welfare' disposals (care orders and supervision orders) and 'punishment' disposals (fines and attendance centre orders). The concept of a sentencing 'tariff' essentially means two things: first, the more serious the offence the more severe will be the sentence, and secondly, this relationship will operate in a fairly consistent and predictable way. It is a concept which has come to be widely accepted in relation to the sentencing of adults and has been well described by Thomas (1979). But for young offenders, where sentencers have the added complication that they must have regard to the welfare of the child and to sentencing options which include welfare measures, the concept of a tariff is less obviously applicable (Tarling et al. 1985: 168).

In any event, for this study the dependent variables were collapsed to five, from twenty two outcome variables, in such a way that enabled the effect of the 'gatekeeping' function of the police on Asian, black and white defendants with respect to their decisions to caution or to prosecute to be assessed. This was reflected in court decisions to acquit or to impose a non-custodial or a social work and probation or a custodial sentence. The collapsed variables were as follows:

Police diversionary measures

These comprised (i) police on-the-street discretion and/or police station decisions to take no further action on suspects of a misdemeanour and (ii) the giving of cautions at a police station (distinguished between 'straight' cautions and those given with 'strings' attached, after consultation with the local multi-agency panel (MAP) which consisted of representatives of the Education Department, Police, Probation and After-Care Service and Social Services, as discussed in chapter three). A caution with 'strings' was meant to be a diversionary measure given to a young offender, which was dependent upon his/her acceptance, first of his/her guilt to a specific offence(s) which s/he was alleged to have committed and secondly, his/her agreement to partake in intermediate treatment activities on a voluntary basis for a specific period of time. It should be noted that the police retain the overall discretion to the giving of cautions (straight or with strings) via MAP.

Acquittals

These were cases dismissed in court because of insufficient evidence.

Court non-custodial sentences

These were cases in which the defendants were bound over in order to keep the peace, as well as those who received absolute and conditional discharges, fines (s.26 CJA'82), compensation orders (s.27 CJA'82; s.35 of the Powers of Criminal Courts Act 1973) and attendance centre orders (s.16 CJA'82).

Court social work and probation sentences

Court social work and probation sentences were primarily community service orders (s.68 subsection 1 of the CJA'82), supervision orders (s.20 subsection 1 of the CJA'82), supervision orders with discretionary intermediate treatment requirements (s.20 CJA'82, previously s.12 of the Children and Young Persons Act 1969), supervision orders with supervised activities requirements (s.20 CJA'82 and previously s.12[3c]b of the 1969 Childrens Act), probation orders, remands in care of the local authority (s.23 subsection 1 of the 1969 Childrens Act), residential care orders (ss.22 and 24 CJA'82 inserted after s.20A subsection of the 1969 Childrens Act) and care orders (s.7 subsection 7, of the Childrens Act 1969).

Custodial sentences

These were cases involving remands in custody, detention centre orders (s.4 CJA'82) and youth custody orders (s.6 CJA,82).

A Table of the principal United Kingdom statutes in the network of offending and its treatment (for young offenders), together with those which introduced changes in the network during the period of the study is also shown on page xiii.

Thus, the sample sizes for the outcome variables were 531 police decisions (31.6% of all arrests), 159 acquittals (9.5% of all arrests or court appearances), 652 court non-custodial sentences (38.8% of all arrests or court appearances), 224 court social work and probation sentences (13.3% of all arrests or court appearances) and 116 custodial sentences (6.9% of all arrests or court appearances).

Data sources

Quantitative data were collected between March 1986 and June 1987. The researcher was granted about one day per week study leave by Brent's Department of Social Services in order to carry out the data collection. The sources were official records from the police (Wembley Youth and Community Section), court sections (Brent and Harrow Social Services), Brent's six Area Social Services Offices, local intermediate treatment centres (Forbes House and Morgan Lodge) and the Probation Service (Kilburn and Wembley). All files for the relevant period of the study were perused, in order to match information obtained inter departmentally.

The process of obtaining qualitative information on policy and practice issues locally was a continuous one achieved through participant observation, by virtue of the researcher being employed as a full-time social worker (Adolescents Team) for Brent between March, 1982 and September, 1988. In that capacity, he assisted adolescents appearing before the youth courts (Magistrates and Crown courts). He was also an emergency social worker who facilitated bail arrangements for youths confined to police custody at police stations in and around London (during out of office hours), in pursuance of s.57 and s.66 of the Police and Criminal Evidence Act 1984 which pertain to young offenders' rights and the police code of practice. Certainly, the method of participant observation was useful in assisting the researcher to gain some insight into the subject under investigation, 'in its natural social setting', the limitations of which can be offset by the use of the other methods and with respect to this study, the utilisation of quantitative data. It was thus possible to conduct unstructured interviews with the police, the local youth law centres, Brent Social Services management, area-based social workers, intermediate treatment social workers and probation officers which were written up in note form.

Bivariate analysis

The hierarchically ordered data was first analysed using the computer Statistical Package for Social Sciences (SPSS-X) 'crosstabulation' and 'mult response' procedures to determine the relationship between the dependent variables and the main independent variable, race. However, as Norusis (1987) has pointed out, such bivariate analyses cannot identify causal relationships but only describe an association between two variables, since row and column percentages in a contingency table do not allow for quantification or testing of that relationship, except when use of various indexes that measure the extent of the association is also made, in conjunction with statistical tests of the null hypothesis of independence measured by chi-square. Nonetheless, chi-squared tests in themselves have some limitations, one of which is the fact that they are affected by sample size, so that with a large sample, significance levels of less than 1% will be common, whether or not a substantively significant relationship exists between the variables (Nie 1975: 224). Without adjustments provided by chi-square based tests, such as the Phi coefficient and Cramer's V, a comparison of chi-square values from tables with different sample sizes and different dimensions would be difficult to make (Norusis 1987: 275). Both Phi and V measure the extent of the association on a range of 0 to 1, where a value of 0 corresponds to no association and a value of 1 to a perfect association.

Multivariate analysis

Thus far, most criminological research on police arrests and sentencing in criminal courts have stressed the limited explanatory value of the data presented, emphasising that causal factors other than ethnicity, age and sex are not so readily available (for example, Stevens and Willis 1979; Walker 1986, 1987a; Home Office Statistical Branch, Bulletins 5/89 and 6/89). What was required then, and what this study did in its attempt to fill the void, was to carry out a multivariate analysis of the data, in order to determine the probability of receiving a particular outcome in a local youth criminal justice system. The process involved comparing each court disposal with police diversionary measures, while simultaneously controlling for the influence of the explanatory variables considered in combination with each other. The method was very useful and important in determining the direction of the relationship of the variables since, as explained above, the bivariate analyses of the nominally measured variables only provide contingency tables showing the distribution of the dependent variable changing across levels of the independent variables, as well as the strength of the association, without making assumptions about the nature of that relationship.

Accordingly, the multivariate analysis of the data presented in this study involved using a Generalised Linear Interactive Modelling (GLIM 3.77) software package. It is a statistical modelling tool for specifying and fitting statistical models to data. It assesses goodness of fit and displays the estimates and predicted values from the model. The statistical models that GLIM can fit are known as 'generalised linear models', and these include linear regression, analysis of variance, log-linear, probit and logit. The logit model technique was the one used in this analysis. Compared with the other models logit is the most suitable for binary responses, that is when the dependent variable is dichotomous, such as the paired dependent variables used in this analysis. For instance, probit models could also have been used to model the variables of interest. However, although such models provide adequate estimates, parameters cannot be used to calculate the expected odds of court disposals as against police diversionary measures as they can in logit models. Moreover, regression techniques are not applicable to the modelling of dichotomous dependent variables.

In order to apply the logit model analyses, a paired response design consisting of four pairs of dependent variables was employed, since GLIM is unable to handle categorical response variables. These were:

a)   police decisions vs acquittals,
b)   police decisions vs court non-custodial sentences,
c)   police decisions vs court social work and probation sentences, and
d)   police decisions vs custodial sentences.

This enabled a set of categorical independent variables to be modelled on the probability of receiving an acquittal or any of the other three categories of court disposals as against police decisions to take no further action or to caution suspected young offenders. In this way, it was possible to establish the variables with the most significant influence on the probability of receiving an outcome coded 1 for the dependent or response variable. Consequently, each of the four categories of court disposals were coded 1 and police decisions coded 0, making each of these paired dependent variables a simple 0/1 dichotomy.

It should be noted that various paired dependent variables were designed in modelling the logit analysis, such as police decisions versus cases dismissed, court non-custodial sentences versus court non-custodial social work and probation sentences and non-custodial sentences versus custodial sentences, in order to reflect the sequence of steps observed in the criminal justice system. However, the paired dependent variable police decisions versus each of the four court outcomes was finally adopted in the analysis.

In essence, there were substantive and statistical reasons for relating each of the court outcomes to police decisions. Firstly, it should be noted that sentencing can take place at any point of the tariff and does not necessarily follow the sequence of the tariff (see, e.g., Moxon et al. (1985), *Juvenile Sentencing: Is There a Tariff?*). This being the case, it seemed logical to design a model that analyses a bivariate probability of a particular court outcome as against the probability of diversion from the courts by the police, consistent with the aim of the study. The relevance of the focus of this kind of analysis was that, differences in impact were compared by type of court disposal, in order to determine at what stage of the court process defendants are more likely to be dealt with by the courts as opposed to the police diverting them from a court appearance. Secondly, the parameter race (the main independent variable for the study) was shown to be consistently significant in determining police decisions to take no further action or to caution defendants in all the final models (except in the over 14s analysis of court non-custodial sentences).

The general logit model itself takes the form

$$\log_e p/(1\text{-}p) = a + B_1X_1 + B_2X_2 + B_3X_3 \ldots$$

where a, B_1, B_2 and B_3... are the coefficients to be estimated and X_1, X_2 and X_3... are the independent variables. In other words, in this equation each explanatory variable is associated with a coefficient that represents the direction and the magnitude of the effects of those variables on the response. However, odds can be substituted for the $p/(1\text{-}p)$ in the equation as follows..

$$\log \text{odds} = \%GM + B_1X_1 + B_2X_2 + B_3X_3 \ldots$$

This is why logit is sometimes called the log odds, being the odds in favour of $Y = 1$, or presence of attribute; that is the court disposal as opposed to police decisions. However, in the logit model, the dependent variable is not the actual value of the variable but the $\log_e$ of the odds. The $\log_e$ of the odds is used rather than the odds itself in order that the dependent variable can take on any value from negative to positive infinity. Clearly, if the odds themselves were used, the dependent variable would be bounded by a zero. Note that in GLIM the coefficient 'a' in the above equation is represented by the parameter %GM. Thus, a range of logit models were fitted to the data using this framework, in order to examine the relationship between the odds of receiving a particular court disposal as against police diversionary measures in the institutional processing of young offenders in the London Metropolitan Police District of Brent, and the influencing factors.

Since the aim of this study was to attempt to provide a global test for each independent variable on the response, the most parsimonious logistic model that could be adequately fitted to the data was one which included all possible association effects. The model contained 75 parameters which were weighted according to age group, that is between the under 14 year old defendants and the over 14 year old defendants (the custodial candidates). Therefore, the analysis involved seven logit models each possessing similar parameters testing the influence of those parameters on each of the four court outcomes as against police decisions. As the under 14s are not eligible for custody, they were excluded from the custodial outcome analysis. Splitting the age groups in this way also meant that differences in the direction and magnitude of the same parameters on the same response variable by age of the defendant could be determined except, of course, in the custody model which applied only to the over 14s.

Nonetheless, the logit model fitted to the data did not provide such a good fit and appeared rather over-parameterised; that is, it contained too many 'aliased' or insignificant parameters associated with it. This applied to all the seven models. Thus, only details of the parameter estimates significantly different from zero are given in the final model adopted. As is usual, a significant parameter is taken to be one with a t-value outside the -1.96 to 1.96 range; and the values are derived from dividing the parameter estimates by their standard error. In the logit models insignificant parameter estimates were set to zero or 'aliased', meaning that those cells had missing data (see Healey 1988: 59).

The model that was finally adopted for this study was from a subsample of police decisions vs custodial sentences by the over 14s, which showed 22 significant parameters from a total of 33 categories of race, type of the primary offence, type of the first offence taken into consideration at the same hearing with the primary offence, the total number of offences dealt with at the same hearing and the number of court appearances or arrests. The variables that were found to be insignificant were SEGP (socio-economic group), SES (employed vs unemployed), RESI (residential area), COES (council estate vs private sector housing), TYP3 and TYP4 Offences (3rd and 4th TICs), COUR (type of court) SIRA (Agency providing the Social Inquiry Report), SIR (type of SIR recommendation), NOSP (SIR with no specific recommendation), NOSI (absence of SIR in cases involving custodial sentences) and APPE (appeals).

Given the fact that much of the sociological theorising about criminality and its causation revolves around sex, race and social class, the finding of no significant association between outcomes and socio-economic groups or status is a surprising result. One reason for this could have been the fact that the contribution of these insignificant variables was assessed in combination with the other variables in the same model, which in turn considered RRAC (Race), TYP1 (the type of the primary offences), RTY2 (the type of the first TICs), NOH (the total number of offences dealt with at the same hearing) and NOCA (the total number of court appearances or arrests) to be better predictors of the bivariate probability of court outcomes as against the probability of police diversionary measures. However, as pointed out in chapter two, evidence of the class/crime and the race/crime inter relationship is contradictory and sometimes inconclusive (e.g., Hirschi 1969; Tittle et al 1978; Braithwaite 1981; Box 1986). Again, as stated in chapter two, most of the evidence used to support predictions of class or socio-economic status differences is drawn from official statistics, although differences of opinion do exist in sociological literature between those who argue in favour of the accuracy of official statistics with respect to class and those who argue that the statistics are artificially inflated as a result of official bias and that they are riddled with error (Merton 1957; Box 1986;). In fact, Box (1986) suggests that:

the vast majority... of research... have been unable to provide evidence supporting a greater involvement in delinquency of lower-class adolescents.

(pp. 78-9).

Moreover, Hood (1992) recently found that a significantly higher proportion of black people were unemployed or were not regularly in employment in his study of race and custodial sentences in the West Midlands, but warns that the amount and reliability of this type of information was very much dependent on whether or not a probation officer had compiled a social inquiry report, and that they had done so much less often for black offenders. At any rate, Field (1990) argued that unemployment was in fact a 'lagging' indicator of crime rates (see chapter three). Thus, the importance of social class is still much debated, and this research has implications for that debate.

There were also no interaction effects significant at the 0.05 level in the final saturated logit models fitted to the data which included all possible association effects and a single interaction effect between race and each of the rest of the control variables. This means that significant interaction between race and the type of the primary offence, race and the type of the first offence taken into consideration at the same hearing with the primary offence, race and the total number of offences dealt with at the same hearing and race and the number of arrests or court appearances did not exist in predicting court sentences as against police diversionary measures. However, it was possible to calculate the expected odds and/or probabilities of the outcomes by racial background of the defendant while simultaneously controlling for the influence of this string of explanatory factors, as explained below.

Parameter estimates obtained from the additive model above of the $\log_e$ odds of each of the four court disposals as opposed to police decisions, can also be expressed as multiplicative effects on the odds of each of the court disposals as opposed to police decisions. Multiplicative effects on the odds of a particular court outcome arise from transformations of the parameter estimates in the model into their exponential values. In other words, the multiplicative odds are a way of calculating the odds for any set of parameters in the models, as this bypasses the need to calculate it from the model equation. Simply, the multiplicative form of the odds is the parameter estimate anti log. In this study, the transformed parameter estimates are shown in Figures A2.1 through A2.7 in Appendix 2 (Note 2). Some writers argue that this allows for a more convenient interpretation of the coefficients to be made (Payne 1987: 206).

It should be noted that the odds is a ratio of the probability that an event occurs over the probability that it will not occur. For example, the odds that the courts will pass an acquittal judgement or impose a non-custodial sentence, or a social work and/or a probation sentence, or a custodial sentence on a particular case as against police decisions, is a ratio of the probability that the courts will acquit that case or impose a non-custodial, or a social work and/or probation, or custodial sentence over the probability that the police will decide to take no further action or to caution that case. Let us take a sample of 100 young offenders where 80 received police decisions and 20 an acquittal. The probability of acquittals in that sample is 20%, but the odds of acquittals rather than police decisions are 20/80 = 0.25. In other words, the young offenders in that sample are one quarter as likely to be acquitted as for the police deciding to take no further action or to caution them.

So the odds are an alternative way of expressing probabilities and can be derived from the latter; thus p/(1-p) = odds, where p is the probability of an acquittal or of any of the other three categories of court sentences. Hence, from the above example, the odds of acquittals or of any of the other court disposals as opposed to police decisions are generally given by 0.20/(1-0.20) = 0.25. Equally probabilities can also be derived from odds; thus p = odds/(1+odds). Therefore, an odds of 0.25 in the above example is the same thing as a probability of 20% given by 0.25/(1+0.25). Probabilities, then, are used in the interpretation of the results from the logit analyses presented in Chapters five through eight.

Another useful way of showing parameter estimates and their odds or probabilities is to represent them graphically, as shown in Figure 4.1 overleaf. Suppose that we were interested in finding out the relationship between the odds of receiving court sentences following prosecution as against the odds of receiving police diversionary measures and defendants' characteristics, and after fitting a logit model to the data, the estimates are given as 1, -1 and -2 for the influence on being prosecuted and receiving court sentences of defendants with A, B and C characteristics, respectively. From the simple additive model, A + B + C characteristics Y (the outcome variable coded 1, that is, being prosecuted and receiving court sentences) would be the %GM = 1 for A, 1 + -1 = 0 for B and 1 + -2 = -1 for C. Thus, the linear predictor in Figure 4.1 (and in the subsequent charts) is that part of the logit model equation to the right of the equals sign and representing the Y coefficients. The larger the value for the linear predictor (that is, towards positive infinity) the closer the probability is to 1, and the smaller the value for the linear predictor (that is, towards negative infinity) the closer the probability is to 0.

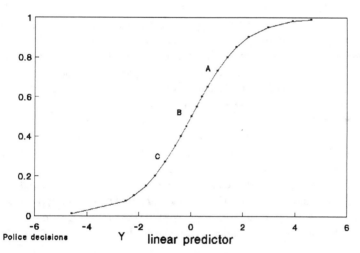

Figure 4.1 Probability of court sentences by defendants' characteristics

The probability values shown in Figure 4.1 are derived from the Y coefficients, thus..

When Y = 1, log odds = A's estimate or the %GM = exp(1)
= 2.72 (anti log)

so that p = 2.72/(1+2.72) = **0.73** for the influence on being prosecuted and receiving court sentences of defendants with A characteristics. Similarly,

63

When Y = 0, log odds = 1 (A's estimate) + -1 (B's estimate)
= exp(0)
= 1 (anti log)

so that $p = 1/(1+1) = \mathbf{0.50}$ for the influence on being prosecuted and receiving court sentences of defendants with B characteristics, and

When Y = -1, log odds = 1 (A's estimate) + -2 (C's estimate)
= exp(-1)
= 0.37 (anti log)

so that $p = 0.37/(1+0.37) = \mathbf{0.27}$ for the influence on being prosecuted and receiving court sentences of defendants with C characteristics.

In other words, the multiplicative effect of comparing A with B characteristics in the linear prediction is to reduce the odds for defendants with A characteristics of being prosecuted and receiving court sentences by a factor of 0.37; that is, the odds become 2.72 (A's odds) times 0.37 (B's odds) = 1.01, or $p = 1.01/(1+1.01) = .5$ or 50%. Similarly, by comparing the same A characteristics with those of C, the effect is to further reduce the odds by a factor of 0.14; that is, the odds become 2.72 (A's odds) times 0.14 (C's odds) = 0.38, or $p = 0.38/(1+0.38) = 0.27$, or 27%.

Accordingly, the plotted result in the example shown in Figure 4.1 suggests that defendants with A characteristics have an increased probability at .73 of receiving a court sentence rather than a police diversionary measure compared to defendants with B or C characteristics, whose probability of receiving such an outcome is .50 and .27 respectively. This means that the probability for defendants with B characteristics of being prosecuted and of receiving court sentences is equal to their probability of receiving police diversionary measures, at 50% compared to defendants with A characteristics. On the other hand, the probability for defendants with C characteristics of being dealt with by way of police diversionary measures rather than court disposals is much higher compared to defendants with A and B characteristics.

Thus, an independent variable whose p is .5 has an equal probability of obtaining either police decisions or court disposals. In these cases the linear predictor is equal to 0, that is the Grand Mean (GM) estimate = 0, or, Y = 0, or, p = 50%. Finally, it should be noted that a positive coefficient in the models indicates over-representation of the variable coded 1, and a negative coefficient (that is, p = <0.5) over-representation of the variable coded 0.

5 Analysing the results: Acquittals

Introduction

The research results presented here, and in chapters six through eight, are from the logit analyses which provided a global test for each independent variable on the response, rather than a series of tests from crosstabular analysis. As stated in the previous chapter, logit surpasses crosstabulation, since it simultaneously estimates the effects of multiple variables.

Factors influencing the odds of acquittal rather than police diversionary measures for the under 14s

The analysis began with an examination of the association between the propensity for young people to be prosecuted by the police and for their cases to be dismissed in the courts on grounds of insufficient evidence rather than receiving police diversionary measures and the influencing factors. Those factors were race, the type of the primary offences committed, the type of the first offences taken into consideration at the same hearing as the primary offences or TICs, the total number of offences dealt with at the same hearing and the number of arrests or court appearances for the 10 - 13 year age group (N = 208). The logit model can also be thought of as representing the relationship between the odds of cases being dismissed in the courts and race, controlling for the influence of the type of primary offences, the type of the first TICs, the total number of offences dealt with at the same hearing and the number of arrests or court appearances. Or, again, as representing the relationship between the odds of cases being dismissed and the type of the primary offences controlling for the influence of race, the type of the first

TICs, the total number of offences dealt with at the same hearing and the number of arrests or court appearances; and so on.

Hence, the model assesses the likelihood of the under 14 year old defendants of being prosecuted and of receiving acquittals in the courts because of weak evidence from the police, rather than the likelihood of the police deciding to take no further action or to caution them, when the independent variables of interest had been controlled for.

Thus, the result shown in Figure A2.1 in Appendix 2 (p. 156), was found after weighting police diversionary measures plus cases dismissed in the courts for all the under 14s and fitting a logit model to the data. In the GLIM scheme, the multiplicative effects corresponding to the first level of each variable are constrained to the value unity, so that all interpretation is made relative to these base categories. In Figure A2.1, for example, the 'constant' parameter estimate -3.112 or 0.04451 (anti log), gives the odds of cases being dismissed in the courts as against police decisions to take no further action or to caution black 10 - 13 year old defendants who were arrested for allegedly committing primary offences of theft or of handling stolen goods, who had no TICs and therefore had only one offence being dealt with, and who were arrested or appearing before the court for the first time, after controlling for the influence of all the other parameters in the model.

In other words, the constant parameter estimate gives the estimated log odds for black under 14s in the model possessing the above mentioned record of offences and arrests or court appearances, whilst the coefficients in the model associated with the other factors represent the increase or decrease in the log odds from this category. Thus, the reference category associated with each variable is set to zero. Positive parameter estimates refer to an increase in the odds of cases dismissed compared to the reference category, whilst negative parameter estimates refer to a decrease in the odds of cases dismissed compared to the reference category.

Thus in relation to race, when the influence of the type of the primary offences, the type of the first TICs, the total number of offences dealt with at the same hearing and that of the number of arrests or court appearances was controlled for in determining the odds of acquittals, the model predicted a negative and highly significant constant (t-value = -4.888, derived from the constant parameter estimate divided by its standard error, that is, -3.112/0.6367), as shown in Figure A2.1. This result meant that black under 14s who were arrested or who appeared before the courts for allegedly committing primary offences of theft or of handling stolen goods for the first time, but who had no TICs, had highly significantly lower odds of receiving acquittals in the courts rather than of receiving police diversionary measures, as it would be expected. This is so, because in recent years, there have been reported increases and encouragement in the use of police cautioning in England and Wales (Home Office 1980; Rutter and Giller 1983; Laycock and Tarling 1984; Mellish 1984; Home Office circular 14/1985). However, the model also suggests that, when compared to the odds of 0.04451 of being prosecuted and of being acquitted in the courts for the above described black children, the odds for both white and Asian children of similar description of being prosecuted and of being acquitted in the courts decreased by factors of 0.67862 and 0.00026, to become 0.04451 x 0.67862 = 0.03021 and 0.04451 x 0.00026 = 0.00001 respectively. However, the differences between the odds of acquittals between black and the other two groups of children were not significant (t-values = -0.533 and -0.123 in the case of white and Asian children respectively). This suggests that all children in the model were treated nearly the same in relation to acquittals as against police diversionary measures.

The model also predicted positive but insignificant results for all children who were arrested or who appeared before the courts charged with primary offences involving conveyances, property, violence and other summary and indictable offences (t-values = 0.335, 0.667, 0.031 and 0.033 respectively). This result meant that the odds for the above described children of being prosecuted and of being acquitted in the courts increased by factors of 1.56189, 1.83437, 1.04108 and 1.04253, to become 0.04451 x 1.56189 = 0.06952 for those who were arrested for having allegedly committed primary offences involving conveyances, 0.04451 x 1.83437 = 0.08165 for property related offences, 0.04451 x 1.04108 = 0.04634 for offences involving violence and 0.04451 x 1.04253 = 0.04640 for other summary and indictable offences compared to the odds of 0.04451 of receiving acquittals for children who were arrested or who appeared in the courts for having allegedly committed primary offences of theft or of handling stolen goods. However, the t-values shown above indicate that the differences between the odds between primary offences of theft or of handling stolen goods and primary offences involving conveyances, property, violence and other summary and indictable primary offences were not significant.

The primary offences result also shows that the odds of being prosecuted and of being acquitted in the courts for those children who were arrested for having allegedly committed primary offences against the police were decreased by a factor of 0.00011, to become 0.04451 x 0.00011 = 0.05E-04 compared to the odds of 0.04451 of acquittals found amongst children who were arrested or who appeared before the courts for having allegedly committed primary offences of theft or of handling stolen goods. However, the difference in the odds between these two groups of children was again not significant (t-value = -0.156).

The result from the analysis of the influence of the type of the first TICs on the response estimates both positive and negative insignificant associations, notwithstanding an increase in the odds of acquittals by a factor of 4359.00893 to become 0.04451 x 4359.00893 = 194.01949 in respect of all children who had offences relating to property as their first TICs compared to the odds of 0.04451 in respect of those children who appeared before the courts without any TICs (t-value = 0.066).

Likewise, the result that was found in respect of the influence of the total number of offences dealt with at the same hearing on the response was also negative and insignificant. This meant that there was an insignificant decrease in the odds of acquittals by factors of 2.31E-04, 1.83E-04 and 1.19E-07 to become 0.04451 x 2.31E-04 = 0.01E-03 in respect of a total of two offences dealt with at the same hearings, 0.04451 x 1.83E-04 = 0.01E-03 for a total of three offences and 0.04451 x 1.19E-07 = 0.05E-07 for a total of four offences dealt with at the same hearings compared to the odds of acquittals of 0.04451 in respect of those children who were arrested with only one offence (t-values = - 0.066, -0.052 and -0.108 respectively).

The only positive and significant result in the model was predicted for all children who were arrested or who appeared before the courts for the fifth time (t-value = 2.836). This suggests that all the under 14s odds of being prosecuted and of being acquitted in the courts increased significantly by a factor of 14.57051 to become 0.04451 x 14.57051 = 0.64853 during their fifth arrest or court appearance compared to the odds of 0.04451 of acquittals during their first arrest or court appearance. However, those children who were arrested or who appeared before the courts for the eighth and the ninth or more time(s) had the highest increases in the odds of being prosecuted and of being acquitted in the courts by factors of 597195.6138 and 498819.7066 to become 0.04451 x 597195.6138 = 26581.177 and 0.04451 x 498819.7066 = 22202.465, respectively compared to the odds of acquittals of only 0.04451 for those who were arrested once, although that result was not statistically significant (t-values = 0.132 and 0.130 respectively). Furthermore, this may indicate a greater readiness on the part of the police to prosecute serious recidivists (see Bazak 1981) even when evidence on current charge(s) on which the courts could convict the children was weak.

The probabilities of acquittals as against the probability of police diversionary measures by race were derived from the constant's multiplicative odds, which were divided by one plus the constant's multiplicative odds, thus:

0.04451/(1+0.04451) = **0.04261** for the influence on acquittals of black children who were arrested or who appeared before the courts for the first time charged with primary offences of theft or of handling stolen goods, but who did not have any TICs at the hearings. The probabilities of acquittals in respect of white and Asian children of similar description were derived from multiplying the constant's multiplicative odds by their (white and Asian) respective multiplicative odds and then dividing the resultant odds by one plus the resultant odds, thus:

0.04451 constant x 0.67862 rrac(2)
= 0.03021

so that p = 0.03021/(1+0.03021) = **0.02932** for the influence on acquittals of similar white children to the above described black children, and

0.04451 constant x 0.00026 rrac(3)
= 0.00001

so that p = 0.00001/(1+0.00001) = **0.00001** for the influence on acquittals of similar Asian children to the above described black children. That is how the probabilities of acquittals in the courts for the constant, controlling for the influence of the other parameters in the model, were calculated. The association in relation to race described above is shown in Figure 5.1.

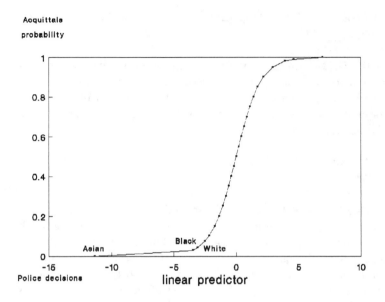

Figure 5.1   Probability of acquittal: Under 14s by race

Thus, the plotted result suggests that all children in the model had a significantly lower probability of being acquitted in the courts as against the probability of receiving police diversionary measures when the stated independent variables had been controlled for.

However, those results also show that there was only a 1% margin of difference in the probabilities of being prosecuted and of being acquitted in the courts in favour of black children compared to white children who were arrested or who appeared before the courts for the first time charged with primary offences of theft or of handling stolen goods, but who had no TICs. The margin of the difference in the probabilities of acquittals between black and Asian children of similar description was slightly larger, at 4%.

The probabilities of receiving acquittals as against the probability of receiving police diversionary measures for the constant, controlling for primary offence type, were derived from:

0.04451 constant x 1.83437 typ1(3)
= 0.08165

so that p = 0.08165/(1+0.08165) = **0.076** for the influence on acquittals of property related primary offences of burglary or of aggravated burglary, or of destroying or damaging property of another, compared to

0.04451 constant x 1.56189 typ1(2)
= 0.06952

so that p = 0.06952/(1+0.06952) = **0.065** for the influence on acquittals of primary offences involving conveyances (offences of unlawful taking of motor vehicles without the owner's consent or lawful authority and/or allowing oneself to be carried in or on it, or of vehicle interference, or of driving without insurance or licence or whilst disqualified or whilst underage), and

0.04451 constant x 1.04253 typ1(8)
= 0.04640

so that p = 0.04640/(1+0.04640) = **0.044** for the influence on acquittals of other summary and indictable primary offences involving fraud, deception, being drunk and disorderly, throwing missiles and breaches of conditions of a current sentence. That is how probabilities of acquittals in the courts for the constant, controlling for the influence of the other types of primary offences in the model, were calculated.

The association in relation to the type of the primary offences described above is shown in Figure 5.2. The plotted result suggests that the probability of being prosecuted and of being acquitted in the courts rather than the probability of receiving police diversionary measures, in respect of all children, was much lower, regardless of the type of the primary offences allegedly committed.

However, when compared to those children who were arrested or who appeared before the courts for having allegedly committed primary offences of theft or of handling stolen goods, those who were arrested for having allegedly committed primary offences relating to property had a higher probability of being acquitted in the courts, whilst the probability of acquittals in respect of those children who were arrested for having allegedly committed the other types of primary offences in the model were lower.

Those children who were arrested for having allegedly committed primary offences which are police defined (offences of attempting to commit a crime and of going equipped for theft or of possession of articles for housebreaking et cetera) had the highest probability of being dealt with by way of police diversionary measures. It can also be seen in Figure 5.2 that the margin of the difference between the probabilities of acquittals between those children who were charged with property related primary offences and those who were charged with police defined offences

70

was 7%, whilst the difference for those who were charged with other primary offences involving conveyances, other summary and indictable offences, violence and theft or handling stolen goods ranged only from 1% to 3%, respectively.

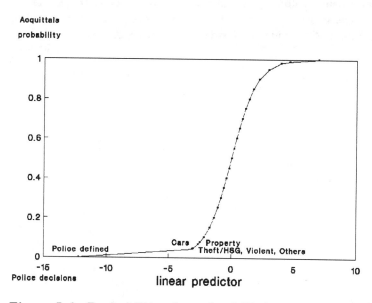

Figure 5.2   Probability of acquittal: Under 14s by type of primary offence

The probabilities of receiving acquittals for the constant, controlling for the number of arrests or court appearances, were derived from

    0.04451 constant x 597195.6138 noca(8)
    = 26581.177

so that p = 26581.177/(1+26581.177) = **0.99996** for the influence on acquittals of the eighth arrest or court appearance compared to

    0.04451 constant x 498819.7066 noca(9)
    = 22202.46514

so that p = 22202.46514/(1+22202.46514) = **0.99995** for the influence on acquittals of the ninth or more arrest(s) or court appearance(s), and

0.04451 constant x 14.57051 noca(5)
= 0.64853

so that p = 0.64853/(1+0.64853) = **0.39340** for the influence on acquittals of the fifth arrest or court appearance. That is how probabilities of acquittals in the courts for the constant, controlling for the influence of the other frequencies of arrests or court appearances in the model, were calculated. The above described association in respect of the number of arrests or court appearances is shown in Figure 5.3.

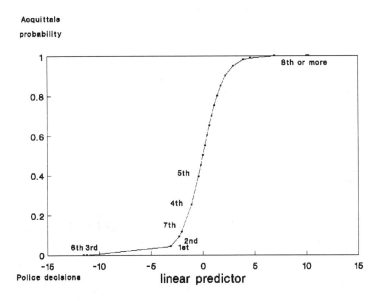

Figure 5.3 Probability of acquittal: Under 14s by number of arrests or court appearances

The plotted result suggests that the probability of being prosecuted and of being acquitted in the courts rather than the probability of receiving police diversionary measures, in respect of those children who were arrested or who appeared before the courts for the eighth or more time(s), was nearly 100% compared to the probability of a similar outcome of only 4% for those who were arrested or who appeared before the courts for the first time. On the other hand, those children who were arrested or who appeared before the courts for the fifth, fourth, seventh, second, first and third, and for the sixth time had probabilities of less than 40% of being acquitted.

72

Conversely, it can be stated from the model that the majority of the under 14s, that is those with a record of arrests or court appearances of less than eight, had higher probabilities of receiving police diversionary measures rather than the probability of being acquitted in the courts. As it is generally assumed that a defendant would be expected to receive a police diversionary measure during their earlier encounter(s) with the police, the lowest probability of 0.00001 of cases dismissed during the sixth arrest is a surprising result.

However, it can be concluded from the above result that the expected probabilities of cases being dismissed in the courts for the under 14s in the model because the police failed to provide the evidence became higher as the frequency of arrests or court appearances increased, when the effect of all the other parameters in the model had been controlled for.

Table A3.1 in Appendix 3 (p. 164) compares the probabilities of being prosecuted and of being acquitted in the courts for the various logical combinations of race, type of primary offences, type of the first TICs, the total number of offences dealt with at the same hearings and the number of arrests or court appearances. However, in order to show strings of variables which positively, as well as significantly, influenced court sentences, the only control variables included in the calculations were all the constant variables, all the primary offences with a positive effect on the response, as well as the number of arrests or court appearances which had a positive and significant effect on the response. These variables were the primary offences of theft or of handling stolen goods, involving motor vehicles, relating to property, involving violence and other summary and indictable primary offences, defendants without any TICs, only one offence dealt with at the hearings and the first, as well as the fifth arrest or court appearance (see the keys in Tables A3.1 and A3.2 in Appendix 3, pages 164 and 165 respectively).

Thus, the estimated probabilities of cases dismissed in the courts as against the probability of receiving police diversionary measures by race, controlling for the influence of the various combinations of variables of interest described above, were derived from:

0.04451 constant x 1.83437 typ1(3) x 14.57051 noca(5)
= 1.18965

so that p = 1.18965/(1+1.18965) = **0.54331** for the influence on acquittals of black children arrested or appearing before the courts for the fifth time, charged with having allegedly committed primary offences involving property, but who did not have any TICs at the hearings. When compared to white children of similar description, the calculation gave a probability of **0.44670** for the influence on acquittals of similar white children to the above described black children. Similarly, the probability of acquittals for similar Asian children was given as **0.03E-02** for the influence on acquittals of similar Asian children to the above described black children. Thus, the probabilities of acquittals as against police diversionary measures by race and any other combination of the control variables shown in Tables A3.1 and A3.2, were calculated in this way.

Table A3.2 in Appendix 3 shows the margins of the difference between the probabilities of being acquitted in the courts as against the probability of receiving police diversionary measures between the three groups of children calculated from the probabilities of the various combinations of the control variables shown in Table A3.1. Clearly, the widest margin of the difference in the probabilities of receiving acquittals in the courts was found between black and Asian children. It was in favour of black children and was followed by the margin of the difference between the probabilities between white and Asian children, in favour of white children. The gap between the probabilities of acquittals between black and white children was somewhat narrower, but in favour of black children.

It can be seen from Table A3.2 that the widest gaps between the probabilities of being acquitted in the courts between the three groups of children became wider only when a fifth arrest or court appearance was included in the calculations, regardless of the influence of the type of primary offences in the model. On the other hand, the gaps between the probabilities between them were much narrower, when arrested or appearing before the courts only for the first time.

Thus, the widest differences between the probabilities of being prosecuted and of being acquitted in the courts as against the probability of receiving police diversionary measures (margins of 54%, 45% and 10% between black and Asian, white and Asian, and black and white children, respectively) were found amongst those children who were arrested or who appeared before the courts for the fifth time without any TICs and charged with primary offences involving property. On the other hand, the narrowest margins of the difference between the probabilities, that is of only 4%, 3% and 1% between the three respective groups of children, were found amongst those who were arrested or who appeared before the courts for the first time without any TICs and charged with primary offences involving theft or handling stolen goods. The differences described above reflect the police tendency to prosecute 'recidivists' arrested for allegedly committing more serious offences, despite insufficient evidence on which to convict them compared to being arrested only once for allegedly committing less serious offences. In those cases the sentencing was almost equal.

Summary

The result obtained from an analysis of the relationship between the odds for all children in the model of being prosecuted and of being dismissed in the courts as against their odds of receiving police diversionary measures suggests that those children who were arrested or who appeared before the courts for the fifth time were significantly more likely to have been acquitted in the courts and less likely to have received police diversionary measures compared to those children who were arrested only once (t-value = 2.836). However, the highest probabilities of such an outcome, that is of nearly 100%, were found amongst those children who were arrested for the eighth and the nineth or more time(s) compared to those who were arrested only once, as well as amongst those who had property related offences as their first TICs compared to those without any TICs, although these results were not significant (t-values = 0.132, 0.130 and 0.066 respectively).

The overall probability of cases being dismissed in the courts due to weak evidence following prosecution by the police was much higher for black children compared to the probabilities of cases dismissed for Asian or white children, notwithstanding the influence of the type of primary offences, type of the first offences which were taken into consideration at the same hearings with the primary offences, the total number of offences dealt with at the same hearing and the number of arrests or court appearances.

The difference between the probabilities applying to the three groups of children suggests that Asian children were less likely to have been acquitted in the courts and more likely to have received police diversionary measures, when compared to the other two groups of children. Likewise, black children were more likely to have been acquitted in the courts rather than to have received police diversionary measures when compared to the other two groups of children. White children, on the one hand, were more likely to have been acquitted in the courts when compared to Asian children and, on the other, they were more likely to have received police diversionary measures when compared to black children.

Factors influencing the odds of acquittal rather than police diversionary measures for the over 14s

The next analysis involved an examination of the relationship between the odds of cases dismissed as against police decisions and race, the type of the primary offences, the type of the first TICs, the total number of offences dealt with at the same hearing and the number of arrests or court appearances for the 461 over 14 year old defendants. Thus, the result shown in Figure A2.2 in Appendix 2 (p. 157) was found after weighting police decisions plus acquittals for all the over 14 year old young persons and fitting a logit model to the data.

It should be noted that the odds and probabilities presented in this and subsequent analyses were calculated in the same way as they were calculated in the under 14s analysis.

It can thus be seen from Figure A2.2 that the model predicted a negative and highly significant constant (t-value = -4.629), meaning that the black young persons who were arrested or who appeared before the courts for the first time charged with having allegedly committed primary offences of theft or of handling stolen goods, but who had no TICs at the hearings, had very significantly lower

75

odds of being prosecuted and of being acquitted in the courts as opposed to the odds of receiving police diversionary measures, as would be expected. The odds were only 0.22515. The model also predicted a negative and significant contribution to the response in respect of white young persons (t-value = -2.079), meaning that when compared to the odds of being acquitted in respect of black young persons described above, the odds of acquittals for similar white young persons in the model decreased significantly from 0.22515 to 0.13587. Asian young persons also had a negative but insignificant estimate associated with them, meaning that the difference between the odds of acquittals between black and Asian young persons was not significant (t-value = -1.125), in spite of the decrease in the odds of acquittals in respect of Asian young persons from 0.22515 to 0.11277.

A positive and significant result was also predicted for all young persons who were arrested or who appeared before the courts charged with primary offences involving violence; that is, offences of assaults occasioning actual or bodily harm, aggravated assaults and malicious wounding, robbery and aggravated robbery and of carrying offensive weapons (t-value = 3.061). This result meant that there was a significant increase in the odds of being acquitted in the courts for those young persons arrested for having allegedly committed primary offences of violence to 0.69978 compared to the odds of 0.22515 of acquittals, in respect of those young persons who were arrested for having allegedly committed primary offences of theft or of handling stolen goods.

The primary offences result also shows insignificant increases in the odds of acquittals as against police diversionary measures for those young persons who were arrested for having allegedly committed primary offences relating to property and police defined offences from 0.22515 for those who were arrested for having allegedly committed primary offences of theft or of handling stolen goods to 0.23076 and 0.29862 (t-values = 0.073 and 0.586 respectively). The other types of primary offences in the model had negative and insignificant estimates associated with them.

The model also predicted a negative and significant result for all young persons who had offences relating to property as their first offence taken into consideration at the same hearings as the primary offences (t-value = -2.027). This meant that, compared to the odds of acquittals in respect of those young persons who were arrested or who appeared before the courts without any TICs, there was a significant decrease in the odds of acquittals in respect of young persons who had offences relating to property as their first TICs, from 0.22515 to 0.00899. The other types of first TICs in the model had both insignificant positive and negative estimates associated with them, notwithstanding the largest increase in the odds of acquittals in the whole model for all those who had offences involving possession of drugs, as their first offence taken into consideration at the same hearings as the primary offences, from 0.22515 to 69.61719.

As regards the influence of the total number of offences dealt with at the same hearing as the primary offences on acquittals as against police diversionary measures, the model predicted positive but insignificant results for all young persons arrested or appearing in the courts with a total of two and three offences dealt with at the same hearings (t-values = 0.747 and 1.479 respectively). This suggests that, when compared to the odds of acquittals for those young persons who appeared before the courts charged with only one offence, there were insignificant increases in the odds of acquittals in respect of all those young persons who were arrested or who appeared before the courts with two and three offences which were dealt with at the same hearings, from 0.22515 to 0.54581 and 1.61286 respectively.

It can be seen from Figure A2.2 that positive and significant results were predicted for all young persons who were arrested or who appeared before the courts for the third, fifth through the eighth time (t- values = 3.214, 3.375, 1.990, 2.784 and 2.790 respectively). The result in respect of those who appeared before the courts for the ninth or more time(s) was also positive but highly significant (t-value = 4.939). This suggests that all the young persons' odds of being acquitted in the courts as against the odds of receiving police diversionary measures increased significantly to 0.71535, 1.03460, 0.70048, 1.39238 and 1.39238 when arrested or appearing before the courts for the third, fifth through the eighth time, respectively, when compared to the odds of 0.22525 of acquittals during their first arrest or court appearance. The increase in the odds of acquittals to 2.75664 for those who appeared before the courts for the ninth or more time(s) was highly significant when compared to the odds of 0.22515 of acquittals during their first arrest or court appearance. It should be noted that the result for those young persons who were arrested twice and four times was also positive but insignificant (t-values = 1.330 and 1.386) respectively.

The association in relation to race for the over 14s who were arrested or who appeared before the courts for the first time charged with having allegedly committed primary offences of theft or of handling stolen goods, but who did not have any TICs at the hearings described on pages 75-6 is shown in Figure 5.4 overleaf. The plotted result suggests that all young persons in the model had significantly lower odds of being acquitted in the courts as opposed to their probability of receiving police diversionary measures, when the independent variables described above had been controlled for. However, those results also show that there was a 6% margin of difference in the probabilities of being acquitted in the courts between black and white young persons, in favour of black young persons. As stated before, that level of difference between them was found to be statistically significant, whilst the 8% margin of difference in the probabilities of acquittals between black and Asian young persons of similar description, again in favour of black young persons, was not.

The association in relation to the type of the primary offences described on page 76 is shown in Figure 5.5. Thus, the plotted result in Figure 5.5 suggests that the probability of being acquitted in the courts, in respect of all young persons, was lower, regardless of the type of the primary offences allegedly committed. However, when compared to those young persons who were arrested or who appeared before the courts for having allegedly committed primary offences of theft or of handling stolen goods, those who were arrested for having allegedly committed primary offences involving violence had a higher probability of being acquitted in the courts, that is of 41%, whilst the probabilities of acquittals in respect of those young persons who were arrested for having allegedly committed the other types of primary offences in the model were less than 23%. Those who were arrested for having allegedly committed primary offences involving possession of drugs had the highest probability of being dealt with by way of police diversionary measures. Their probability of receiving an acquittal in court was slightly less than 10%, when compared with those arrested for committing other types of primary offences.

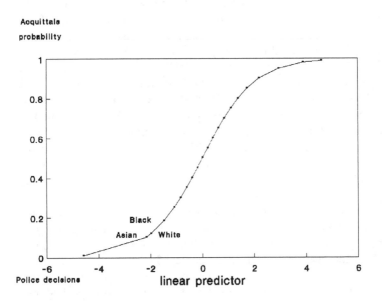

Figure 5.4   Probability of acquittal: Over 14s by race

It can thus be seen in Figure 5.5 that the margin of the difference between the probabilities of acquittals between those young persons who were charged with primary offences involving violence and those who were charged with possession of drugs was found to be 32%, whilst that difference in relation to those who were charged with primary offences which were police-defined, relating to property, involving theft or handling stolen goods, motor vehicles, other summary and indictable primary offences and primary offences against the police, ranged from 18% to 31% respectively. This suggests that those over 14s who were arrested or

78

who appeared before the courts for having allegedly committed primary offences involving violence were much more likely to have been acquitted in the courts compared to the likelihood of a similar outcome in respect of those over 14s who were arrested with having allegedly committed the other types of primary offences shown in the model.

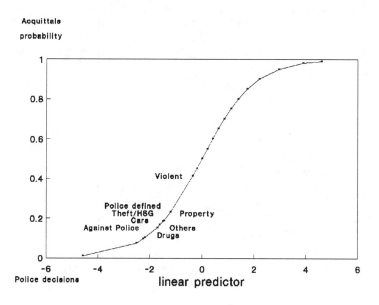

Figure 5.5   Probability of acquittal: Over 14s by type of primary offence

The association in relation to the type of the first TICs described on page 76 is shown in Figure 5.6. The plotted result suggests that the probability of being acquitted in respect of those young persons who appeared before the courts with offences involving possession of drugs and violence as first TICs was nearly 100% and 55% respectively, when compared to the probability of acquittals of only 18% in respect of those young persons who appeared before the courts without any TICs. Thus, the margin of the difference in the probabilities of acquittals between those over 14s who appeared before the courts with offences of possession of drugs and those who appeared with offences involving violence as their first TICs was 43%. That margin of difference in respect of those over 14s who appeared before the courts without any TICs, or with police defined offences, theft or handling stolen goods, motor vehicles, other summary and indictable offences and property related offences as their first TICs, increased from 80% to 98% respectively.

The association in respect of the number of arrests or court appearances described on page 77 is shown in Figure 5.7 overleaf.

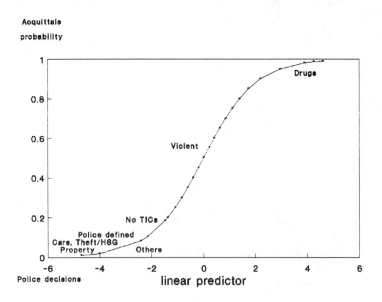

Figure 5.6   Probability of acquittal: Over 14s by type of first TIC

The plotted result in Figure 5.7 suggests that the probability for all the young persons in the model of being acquitted rather than the probability of receiving police diversionary measures increased as the frequency of arrests or court appearances increased. Those who were arrested or who appeared before the courts for the ninth or more time(s) were found to have had a higher probability of being acquitted, that is of 73% compared to the probabilities of acquittals in respect of those who appeared before the courts during other times. This result reflects the reluctance on the part of the police to use cautions on people who keep offending (see Laycock and Tarling 1984), allied to their inability to get evidence.

It can also be seen in Figure 5.7 that the margin of the difference between the probabilities of acquittals between those over 14s who were arrested or who appeared before the courts for the ninth or more time(s) and those who were arrested or who appeared before the courts for the first time was found to be 55%, whilst that difference in respect of those young persons who were arrested or who appeared before the courts for the eighth, seventh, fifth, third, sixth, fourth and the second time was found to have ranged from 15% to 47% respectively.

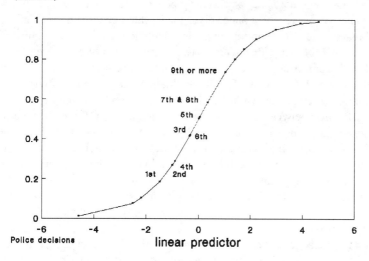

**Figure 5.7 Probability of acquittal: Over 14s by number of arrests
or court appearances**

Table A3.3 in Appendix 3 (p. 166) compares the probabilities of being acquitted for the various logical combinations of race, type of primary offences, type of the first TICs, the total number of offences dealt with at the same hearings and the number of arrests or court appearances. However, the only control variables included in the calculations were all the constant variables, all the primary offences with a positive, as well as a positive and significant effect on the response and all arrests or court appearances which had positive and significant effects on the response. These variables were the primary offences of theft or of handling stolen goods, involving motor vehicles, violence and those which were police defined, defendants without any TICs, only one offence dealt with at the hearings and the first, third, fifth through nineth or more arrest(s) or court appearance(s) (see the keys in Tables A3.3 and A3.4 in Appendix 3, pages 166 and 167 respectively).

Probabilities of cases dismissed in the courts as against the probability of receiving police diversionary measures by race controlling for the influence of the various combinations of variables of interest described above, were estimated by multiplying the constant's multiplicative odds by the parameter estimate's multiplicative odds, as in the under 14s analysis.

Table A3.3 shows that, when compared to black young persons, both Asian and white young persons in the model were more likely to have received police diversionary measures. Thus, they were less likely to have had their cases dismissed in the courts, notwithstanding the combination of the control variables included in the calculations. On the other hand, black young persons were more likely to have been acquitted than to have received police diversionary measures, again irrespective of the combination of the control variables included in the calculations. For example, the margin of the difference between the probabilities of acquittals between black and Asian young persons who were arrested or who appeared before the courts without any TICs, for the fifth time charged with primary offences of theft or of handling stolen goods, was 17%. For primary offences involving motor vehicles the difference between them was also found to be 17%; for offences involving violence, 15%; and for offences which were police-defined the difference was also 17%. When compared with the probabilities of acquittals for equivalent white young persons, that margin of the difference between the probabilities of acquittals between black and white young persons was found to be slightly smaller, that is a difference of 12% for theft or handling stolen goods, 13% for offences involving motor vehicles, 10% for offences involving violence and 13% for offences which were police defined.

Table A3.4 in Appendix 3 shows the margins of the difference between the probabilities of being acquitted in the courts as against the probability of receiving police diversionary measures between the three groups of young persons in the model, calculated from the probabilities of the various combinations of the control variables shown in Table A3.3. Clearly, the widest margin of difference in the probabilities of receiving acquittals in the courts was found between black and Asian young persons, in favour of black young persons, followed by the margin of difference between the probabilities for black and white young persons, again in favour of black young persons. The gap between the probabilities of acquittals between white and Asian young persons was found to be narrower, but in favour of white young persons. Thus, the widest margins of the difference between the probabilities of being acquitted in the courts (margins of 17%, 13% and 5% between black and Asian, black and white, and white and Asian young persons, respectively) were found amongst the following young persons:

a) those who appeared before the courts for the fifth time without any TICs charged with police defined primary offences, that is offences of attempting to commit crime, or of going equipped for theft, or of possession of articles for housebreaking, et cetera, and

b) those who appeared before the courts for the seventh and eighth time without any TICs charged with primary offences involving theft or handling stolen goods and property (burglary, aggravated burglary and destroying or damaging property of another).

The difference suggests a greater willingness on the part of the police to prosecute black over 14 year old 'recidivists' whom they suspected of attempting to commit offences and those arrested for allegedly committing offences involving theft or handling stolen goods, but without providing sufficient evidence to secure their conviction, when compared to their white and Asian counterparts.

On the other hand, the narrowest margins of the difference between the probabilities, that is of 8%, 6% and 2% between the three respective groups of young persons in the model, were found amongst those who were arrested or who appeared before the courts for the first time without any TICs charged with primary offences involving theft or handling stolen goods. In this case the difference suggests a concern for equitable sentencing.

Summary

The result which was obtained from an analysis of the relationship between the odds of all the young persons in the model being dismissed in the courts as against the odds of receiving police diversionary measures suggests that only those young persons who were arrested for having allegedly committed primary offences involving violence were significantly more likely to have been acquitted in the courts and less likely to have received police diversionary measures compared to those who were arrested for having allegedly committed primary offences of theft or of handling stolen goods (t-value = 3.061). A similar result was also found amongst those young persons who were arrested or who appeared before the courts for the third, fifth through ninth or more time(s) when compared to those who were arrested or who appeared before the courts only once (t-values = 3.214, 3.375, 1.990, 2.784, 2.790 and 4.939 respectively). However, the highest probability of such an outcome, that is of nearly 100%, was found amongst those young persons who had offences involving possession of drugs taken into consideration as their only previous offence at the same hearings as the primary offences compared to those who appeared before the courts without any TICs, although that result was not statistically significant (t-value = 0.683).

However, the overall probability of cases being dismissed in the courts due to insufficient evidence following prosecution by the police was much higher for black young persons compared to the probabilities of cases dismissed for Asian and white young persons, notwithstanding the influence of the type of primary offences, the type of the first offences which were taken into consideration at the same hearings with the primary offences, the total number of offences dealt with at the same hearing and the number of arrests or court appearances included in the calculations. This implies that the police were much more prepared to prosecute black young persons even on weak evidence and were comparatively more lenient towards white and Asian young persons, regardless of the control variables included in the calculations. Moreover, the difference in the probability of being acquitted between the three groups of young persons suggests that Asian young persons were less likely to have been acquitted in the courts and more likely to have received police diversionary measures, when compared to the other two groups of young persons. Likewise, black young persons were more likely to have been acquitted in the courts rather than to have received police diversionary measures when compared to the other two groups of young persons. In fact, the difference between the probabilities of being acquitted in the courts between black and white young persons was found to have been significant. White young persons, on the other hand, were more likely to have been acquitted in the courts when compared to Asian young persons and, on the other, they were significantly more likely to have received police diversionary measures when compared to their black counterparts. Finally, the trend in the probabilities of acquittals in favour of black young persons was consistent with that observed in the under 14s analysis.

6 Court non-custodial sentences

Introduction

This chapter examines the relationship between the odds of court non-custodial sentences against police decisions and race, the type of the primary offences, the type of the first TICs, the total number of offences dealt with at the same hearing and the number of arrests or court appearances. The model thus makes a direct comparison of the association between the propensity for young people to be prosecuted, convicted and then conditionally discharged or bound over in order to keep the peace or fined or being ordered to pay compensation or to receive an attendance centre order in court as opposed to the propensity for the police deciding to take no further action or to caution them, and the influencing factors on these decisions.

It should be noted that the largest number of observations were provided by this model for both age groups compared to the number of observations from the other five models (N = 347 for the under 14s and 794 for the over 14s).

Factors influencing the odds of court non-custodial sentences rather than police diversionary measures for the under 14s

The next analysis involved examining the relationship between the odds of court non-custodial sentences as opposed to police diversionary measures and the influencing factors mentioned above for the 347 under 14 year old defendants. Thus, the result shown in Figure A2.3 in Appendix 2 (p. 158) was found after weighting police decisions plus court non-custodial sentences for all the under 14s and fitting a logit model to the data.

It can thus be seen from Figure A2.3 that the model predicted a negative and highly significant constant (t-value = -5.469) meaning that the black under 14s who were arrested or who appeared before the court for the first time having allegedly committed primary offences of theft or of handling stolen goods, but who had no TICs at the hearing had very significantly lower odds of being prosecuted and then of receiving non-custodial sentences in the courts as opposed to the police deciding to take no further action or to caution them. The odds were 0.20454. The other two race variables had insignificant estimates associated with them, despite the increase in the odds of court non-custodial sentences from 0.20454 for black children described above to 0.25130 in respect of similar Asian children (t-value = 0.268).

The model also predicted a negative and significant result for all the children arrested with having allegedly committed primary offences which are police-defined, that is with offences of going equipped for theft or of possession of articles for housebreaking or of attempting to commit a crime (t-value = -2.081). This meant that such children's odds of receiving a court non-custodial sentence rather than of receiving a police diversionary measure decreased significantly to become 0.01669 when compared to the odds of 0.20454 for those who were arrested for having allegedly committed primary offences of theft or of handling stolen goods. The other types of primary offences had insignificant estimates associated with them, notwithstanding the increase in the odds by a factor of 624.53040 to become 127.74145 for all the children who were arrested with primary offences against the police, that is of assaulting or of obstructing the police in the execution of their duty, or of using threatening, abusive or insulting words or behaviour (t-value = 0.286).

The result from the analysis of the influence of the type of the first TICs on the response shows both positive and negative insignificant estimates associated with them, notwithstanding increases in the odds of receiving non-custodial sentences in the courts from the odds of 0.20454 for those children who appeared before the courts without any TICs, to become 0.75882 for all children who had offences of theft or of handling stolen goods as their first TICs, 3.78108 for those who had offences involving motor vehicles their first TICs, 0.48871 for those who had offences relating to property as their first TICs, 1.03666 for those who had offences involving violence as their first TICs and 2.86340 in respect of all children who had other summary and indictable offences taken into consideration, as their first TICs at the same hearing as the primary offences (t-values = 0.816, 1.511, 0.542, 1.022 and 1.301 respectively).

Likewise, the result that was found in respect of the influence of the total number of offences that were dealt with at the same hearing on the response was both negative and positive, but insignificant, regardless of an increase in the odds of non custodial sentences in the courts from 0.20454 in respect of the influence of only one offence on the response to 0.33191 in respect of a total of four offences which were dealt with at the same hearings (t-value = 0.285).

However, the only positive and highly significant and significant result was that

86

which was predicted for all the children who were arrested or who appeared before the courts for the second through fourth and fifth through seventh time (t-values = 7.008, 5.418 and 4.606 and 2.828, 2.819 and 2.195 respectively). This suggests that, when compared to the odds of being prosecuted and of receiving non-custodial sentences in the courts as opposed to the police deciding to take no further action or to caution those children who were arrested or who appeared before the courts for the first time, there were highly significant increases in the odds of being prosecuted and of receiving non-custodial sentences in the courts from 0.20454 to become 2.03604 in respect of those who were arrested or who appeared before the courts for the second time, 2.46948 for those who were arrested for the third time and 4.49519 for those arrested for the fourth time. For those who were arrested for the fifth through the seventh time, the increase from 0.20454 to become 1.33644, 2.44980 and 6.24018 respectively, was also significant. It should be noted that all the children who were arrested or who appeared before the courts for the eighth or ninth or more time(s) had the highest odds in the model of being prosecuted and of receiving non-custodial sentences in the courts, although the increase in the odds from 0.20454 to become 1002.25554 and 569.07275 was not significant (t-values = 0.378 and 0.352 respectively).

The relationship in relation to race for the under 14s described on pages 85-6 is shown in Figure 6.1.

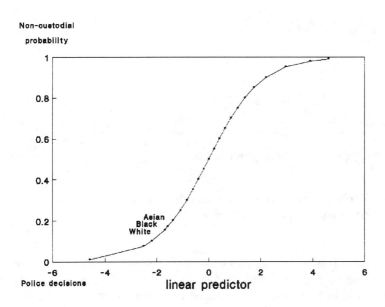

Figure 6.1   Probability of court non-custodial sentences: Under 14s by race

The plotted result clearly shows that all the children in the model had a higher probability of receiving a police decision to take no further action or to caution them as against the probability of being prosecuted and of receiving a non-custodial sentence in the courts when the above variables had been controlled for.

However, the probability of non-custodial sentences for Asian children was the highest in the model compared to their black and white counterparts, although the margin of the difference between the probabilities is only 3% and 5% respectively. On the other hand, the probability of receiving police diversionary measures as opposed to being prosecuted and receiving non-custodial sentences in the courts was higher for white children compared to the probabilities of black and Asian children.

The relationship in relation to the type of the primary offences described on page 86 is shown in Figure 6.2.

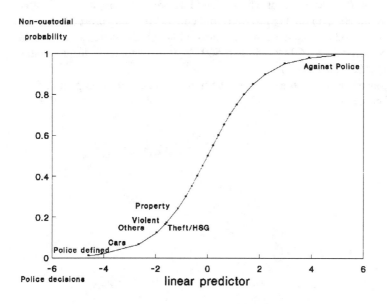

**Figure 6.2   Probability of court non-custodial sentences: Under 14s
by type of primary offence**

The plotted result in Figure 6.2 suggests that when compared to children who were arrested for having allegedly committed primary offences of theft or of handling stolen goods, those children who were arrested for having allegedly committed primary offences against the police (assaulting or obstructing the police in the execution of their duty, or using threatening, abusive or insulting words or behaviour) had a nearly 100% probability of being prosecuted, convicted and of receiving a court non-custodial sentence rather than the probability of receiving a police diversionary measure.

It can also be seen in Figure 6.2 that the rest of the children in the model who were arrested for having allegedly committed the other types of the primary offences involving property, or theft or handling stolen goods, or violence, or other summary and indictable offences, or motor vehicles, or police defined offences had probabilities of being prosecuted and of receiving non-custodial sentences in the courts of less than 24%. The lowest probabilities of such an outcome, that is of only 7% and 2%, were found to have been amongst those children who were arrested for having allegedly committed primary offences involving motor vehicles (unlawful taking of motor vehicles without the owner's consent or lawful authority and/or for allowing themselves to be carried in or on it, or for vehicle interference, or for driving without insurance or licence or whilst disqualified or underage) and amongst those arrested for having allegedly committed police defined primary offences (going equipped for theft or of possession of articles for housebreaking, or of attempting to commit a crime) respectively, when compared with children who were arrested for having allegedly committed primary offences of theft or of handling stolen goods. Consequently, these children were more likely to receive police diversionary measures compared to the likelihood of such an outcome in respect of those arrested for having allegedly committed primary offences against the police.

The association in respect of the number of arrests or court appearances described on pages 86-7 is shown in Figure 6.3. The plotted result suggests that, when compared to children who were arrested or who appeared before the courts for the first time, those children in the model who were arrested or who appeared before the courts more than once had much higher probabilities of being prosecuted, convicted and of receiving court non-custodial sentences. Figure 6.3 also shows that the probabilities of non-custodial sentences increased as the frequency of arrests or court appearances increased. Only those children who were arrested or who appeared before the courts for the first time had a much lower probability, that is of only 17% of being prosecuted and of receiving a non-custodial sentence, whilst the probabilities for those who were arrested or who appeared before the courts for the eighth or more times was nearly 100%. The probabilities of court non-custodial sentences for those children who were arrested or who appeared before the courts during other times ranged from 57% to 86%.

Table A3.5 in Appendix 3 (p. 168) compares the probabilities of receiving court non-custodial measures by race and the various logical combinations of the control variables for all the children in the model. However, the only control variables included in the calculations were all the constant variables, all the primary offences which had positive effects on the response and all arrests or court appearances which had both positive and significant effects on the response. These variables were primary offences of theft or of handling stolen goods, as well as those relating to property and those against the police, children without TICs, only one offence dealt with at the hearing and the first through seventh arrest or court appearance (see the keys in Tables A3.5 and A3.6 in Appendix 3, pages 168 and 169 respectively).

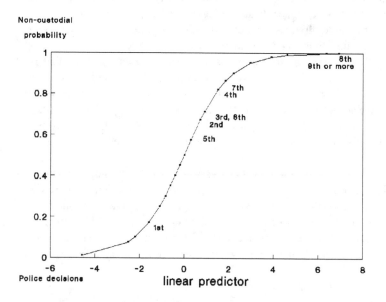

Figure 6.3 Probability of court non-custodial sentences: Under 14s by number of arrests or court appearances

It can be seen from Table A3.5 that the group with the highest probability of having been prosecuted, convicted and of having received court non-custodial sentences as against the probability of receiving police diversionary measures were Asian children, irrespective of the different combinations of the control variables included in the calculations.

Table A3.6 in Appendix 3 shows the margins of the difference between the probabilities of being prosecuted, convicted and of receiving non-custodial sentences in the courts as against the probability of receiving police diversionary measures between the three groups of children in the model, which were calculated from the probabilities of the various combinations of the control variables shown in Table A3.5. Clearly, the widest margin of difference in the probabilities of receiving court non-custodial sentences was found to have been between Asian and white children, in favour of Asian children, followed by the margin of the difference between the probabilities between Asian and black children, again in favour of Asian children. The gap between the probabilities of court non-custodial sentences between black and white children was found to have been narrower, but in favour of black children.

Thus, the widest margins of the difference between the probabilities of being prosecuted, convicted and of receiving court non-custodial sentences (margins of 8%, 5%, and 3% between Asian and white, Asian and black, and black and white children, respectively), were found amongst those children who were arrested or who appeared before the courts for the fifth time without any TICs charged with primary offences involving theft or handling stolen goods. On the other hand, the margin of the difference between the probabilities of receiving a court non-custodial sentence between the three groups of children who were arrested for allegedly committing primary offences against the police was found to be almost zero, regardless of the number of times that they were arrested or appeared before the courts. In this case this result suggests that all the children in the model were sentenced equally when the type of the primary offence with which they were charged was an offence against the police.

Summary

The result obtained from an analysis of the relationship between the odds of all children being prosecuted, convicted and of receiving non-custodial sentences in the courts as against the odds of receiving police diversionary measures suggests that only those children who were arrested or who appeared before the courts for the second through the seventh time were very significantly and significantly more likely to have received court non-custodial sentences and less likely to have received police diversionary measures (t-values = 7.008, 5.418, 4.606, 2.828, 2.819 and 2.195 respectively). However, the model predicted that those children who were arrested or who appeared before the courts for the eighth and the nineth or more time(s) had the highest probability of nearly 100% of being prosecuted, convicted and of receiving non-custodial sentences in the courts when compared to those who were arrested only once, although that result was not statistically significant (t-values = 0.378 and 0.352 respectively). This suggests that the police were nearly always prosecuting serious 'recidivists' and securing convictions which resulted in their receiving non-custodial sentences in the courts.

The model also predicted that those children who were arrested for having allegedly committed primary offences of assaulting or obstructing the police in the execution of their duty and of using threatening, abusive or insulting words or behaviour had a nearly 100% probability of being prosecuted, convicted and of receiving non-custodial sentences in the courts rather than the probability of receiving police diversionary measures when compared to those children who were arrested for having allegedly committed primary offences of theft or of handling stolen goods. Although that result was not statistically significant (t-value = 0.286), it meant that all those children who were charged with primary offences against the police were, again, nearly always prosecuted by the police, convicted and receiving court non-custodial sentences. On the other hand, those children who were arrested for having allegedly committed police defined primary offences of going equipped for theft or of possessing articles for housebreaking and of attempting to commit a crime received significantly more police diversionary measures as opposed to being prosecuted (t-value = -2.081). This could reflect police reluctance to prosecute defendants arrested for having allegedly committed offences that are difficult to prove in court.

However, the overall probability of being prosecuted, convicted and of receiving court non-custodial sentences as against the probability of receiving police diversionary measures was higher for Asian children compared to the probabilities of court non-custodial sentences for white and black children, notwithstanding the influence of the type of primary offences, the type of the first offences which were taken into consideration at the same hearings with the primary offences, the total number of offences dealt with at the same hearing and the number of arrests or court appearances included in the calculations.

The difference in the probabilities between the three groups of children in the model suggests that Asian children were less likely to have received police diversionary measures and more likely to have received non-custodial sentences in the courts compared to their white and black counterparts. Likewise, black children were slightly less likely to have received police diversionary measures and slightly more likely to have been prosecuted, convicted and to have received court non custodial sentences compared to their white counterparts.

Factors influencing the odds of court non-custodial sentences rather than police diversionary measures for the over 14s

The next analysis involved an examination of the relationship between the odds of non-custodial sentences as opposed to police decisions for the 794 over 14 year old defendants and the same influencing factors as those used in the under 14s analysis described above. Accordingly, the result shown in Figure A2.4 in Appendix 2 (p. 159) was found after weighting police decisions plus court non-custodial sentences for all the over 14s and fitting a logit model to the data.

It can thus be seen from Figure A2.4 that the model predicted a negative and insignificant constant (t-value = -0.752). This meant that the black over 14s who were arrested or who appeared before the courts for the first time with having allegedly committed primary offences of theft or of handling stolen goods, but who had no TICs at the hearing, had insignificant lower odds of being prosecuted, convicted and of receiving non-custodial sentences in the courts as against the odds of receiving police diversionary measures. The odds were 0.85522. The other two race variables also had negative and insignificant estimates associated with them, in spite of decreases in the odds of court non-custodial sentences from 0.85522 for black young persons described above to 0.62852 and 0.60182, in respect of white and Asian young persons who had a similar record of arrests or of court appearances and of the type of primary offences as the black young persons described above (t-values = -1.875 and -0.967 respectively).

The model also predicted a negative and significant result for all young persons arrested with having allegedly committed other summary and indictable primary offences; that is, with offences involving fraud, deception, arson, being drunk and disorderly, throwing missiles and breaches of conditions of an original sentence (t-value = -2.338). This meant that the odds for such young persons of receiving court non-custodial sentences as opposed to receiving police diversionary measures decreased significantly to become 0.40718 when compared to the odds of 0.85522 for those who were arrested with having allegedly committed primary offences of theft or of handling stolen goods. The other types of primary offences in the model had insignificant estimates associated with them, either positively or negatively.

However, the model did predict some positive and significant results for all young persons who had offences involving conveyances and violence taken into consideration, as their first TICs at the same hearing as the primary offences (t-values = 1.968 and 2.417 respectively). This result meant that, when compared to the odds of 0.85522 of receiving court non-custodial sentences for those young persons who did not have any TICs at the hearings, such young persons' odds of receiving non-custodial sentences in the courts rather than police diversionary measures increased significantly to become 2.58986 and 13.25803 respectively. The other types of first TICs in the model had both positive and negative insignificant estimates associated with them, notwithstanding the largest increases in the odds of non-custodial sentences in the whole model for all those young persons who had offences against the police and of possession of drugs as their first TICs, from 0.85522 to 311.87531 and 245.57526 respectively.

As regards the influence of the total number of offences dealt with at the same hearing as the primary offences on court non-custodial sentences as against police diversionary measures, the model predicted both negative and positive insignificant results in respect of those young persons who were arrested or who appeared in the courts with a total of two and three offences which were dealt with at the same hearings when compared to the odds of those who were arrested or who appeared in the courts with just one offence (t-values = -0.307 and 0.476 respectively).

The other positive and significant results were predicted for all young persons who were arrested or who appeared before the courts for the second through the seventh and the nineth or more time(s) (t-values = 3.697, 3.783, 2.564, 2.792, 3.126, 2.861 and 2.534 respectively). This suggests that when compared to the odds of being prosecuted, convicted and of receiving court non-custodial sentences for those young persons who were arrested or who appeared before the courts for the first time, the odds increased significantly from 0.85522 to become 1.93945 for the second arrest, 2.14192 for the third arrest, 1.66031 for the fourth arrest, 2.15395 for the fifth arrest, 2.75276 for the sixth arrest, 3.35887 for the seventh arrest and 2.49829 for the ninth or more arrest(s). The increase in the odds of court non custodial sentences during the eighth arrest or court appearance was not significant (t- value = 1.314).

The association in relation to race for the over 14s who were arrested or who appeared before the courts for the first time without any TICs charged with having allegedly committed primary offences of theft or of handling stolen goods described on pages 92-3 is shown in Figure 6.4.

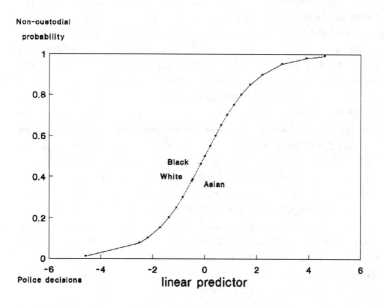

Figure 6.4 Probability of court non-custodial sentences: Over 14s by race

The plotted result suggests that all the over 14 year old defendants in the model had a slightly higher probability of receiving a police decision to take no further action or to caution them rather than the probability of being prosecuted, convicted and of receiving a non-custodial sentence in the courts when the variables of interest had been controlled for. However, the probability of such an outcome was found to be higher for both white and Asian young persons and lower for black young persons. Conversely, this result meant that black young persons' probability of being prosecuted, convicted and of receiving non-custodial sentences in the courts rather than the probability of receiving police diversionary measures was higher compared to the probabilities of their white and Asian counterparts, by a margin of 7% and 8% respectively.

The relationship in relation to the type of the primary offences described on page 93 is shown in Figure 6.5. The plotted result in Figure 6.5 suggests that only

94

those young persons who were arrested for having allegedly committed primary offences against the police had a higher probability, at 55%, of receiving court non custodial sentences as against the probability of receiving police diversionary measures. On the other hand, the probability of receiving a similar outcome in respect of those young persons who were arrested for having allegedly committed the other types of primary offences in the model was found to be below 50%, and ranging from 29% for other summary and indictable offences to 49% for primary offences involving possession of drugs.

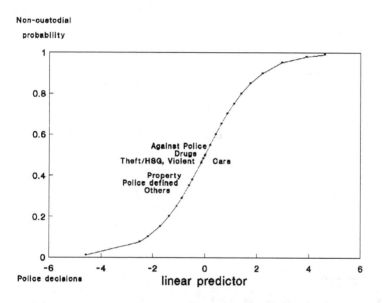

Figure 6.5 Probability of court non-custodial sentences: Over 14s by type of primary offence

Thus, all young persons who were arrested for having allegedly committed other summary and indictable primary offences (fraud, deception, arson, being drunk and disorderly, throwing missiles and breaches of a current sentence) were more likely to receive a police decision to take no further action or to caution them compared to the likelihood of a similar outcome for those arrested for having allegedly committed the other types of the primary offences in the model, in particular offences against the police.

The relationship in respect of the type of the first offences which were taken into consideration at the same hearing as the primary offences described on page 93 is shown in Figure 6.6. The graph shows that those young persons who had no TICs

95

at the hearings and those with police defined offences as their first TICs had a lower probability, at 46%, of being prosecuted, convicted and of receiving non custodial sentences in the courts compared to those who were arrested or who appeared in court charged with the other types of first TICs in the model. Alternatively, those young persons who had offences involving property, theft or handling stolen goods, other summary and indictable offences, conveyances, violence, possession of drugs and offences against the police as their first TICs had probabilities of being prosecuted, convicted and of receiving court non-custodial sentences which ranged from 54% to nearly 100%.

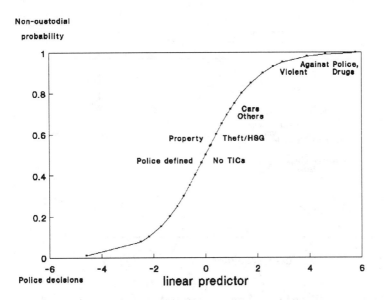

Figure 6.6   Probability of court non-custodial sentences: Over 14s by type of first TIC

The relationship in respect of the number of arrests or of court appearances described on pages 93-4 is shown in Figure 6.7. The plotted result suggests that when compared to young persons who were arrested or who appeared before the courts for the first time, those young persons who were arrested or who appeared before the courts more than once without any TICs charged with primary offences of theft or of handling stolen goods had higher probabilities of being prosecuted, convicted and of being conditionally discharged, or of being bound over in order to keep the peace, or of being fined or ordered to pay compensation, or of receiving an attendance centre order in the courts rather than the probability of receiving police diversionary measures. In fact the probabilities ranged from 62% to 77%, the highest being for those young persons who were arrested or who appeared before the courts for the ninth or more time(s) and for the sixth and the seventh time. Only those young persons who were arrested for the first time were slightly more likely to have received police diversionary measures as against the likelihood of receiving court non-custodial sentences compared to when they were arrested more than once.

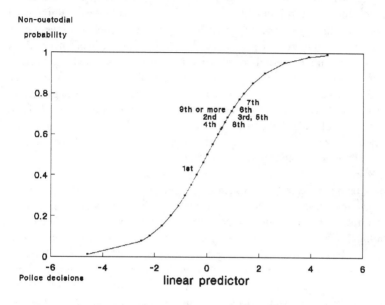

Figure 6.7   Probability of court non-custodial sentences: Over 14 s
by number of arrests or court appearances

Table A3.7 in Appendix 3 (pp. 170-1) compares the probabilities of court non custodial sentences by race and the various logical combinations of race, types of primary offences, types of first TICs, the total number of offences dealt with at the same hearing and the number of arrests or court appearances for all young persons in the model. However, the only control variables included in the calculations were all the constant variables, all the primary offences which had positive results, all offences which had a positive and significant effect on the response which were taken into consideration at the same hearing as the primary offences as first TICs and all arrests or court appearances, again only those which had positive and significant effects on the response. These variables were primary offences of theft or of handling stolen goods, as well as those involving motor vehicles, violence, offences against the police and possession of drugs, defendants without TICs, offences involving motor vehicles, as well as those involving violence as the first TICs, one and two offences dealt with at the same hearing and the first through seventh and the nineth or more arrest(s) or court appeareance(s) (see the keys in Tables A3.7 and A3.8 in Appendix 3, pages 170-1 and 172-3 respectively).

It can also be shown in Table A3.7 that all young persons in the model were more likely to have been prosecuted, convicted and to have received court non custodial sentences and less likely to have received police diversionary measures as the frequency of their arrests or court appearances increased from one, regardless of the combination of the control variables included in the calculations. Although all young persons would have been expected to receive more police diversionary measures during their first arrest, irrespective of the type of primary offences, black young persons in the model were more likely to have been prosecuted and to have received court non-custodial sentences when primary offences against the police were included in the calculation. On the other hand, white and Asian young persons were more likely to have received police diversionary measures and less likely to have been prosecuted for the same offence. This implies a harsher response on the part of the police towards black young persons whom they arrested for the first time for allegedly committing offences against them.

Table A3.8 in Appendix 3 shows the margins of the difference between the probabilities of being prosecuted, convicted and of receiving non-custodial sentences in the courts as against the probability of receiving police diversionary measures between the three groups of young persons in the model, which were calculated from the probabilities of the various combinations of the control variables shown in Table A3.7. Clearly, the widest margin of difference in the probabilities of receiving court non-custodial sentences was found between black and Asian young persons, in favour of black young persons, followed by the margin of the difference between the probabilities between black and white young persons, again in favour of black young persons. The gap between the probabilities of court non-custodial sentences between white and Asian young persons was very narrow, but in favour of white young persons.

Thus, the widest margins of the difference between the probabilities of being prosecuted and of receiving court non-custodial sentences (margins of 9%, 8% and 1% between black and Asian, black and white, and white and Asian young persons, respectively) were found amongst all those young persons who were arrested or who appeared before the courts only once, regardless of the type of primary offences. On the other hand, the narrowest margins of the difference between the probabilities, that is of only 1%, 1% and nearly zero between the three respective groups of young persons, were found amongst the following young persons:

a)   those who were arrested or who appeared before the courts for the third, fifth through seventh and nineth or more time(s) with two offences that were dealt with at the same hearing, that is with primary offences involving theft or handling stolen goods and with offences involving violence which were taken into consideration, and

b)   those who were arrested or who appeared before the courts for the second
        through seventh and nineth or more time(s) with two offences that were
        dealt with at the same hearing, that is with primary offences against the
        police and with offences involving violence which were taken into
        consideration.

The result described above suggests that all young persons in the model were
sentenced equally vis-a-vis non-custodial sentences when arrested or appearing
before the courts more often than once with offences involving violence as their
first TICs.

Summary

The result obtained from an analysis of the relationship between the odds of being
prosecuted, convicted and of receiving court non-custodial sentences against the odds
of receiving police diversionary measures and the independent variables of interest
for the over 14 year old defendants suggests that those young persons who were
arrested or appearing before the courts charged with offences involving conveyances
and violence as their first TICs were significantly more likely to have been
prosecuted and to have received court non-custodial sentences compared to those
young persons without TICs (t-values = 1.968 and 2.417 respectively). However,
the highest probabilities of such an outcome, of nearly 100%, were found amongst
those young persons who were arrested for having allegedly committed offences
against the police, as well as for possession of drugs as their first TICs, although
that result was not significant (t-values = 1.294 and 0.720 respectively). It should
be noted that the under 14s analysis described earlier also showed a probability of
nearly 100% of prosecutions and court non-custodial sentences amongst those
children who were also arrested with primary offences against the police. This,
again, reflects the seriousness with which the police treat offences against them;
that is, their propensity to prosecute such cases than to take no further action or to
caution the defendants.

Those who were arrested or who appeared in the courts for the second through the
seventh time and the nineth or more time(s) were also significantly more likely to
have been prosecuted and to have received court non-custodial sentences compared to
those young persons who were arrested or who appeared before the courts for the
first time (t-values = 3.697, 3.783, 2.564, 2.792, 3.126, 2.861 and 2.534
respectively). It should also be noted that the under 14s analysis also showed
positive and significant as well as highly significant results in relation to a second
through a seventh arrest or court appearance. In this respect, the number of arrests
or court appearances appeared to have been more important than race, type of the

primary offences, type of the first TICs and the total number of offences dealt with at the same hearing in determining prosecutions and court non-custodial sentences for both age groups of the defendants.

However, the overall probability of being prosecuted, convicted and of receiving court non-custodial sentences was higher for black young persons compared to their white and Asian counterparts, notwithstanding the influence of the control variables of interest included in the calculations.

The difference between the probabilities between the three groups of young persons in the model suggests that black young persons were less likely to have received police diversionary measures and more likely to have been prosecuted, convicted and to have received non-custodial sentences in the courts compared to their Asian and white counterparts. Likewise, white young persons were slightly less likely to have received police diversionary measures and slightly more likely to have received court non-custodial sentences compared to their Asian counterparts. However, the under 14s analysis discussed above showed a different trend in that it was the Asian children who were more likely than black or white children to have been prosecuted instead of receiving police diversionary measures.

7 Court social work and probation sentences

Introduction

This chapter examines the relationship between the odds for the different racial groups of receiving court social work and probation sentences as against police diversionary measures and race, the type of the primary offences, the type of the first TICs, the total number of offences dealt with at the same hearing and the number of arrests or court appearances. Hence, the model makes a direct comparison of the association between the propensity for young offenders to receive community service orders, supervision orders, supervision orders with discretionary intermediate treatment requirements, supervision orders with supervised activities requirements, probation orders, remands in care of the Local Authority, residential care orders and full care orders in the courts as against their propensity to receive no further action or cautions from the police and the influencing factors.

Factors influencing the odds of court social work sentences rather than police diversionary measures for the under 14s

The analysis presented here involved an examination of the relationship between the odds of receiving social work sentences in the courts as opposed to the odds of receiving police diversionary measures and the influencing factors mentioned above for the 247 under 14 year old defendants. Accordingly, the result shown in Figure A2.5 in Appendix 2 (p. 160) was found after weighting police decisions plus social work sentences for all the under 14s and fitting a logit model to the data.

It can thus be seen from Figure A2.5 that the model predicted a negative and highly significant constant (t-value = -6.466). This meant that black children in the model who were arrested or who appeared before the courts for the first time, having allegedly committed primary offences of theft or of handling stolen goods, had very significantly lower odds of receiving social work sentences in the courts as against the odds of receiving police diversionary measures. The odds were 0.03916. The other two race variables had positive but insignificant estimates associated with them (t-values = 0.009 and 1.157, in respect of white and Asian children respectively). This meant that there were insignificant increases in the odds of receiving court social work sentences from 0.03916 for black children to 0.03932 and 0.12257 in respect of white and Asian children, respectively.

The model also predicted positive but insignificant results for all children who were arrested for having allegedly committed primary offences relating to property, violence, as well as primary offences against the police (t-values = 1.566, 0.219 and 1.343 respectively). This meant that the increase in such children's odds of receiving social work sentences in the courts as against the odds of receiving police diversionary measures, from 0.03916 for those who were arrested for having allegedly committed primary offences involving theft or handling stolen goods to 0.08847 for offences relating to property, 0.04638 for offences involving violence and 89.46975 for offences against the police, was not significant. The other types of primary offences in the model, that is those involving motor vehicles, police defined offences and other summary and indictable offences, had negative and insignificant estimates associated with them (t-values = - 0.502, -0.262 and -0.476 respectively).

The influence of the type of the first TICs shows positive but insignificant estimates associated with offences involving theft or handling stolen goods, motor vehicles, property, violence and offences against the police as first TICs (t-values = 0.184, 0.012, 0.404, 1.079 and 0.504 respectively). Offences which were police defined and other summary and indictable offences had negative and insignificant estimates associated with them (t-values = -0.417 and -0.119 respectively). This result meant that there were no significant increases or decreases in the odds of receiving social work sentences in the courts, regardless of the influence of the type of the first offences which were taken into consideration at the same hearing as the primary offences when compared to the odds of 0.03916 of receiving a similar outcome in respect of those children who appeared before the courts without any TICs.

The influence of the total number of offences that were dealt with at the same hearing was positive but insignificant for three and four offences that were dealt with at the same hearing (t-values = 0.611 and 0.700 respectively), as well as negative and insignificant for two offences which were dealt with at the same hearing as the primary offences (t-value = -0.056). This result meant that there were no significant increases or decreases in the odds of receiving social work sentences in the courts, when compared to the odds of 0.03916 of receiving a similar outcome for those children who were arrested or who appeared before the courts with only one offence that was dealt with.

Lastly, the model predicted positive, highly significant and significant results for all children who were arrested or who appeared before the courts for the second and third time and for the fourth, sixth, and seventh times (t-values = 4.472, 4.657 and 3.117, 2.177 and 2.704 respectively). This suggests that there were highly significant and significant increases in the odds of receiving social work sentences in the courts as against the odds of receiving police diversionary measures, from 0.03916 in respect of those children who were arrested or who appeared before the courts only once to 0.36346 for children who were arrested for the second time, 0.67429 for those who were arrested for the third time, 0.68791 for those who were arrested for the fourth time, 0.59924 for those who were arrested for the sixth time and 1.62077 for children who were arrested for the seventh time. However, it should be noted that the highest increase in the odds of receiving social work sentences in the whole model, by a factor of 66171.16017 to become 2591.26263, was found amongst those children who were arrested or who appeared before the courts for the ninth or more time(s), although that increase was not significant (t-value = 0.492). Similarly, the increase in the odds of receiving social work sentences amongst those children who were arrested or who appeared before the courts for the fifth time was also insignificant (t-value = 0.744).

The association in relation to race described on pages 101-2 is shown in Figure 7.1.

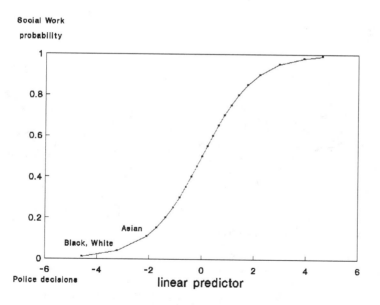

Figure 7.1   Probability of court social work sentences: Under 14s by race

The plotted result clearly shows that all children in the model had a higher probability of receiving a police diversionary measure rather than the probability of receiving a social work sentence in the courts when the variables of interest had been controlled for. However, the probability of such an outcome was found to have been higher for both white and black children compared to the probability of Asian children who were, in fact, found to have had the highest probability of receiving court social work sentences following prosecution by the police compared to their white and black counterparts. Thus, the model suggests that the margin of the difference between the probabilities of receiving court social work sentences as against the probability of receiving police diversionary measures between Asian and the other two groups of children was 7%.

The relationship in relation to the type of the primary offences described on page 102 is shown in Figure 7.2.

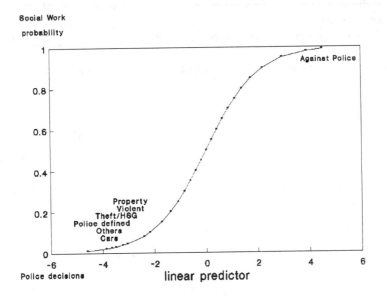

Figure 7.2 Probability of court social work sentences: Under 14s by type of primary offence

This suggests that, when compared to children who were arrested or who appeared before the courts for having allegedly committed primary offences of theft or of handling stolen goods, those children who were arrested for having allegedly committed primary offences against the police had the highest probability (nearly 100%) of having received social work sentences in the courts as against the probability of receiving police diversionary measures. On the other hand, those who were arrested for having allegedly committed primary offences involving motor vehicles had the lowest probability of receiving social work sentences (only 2%). Thus, the margin of the difference between the probability of receiving social work sentences in the courts as against the probability of receiving police diversionary measures between children who were arrested for having allegedly committed primary offences against the police and those who were arrested or who appeared before the courts for having allegedly committed the other types of the primary offences in the model was very high; that is, margins of difference ranging from 91% to 97%.

The association in respect of the number of arrests or court appearances described on page 103 is shown in Figure 7.3.

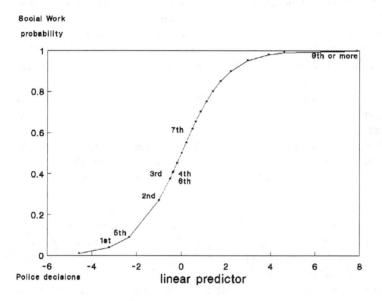

Figure 7.3   Probability of court social work sentences: Under 14s by number of arrests or court appearances

The plotted result suggests that those children who were arrested or who appeared before the courts for the ninth or more time(s) and for the seventh time were more likely to have received social work sentences in the courts and less likely to have received a no further action or caution from the police. On the other hand, those who were arrested or who appeared before the courts for the fourth, third, sixth, second, fifth and for the first time were less likely to have received social work

105

sentences and more likely to have received police diversionary measures.

However, when compared to those children who were arrested or who appeared before the courts for the first time, those children who were arrested or who appeared before the courts more than once were found to have had higher probabilities of receiving social work sentences in the courts as against the probability of having received police diversionary measures. In fact, the probabilities of receiving court social work sentences increased as the frequency of arrests or court appearances increased; that is, from a probability of 4% of receiving social work sentences in respect of those children who were arrested or who appeared before the courts for the first time to a probability of nearly 100% of receiving a similar outcome in respect of those who were arrested or who appeared before the courts for the ninth or more time(s).

Figure 7.3 also shows that the margin of the differences between the probabilities of receiving social work sentences between those children who were arrested or who appeared before the courts for the ninth or more time(s) and those who were arrested or who appeared before the courts for the seventh, fourth, third, sixth, second, fifth and for the first time was 38%, 59%, 60%, 62%, 73%, 91% and 96% respectively. Thus, there were very wide margins of the difference in the probabilities of having received social work sentences in the courts found between those children who were arrested or who appeared before the courts for the ninth or more time(s) and those whose frequency of arrests or court appearances was less than nine times.

Table A3.9 in Appendix 3 (p. 174) compares the probabilities of receiving social work sentences in the courts as against the probability of receiving police diversionary measures by race and the various logical combinations of the control variables for all children in the model. However, the only control variables included in the calculations were all the constant variables, all the primary offences which had a positive effect on the response and all arrests or court appearances which had both positive and significant effects on the response. These variables were primary offences of theft or of handling stolen goods and those involving property, violence and offences against the police, children who had no TICs, only one offence that was dealt with at the hearings and the first through the fourth and the sixth through the seventh arrest or court appearance (see the keys in Tables A3.9 and A3.10 in Appendix 3, pages 174 and 175 respectively).

Table A3.9 suggests that the group with the highest probability of having received social work sentences in the courts were Asian children, irrespective of the different combinations of the control variables included. The only exception was when all the children were arrested or appeared before the courts for the second, third, fourth, sixth and seventh time charged with offences against the police. In those cases, all the children in the model had an equal probability of nearly 100% of receiving social work sentences in the courts as against the probability of receiving police diversionary measures. This implies that all defendants arrested for allegedly committing offences against the police were certainly more likely to be

106

prosecuted and to be treated the same in court, regardless of their racial background or their number of arrests or court appearances.

However, as stated on page 103, the probability of receiving court social work sentences as opposed to the probability of receiving police diversionary measures in respect of all children in the model increased significantly during their second, third, fourth, sixth and seventh arrest or court appearance. The highest probability of such an outcome was found amongst children who were arrested or who appeared before the courts for the ninth or more time(s) compared to those children who were arrested or who appeared before the courts only once.

Table A3.10 in Appendix 3 shows the margins of the difference between the probabilities of receiving social work sentences in the courts as opposed to the probability of receiving police diversionary measures between the three groups of children in the model, which were calculated from the probabilities of the various combinations of the control variables shown in Table A3.9. Clearly, the widest margin of the difference in the probabilities of receiving social work sentences was found between Asians and the other two groups of children. On the other hand, the gap between the probabilities between Asian and white children was the same as the gap between Asian and black children, whilst the gap between the probabilities of receiving court social work sentences between black and white children was nearly zero.

Thus, the widest margins of the difference between the probabilities of receiving social work sentences in the courts (margins of 28%, 28% and 0.001 between Asian and white, Asian and black, and white and black children, respectively) were found amongst children who appeared before the courts for the third and the sixth time without any TICs charged with primary offences involving theft or handling stolen goods. Other wider margins of difference between the probabilities (margins of 27%, 27% and 0.001 between the three respective groups of children) were also found amongst the following under 14s:

a)   those who appeared before the courts for the second time without any TICs charged with primary offences involving theft or handling stolen goods, property and violence,

b)   those who appeared before the courts for the third time without any TICs charged with primary offences involving violence,

c)   those who appeared before the courts for the fourth time without any TICs charged with primary offences involving theft or handling stolen goods and violence, and

d)   between those who appeared before the courts for the sixth time without any TICs charged with primary offences involving violence.

It was also found that there was almost no difference between the probabilities of receiving social work sentences in the courts as opposed to the probability of receiving police diversionary measures between the three groups of children who were charged with primary offences against the police, irrespective of the number of their arrests or court appearances for that type of primary offence. This suggests a stricter but equal treatment of defendants arrested with offences against the police from the police and the courts.

Summary

The result obtained from an analysis of the relationship between the odds of all children receiving social work sentences in the courts as against the odds of receiving police diversionary measures and race, type of primary offences allegedly committed, type of the first offences which were taken into consideration at the same hearing as the primary offences, the total number of offences dealt with at the same hearing and the number of arrests or court appearances suggests that Asian children were more likely than black children to have received social work sentences in the courts. These include supervision orders, supervision orders with discretionary intermediate treatment requirements, supervision orders with supervised activities requirements, residential and care orders. They were less likely to have received police diversionary measures, notwithstanding the influence of the control variables mentioned above. However, the difference between the probabilities of receiving social work sentences between black and Asian children was not significant (t-value = 1.157). On the other hand, white children were very slightly more likely than black children to have received social work sentences as opposed to receiving police diversionary measures, although the difference between the probabilities of receiving social work sentences between black and white children was also insignificant (t-value = 0.009).

The model also predicted that the only children who had an increased probability of receiving social work sentences in the courts and a decreased probability of receiving police diversionary measures were those charged with primary offences against the police. Those who were charged with primary offences involving property, violence, theft or handling stolen goods, police defined offences, other summary and indictable offences and motor vehicles had an increased probability of having received police diversionary measures and a decreased probability of having received social work sentences. However, the increase in the probability of receiving court social work sentences in respect of those children who were charged with primary offences against the police was insignificant (t-value = 0.343).

Lastly, the model predicted that when compared to children who were arrested or who appeared before the courts for the first time, those who were arrested or who appeared before the courts for the second and the third time, as well as for the fourth, sixth and the seventh time were found to have been highly significantly and significantly more likely to have received social work sentences in the courts as opposed to receiving police diversionary measures (t-values = 4.472, 4.657, 3.117, 2.177 and 2.704 respectively).

It was also found that the gap between the probabilities of receiving social work sentences between Asian and white children was the same as the gap that was found between Asian and black children, whilst the gap between the probabilities of receiving social work sentences as against the probability of receiving police diversionary measures between black and white children was almost zero, regardless of the influence of the control variables included in the calculations.

Factors influencing the odds of court social work and probation sentences rather than police diversionary measures for the over 14s

The next analysis involved an examination of the relationship between the odds of receiving social work and probation sentences in the courts (community service orders, supervision orders, supervision orders with discretionary intermediate treatment requirements, supervision orders with supervised activities requirements, probation orders, remands in care of the Local Authority, residential care orders and care orders) as against the odds of receiving police diversionary measures for the 491 over 14 year old defendants and the same influencing factors as those used in the under 14s analysis described above. Thus, the result shown in Figure A2.6 in Appendix 2 (p. 161) was found after weighting police decisions plus social work and probation sentences for all the over 14s and fitting a logit model to the data.

It can be seen from Figure A2.6 that the model predicted a negative and highly significant constant (t-value = -5.867). This meant that black young persons, who were arrested or who appeared before the courts for the first time with having allegedly committed primary offences of theft or of handling stolen goods, but who had no TICs at the hearings, had highly significantly lower odds of receiving social work and probation sentences in the courts as against the odds of receiving police diversionary measures. The odds were 0.12619. One of the other two race variables was associated with a negative and insignificant estimate, while the other was associated with a positive and also insignificant estimate (t-values = -1.143 and 0.193 in respect of white and Asian young persons respectively). This meant that there was an insignificant decrease in the odds of receiving court social work and probation sentences from 0.12619 for black young persons to 0.09562 in respect of white young persons. Similarly, there was an insignificant increase in the odds of receiving court social work and probation sentences to 0.13856 in respect of Asian young persons when compared to the odds of receiving a similar outcome in respect of black young persons in the model.

The model also predicted negative and insignificant results for all young persons, irrespective of the type of the primary offences with which they were arrested or appeared before the courts, except for those who were arrested or who appeared before the courts charged with having allegedly committed primary offences relating to property. In those cases the model predicted a positive but also an insignificant result for them. The t-values in respect of the influence of primary offences involving motor vehicles, violence, police defined offences, offences against the police, possession of drugs, other summary and indictable offences and property related primary offences on the response were -1.821, -0.098, -0.504, -0.914, -1.138, -1.212 and 0.278 respectively.

The above result meant that the decrease in the odds of receiving social work and probation sentences from 0.12619 for those young persons charged with primary offences involving theft or handling stolen goods to 0.06233 for offences involving motor vehicles, 0.12065 for offences involving violence, 0.09769 for police defined offences, 0.06493 for offences against the police, 0.02960 for offences involving possession of drugs and to 0.07059 for other summary and indictable primary offences was not significant. Likewise, the increase in the odds of receiving court social work and probation sentences, from 0.12619 to 0.13786 in respect of those young persons who were charged with having allegedly committed primary offences relating to property, was insignificant.

The influence of the type of the first TICs on the response shows a positive and highly significant estimate associated with offences involving motor vehicles as first TICs (t-value = 4.422), as well as positive and significant estimates associated with offences involving theft or handling stolen goods, property, violence, police defined offences and other summary and indictable offences (t-values = 3.490, 3.793, 3.616, 2.054 and 3.074 respectively). This meant that, when compared to the odds of receiving social work and probation sentences in respect of young persons who had no TICs, there were highly significant or significant increases in the odds of receiving court social work and probation sentences, from 0.12619 to 2.60657 for offences involving motor vehicles as first TICs, 0.89856 for offences involving theft or handling stolen goods, 1.10964 for offences relating to property, 11.22377 for offences involving violence, 0.65641 for police defined offences and to 1.68377 for other summary and indictable offences, taken into consideration, as their first TICs.

However, it should be noted that those young persons who appeared before the courts arrested with offences involving possession of drugs and those against the police as their first TICs, had the highest, albeit insignificant, increase in the odds of receiving social work and probation sentences in the model, from 0.12619 for those young persons who appeared before the courts without any TICs to 4064.44885 in respect of offences involving possession of drugs as first TICs and 604.27744 in respect of offences against the police as first TICs (t- values = 1.167 and 0.619 respectively).

The influence of the total number of offences that were dealt with at the same hearing was negative and significant for two offences that were dealt with at the same hearing and also negative but insignificant for three offences that were dealt with at the same hearing (t-values = -2.145 and -0.257 respectively). This meant that there was a significant decrease in the odds of receiving social work and probation sentences for those young persons who appeared before the courts with a total of two offences, from 0.12619 for those who appeared before the courts charged with only one offence to 0.03988. The decrease in the odds of receiving social work and probation sentences in respect of those young persons who appeared before the courts with a total of three offences that were dealt with at the same hearing, from 0.12619 to 0.10688, was not significant.

When compared to the result that was obtained from the analysis of the influence of the type of the first TICs on the response described above, the result from the model suggests that it was the type of the first offences which were taken into consideration at the same hearing as the primary offences which were more important in influencing court social work and probation sentences in respect of the over 14s in the model rather than the total number of offences that were dealt with at the same hearings.

Lastly, the model predicted positive and highly significant and significant results for all young persons who were arrested or who appeared before the courts for the third, sixth, ninth or more time(s) and for the second, fourth, fifth, seventh and the eighth time (t-values = 3.957, 3.935, 4.511 and 2.384, 3.727, 3.391, 3.673 and 2.121 respectively). This suggests that there were highly significant as well as significant increases in the odds of receiving social work and probation sentences as against the odds of receiving police diversionary measures, from 0.12619 for those young persons who were arrested or who appeared before the courts for the first time, to 0.56385 for the third arrest, 0.95890 for the sixth arrest, 1.46673 for the ninth or more arrest(s), 0.31047 for the second arrest, 0.57123 for the fourth arrest, 0.64793 for the fifth arrest, 1.15146 for the seventh arrest and to 0.55546 for those who appeared before the courts for the eighth time.

The association in relation to race described on page 109 is shown in Figure 7.4. The plotted result clearly shows that all the young persons in the model had a higher probability of having received police diversionary measures rather than the probability of receiving social work and probation sentences in the courts, when the variables of interest had been controlled for. However, the probability of such an outcome was found to have been higher for white young persons compared to their black and Asian counterparts. On the other hand, the highest probability of having received social work and probation sentences was found amongst Asian young persons compared to their black and white counterparts. The model thus suggests that the margin of the difference between the probabilities of receiving social work and probation sentences as against the probability of receiving police diversionary measures between Asian and black young persons was very small; that is, a difference of only 1%, whilst the difference between the probabilities between Asian and white young persons was almost 4%.

The relationship in relation to the type of the primary offences described on pages 109-10 is shown in Figure 7.5. The plotted result in Figure 7.5 suggests that all the young persons in the model had a higher probability of having received

111

police diversionary measures rather than the probability of receiving social work and probation sentences, regardless of the type of the primary offences with which they were arrested. However, when compared to young persons who were arrested or who appeared before the courts for having allegedly committed primary offences of theft or of handling stolen goods, those young persons who were arrested or who appeared before the courts for having allegedly committed primary offences relating to property had the highest probability, at 12%, of having received social work and probation sentences. On the other hand, those young persons who were arrested or who appeared before the courts for having allegedly committed primary offences involving possession of drugs had the lowest probability (only 3%) of receiving court social work and probation sentences.

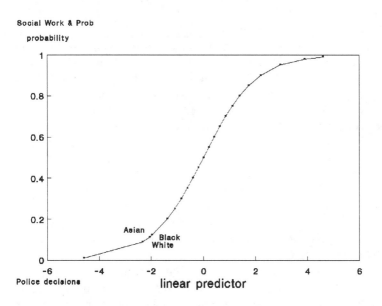

Figure 7.4 Probability of court social work and probation sentences: Over 14s by race

However, as shown in Figure 7.5, the margin of the difference between the probabilities of receiving court social work and probation sentences between those young persons who were arrested with primary offences relating to property and those who were arrested with primary offences involving theft or handling stolen goods, violence and police defined offences was very small, that is, a margin of difference of only 1% to 3% respectively. On the other hand, the margins of the difference between the probabilities between those young persons who were arrested

112

with primary offences involving other summary and indictable offences, offences against the police, motor vehicles and possession of drugs were slightly wider, that is, margins of difference ranging from 5% to 9% respectively.

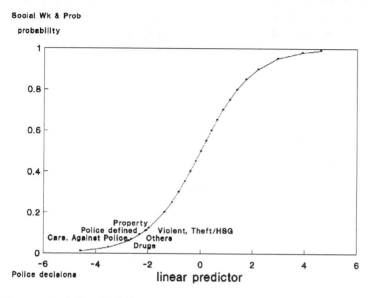

**Figure 7.5 Probability of court social work and probation sentences:
Over 14s by type of primary offence**

The association in relation to the type of the first TICs described on page 110 is shown in Figure 7.6. The plotted result in Figure 7.6 shows that those young persons who had first offences involving possession of drugs, offences against the police, violence, motor vehicles and other summary and indictable offences taken into consideration at the same hearings as the primary offences were found to have been more likely to have received social work sentences in the courts and less likely for the police to have taken no further action or to have cautioned them. On the other hand those who had first offences involving theft or handling stolen goods and police defined offences taken into consideration at the same hearings as the primary offences, as well as those who had no TICs at the hearings, were found to have been more likely to have received police diversionary measures and less likely to have received social work and probation sentences.

However, when compared to those young persons who appeared before the courts without any TICs, those who had first offences involving possession of drugs and offences against the police taken into consideration had the highest probabilities (nearly 100%) of having received social work and probation sentences in the courts as against the probability of receiving police diversionary measures. Similarly, those who had first offences involving violence taken into consideration also had a very high probability (92%) of having received court social work and probation sentences. On the other hand, those young persons who appeared before the courts without any TICs had the lowest probability (11%) of receiving social work sentences, but were more likely to have received police diversionary measures compared to those who appeared before the courts with TICs.

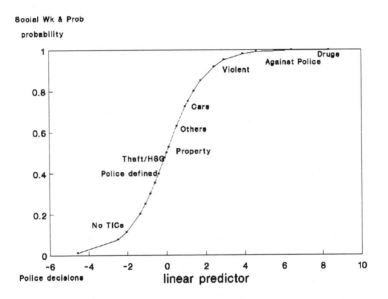

Figure 7.6 Probability of court social work and probation sentences: Over 14s by type of first TIC

The margin of the differences between the probabilities of receiving social work and probation sentences between those young persons who had offences involving possession of drugs as their first TICs and those who had offences against the police, offences involving violence, motor vehicles, other summary and indictable offences, property, theft or handling stolen goods and police defined offences as their first TICs, as well as between those who appeared before the courts without any TICs, was found to be one hundredeth of one percent, 8%, 28%, 37%, 47%, 53%, 60% and 89% respectively. Thus, there was almost no difference between the probabilities of receiving social work and probation sentences between those young persons who had offences of possession of drugs taken into consideration at the

114

same hearings as the primary offences and those who had offences against the police as their first TICs. However, the widest margins of the difference in the probabilities of social work and probation sentences, which ranged from 53% to 89%, were found between those young persons who had possession of drugs as their first TICs and those who had theft or handling stolen goods and police defined offences as their first TICs respectively, as well as between those who appeared before the courts without any TICs.

The association in respect of the number of arrests or court appearances described on page 111 is shown in Figure 7.7.

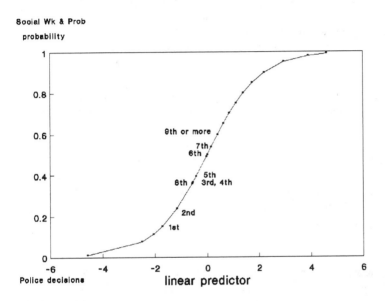

Figure 7.7 Probability of court social work and probation sentences: Over 14 s by number of arrests or court appearances

The plotted result suggests that only those young persons who were arrested or who appeared before the courts for the ninth or more time(s) and for the seventh time were more likely to have received social work and probation sentences in the courts and less likely to have received a no further action or caution from the police. On the other hand, those who were arrested or who appeared before the courts for the sixth, fifth, fourth, third, eighth, second and for the first time were less likely to have received social work and probation sentences and more likely to have received police diversionary measures. Figure 7.7 also shows that those young persons who were arrested or who appeared before the courts more than once were

115

found to have had higher probabilities of receiving social work and probation sentences as against the probability of receiving police diversionary measures when compared to those who were arrested or who appeared before the courts for the first time. In fact, the probabilities of receiving social work and probation sentences increased as the frequency of arrests or court appearances increased; that is, from a probability of 11% of receiving social work and probation sentences in respect of those young persons who were arrested or who appeared before the courts for the first time to a probability of nearly 60% of receiving a similar outcome in respect of those who were arrested or who appeared before the courts for the ninth or more time(s). However, the lower probability of receiving social work and probation sentences in respect of young persons who were arrested or who appeared before the courts for the eighth time was an exception to the above trend.

Thus, the margin of the difference between the probabilities between those young persons who were arrested or who appeared before the courts for the ninth or more time(s) and those who were arrested or who appeared before the courts for the seventh time was smaller compared to the margins of the difference between the probabilities between those who were arrested or who appeared before the courts for the nineth or more time(s) and those who were arrested or who appeared before the courts at other times, which were wider.

Table A3.11 in Appendix 3 (p. 176) compares the probabilities of receiving social work and probation sentences as against the probability of receiving police diversionary measures by race and the various logical combinations of the control variables for all young persons in the model. However, the only control variables included in the calculations were all the constant variables, primary offences which had a positive effect on the response, first offences which were taken into consideration at the same hearings as the primary offences, which had a positive and highly significant effect on the responce, up to a total of two offences that were dealt with at the same hearings, and all arrests or court appearances which had both positive and significant effects on the response. These variables were primary offences involving theft or handling stolen goods and those relating to property, young persons who had no TICs, offences involving motor vehicles as first TICs, up to a total of two offences that were dealt at same hearings, and the first through the ninth or more arrest(s) or court appearance(s) (see the keys in Tables A3.11 and A3.12 in Appendix 3, pages 176 and 177 respectively).

Table A3.11 suggests that the group with the highest probability of having received social work and probation sentences in the courts were Asian young persons, irrespective of the different combinations of the control variables included in the calculations. However, as stated before, all those young persons who were charged with primary offences involving property had a slightly higher probability of having received social work and probation sentences compared to those who were charged with primary offences involving theft or handling stolen goods. Likewise, all those young persons who had two offences dealt with at the same hearings as the primary offences, that is those who had offences involving motor vehicles as

116

their first TICs, were found to have had much higher probabilities of having received social work and probation sentences compared to those who had no TICs. It should be noted that autocrime was considered by the local agencies as a serious offence, hence the tendency for the police to prosecute and for social workers and probation officers to recommend social work and probation sentences in court for those young persons involved in this type of offence. In any event, the probabilities of social work and probation sentences increased as the frequency of arrests or court appearances increased, regardless of the influence of the type of primary offence, type of the first TIC and the total number of offences that were dealt with at the same hearings.

Table A3.12 in Appendix 3 shows the margins of the difference between the probabilities of receiving social work and probation sentences in the courts as opposed to the probability of receiving police diversionary measures between the three groups of young persons, after controlling for the influence of the various variables of interest. The widest margin of the difference in the probabilities of receiving social work and probation sentences was between Asian and white young persons, in favour of Asian young persons, followed by the margin of the difference between the probabilities between black and white young persons, in favour of black young persons. The gap between the probabilities between Asian and black young persons was very narrow, that is, slightly in favour of Asian young persons.

Thus, the widest gaps between the probabilities of receiving social work and probation sentences between the three groups of young persons (gaps of 9%, 7% and 2% between Asian and white, black and white, and Asian and black young persons, respectively) were found amongst the following young persons:

a)   those who appeared before the courts for the first time with a total of two offences that were dealt with at the same hearing; that is, those who were charged with primary offences involving theft or handling stolen goods and property and who had offences involving motor vehicles taken into consideration at the same hearing as the primary offences as their first TICs,

b)   those who appeared before the courts for the fifth time without any TICs charged with primary offences relating to property,

c)   those who appeared before the courts for the sixth, seventh and for the ninth or more time(s) without any TICs charged with primary offences involving theft or handling stolen goods and property.

This result implies that the police and the courts treated the young defendants differently when arrested with offences involving theft or handling stolen goods, property and motor vehicles, regardless of the number of times they had previously been arrested or appeared before the courts.

Summary

The result that was obtained from the social work and probation sentences analysis suggests that Asian young persons were more likely than their white and black counterparts to have received social work and probation sentences (supervision orders, supervision orders with discretionary intermediate treatment requirements, supervision orders with supervised activities requirements, community service orders and probation orders) and less likely for the police to have taken no further action or to have cautioned them, notwithstanding the influence of the control variables of interest. However, the difference between the probabilities of receiving social work and probation sentences between black and Asian young persons, that is in favour of Asian young persons, was not significant (t-value = 0.193). On the other hand, the difference between the probabilities of receiving social work and probation sentences between black and white young persons, that is in favour of black young persons, was also not significant (t-value = -1.143).

The model also predicted that all young persons were more likely to have received police diversionary measures and less likely to have received social work and probation sentences, irrespective of the type of primary offences for which they were arrested. However, those young persons who were arrested and charged with primary offences relating to property were found to have had an increased probability of receiving social work and probation sentences when compared to those young persons who were arrested and charged with other types of primary offences in the model, although that increase was not significant (t- value = 0.278).

It was also predicted in the model that those young persons who had offences involving possession of drugs, offences against the police, violence, motor vehicles, other summary and indictable offences and property related offences taken into consideration at the same hearing as the primary offences as their first TICs, were more likely to have received social work and probation sentences in the courts and less likely to have received police diversionary measures. On the other hand, those young persons who had offences involving theft or handling stolen goods and police defined offences as their first TICs, as well as those young persons who appeared before the courts without any TICs, were found to have been more likely to have received police diversionary measures and less likely to have received social work and probation sentences. Again, the above result suggests that the police and the courts were more likely to be stricter in their treatment of defendants who were arrested with more serious offences than they did with less serious ones.

However, the increase in the probability of receiving social work and probation sentences was significant in respect of those young persons who had offences involving theft or handling stolen goods, motor vehicles, property, violence, police defined offences and other summary and indictable offences as their first TICs when compared to the probability of receiving a similar outcome in respect of those young persons who appeared before the courts without any TICs (t-values = 3.490, 4.422, 3.793, 3.616, 2.054 and 3.074 respectively).

The result that was found in respect of young persons who appeared before the courts with a total of two offences that were dealt with at the same hearing was negative but significant (t-value = -2.145). When compared with the result that was found from the analysis of the influence of the first TICs on the response, this result suggests that the total number of offences that were dealt with at the same hearing was less important in influencing court social work and probation sentences than the type of the first offences which were taken into consideration at the same hearing as the primary offences, which were found to have been more important in determining those outcomes.

Lastly, the model predicted that those young persons who were arrested or who appeared before the courts for the ninth or more time(s) and for the seventh time were more likely to have received social work and probation sentences in the courts and less likely to have received police diversionary measures. On the other hand, those young persons who were arrested or who appeared before the courts for the sixth, fifth, fourth, third, eighth, second and for the first time were more likely to have received police diversionary measures and less likely to have received social work and probation sentences. However, when compared to those young persons who were arrested or who appeared before the courts for the first time, there were significant increases in the probabilities of receiving social work and probation sentences in respect of all those young persons who were arrested or who appeared before the courts more than once (t-values = 2.384, 3.957, 3.727, 3.391, 3.935, 3.673 and 2.121, in respect of the second through the eighth arrest or court appearance, respectively). The increase in the probability of receiving social work and probation sentences in respect of those young persons who were arrested or who appeared before the courts for the ninth or more time(s) was highly significant (t-value = 4.511). Moreover, the probability of receiving social work and probation sentences in the courts as opposed to the probability of receiving police diversionary measures increased as the frequency of arrests or court appearances increased.

It was also found that the gap between the probabilities of receiving social work and probation sentences between Asian and white young persons was greater than the gap between the probabilities of receiving a similar outcome between Asian and black young persons, regardless of the influence of the control variables included in the calculations. There was also a bigger gap between the probabilities of receiving social work and probation sentences between black and white young persons, in favour of black young persons. The smallest gap between the probabilities of receiving social work and probation sentences as against the probability of receiving police diversionary measures was between Asian and black young persons, that is very slightly in favour of Asian young persons in the model, again regardless of the influence of the same control variables which were included in the calculations.

8 Custodial sentences

Introduction

This last results chapter examines the relationship between the odds of custodial sentences as against police diversionary measures and race, the type of the primary offences, the type of the first TICs, the total number of offences dealt with at the same hearing and the number of arrests or court appearances. Accordingly, the model makes a direct comparison of the association between the propensity for young persons to receive custodial sentences in court, that is remands in custody, detention and youth custody orders, as opposed to the propensity to receive no further action or cautions from the police and the influencing factors. The analysis presented here pertains only to the over 14s, since the under 14s are by law not eligible for custodial sentencing.

Factors influencing the odds of custodial sentences rather than police diversionary measures for the over 14s

The result shown in Figure A2.7 in Appendix 2 (p. 162) was found after weighting police decisions plus custodial sentences for all the 436 over 14s and fitting a logit model to the data.

It can thus be seen from Figure A2.7 that the model predicted a negative and highly significant constant (t-value = -6.127). This meant that the black young persons who were arrested or who appeared before the courts for the first time with having allegedly committed primary offences of theft or handling stolen goods, but who had no TICs at the hearings, had highly significantly lower odds of receiving custodial sentences as against receiving police diversionary measures, as it would be expected. The odds were 0.02864. The other two race variables also had negative

120

estimates associated with them, but those relating to white young persons were found to be significant (t-value = -2.289). This meant that there was a significant decrease in the odds of receiving custodial sentences for white young persons of similar description to black young persons, from 0.02864 to 0.01280. The decrease in the odds of receiving custodial sentences in respect of similar Asian young persons, from 0.02864 to 0.01704, was not significant (t-value = -0.781).

The model also predicted positive and significant results for all young persons arrested for having allegedly committed primary offences relating to property, as well as those involving violence (t-values = 2.644 and 3.277 respectively). This result meant that such young persons' odds of receiving custodial sentences as opposed to the odds of receiving police diversionary measures increased significantly, from 0.02864 in respect of those arrested with primary offences involving theft or handling stolen goods to 0.09779 for property related primary offences and 0.16285 for those arrested with primary offences involving violence. The other types of primary offences in the model had negative and insignificant estimates associated with them.

The influence of the type of the first TICs on the response shows both positive and highly significant estimates in relation to the influence of offences involving motor vehicles and those involving violence as first TICs (t-values = 5.065 and 4.271 respectively). This meant that, when compared to the odds of receiving custodial sentences in respect of those young persons who had no TICs, there were highly significant increases in the odds of receiving custodial sentences, from 0.02864 to 3.50450, in respect of those young persons who had offences involving motor vehicles as their first TICs, and to 9.09795 in respect of those who had offences involving violence as their first TICs.

Positive and significant estimates were also found to be associated with offences of theft or of handling stolen goods, those relating to property, those which were police defined and other summary and indictable offences as first TICs (t-values = 3.789, 3.747, 3.100 and 2.771 respectively). This also meant that, when compared to the odds of receiving custodial sentences in respect of those young persons who had no TICs, there were significant increases in the odds of receiving custodial sentences, from 0.02864 to 0.50110, in respect of those young persons who had offences involving theft or handling stolen goods as their first TICs, 0.42744 in respect of those who had offences relating to property as their first TICs, 0.85903 in respect of those who had police defined offences as their first TICs, and to 0.77496 in respect of those who had other summary and indictable offences as their first offences taken into consideration at the same hearings as the primary offences.

However, it should be noted that those young persons who appeared before the courts arrested with offences of possession of drugs and those against the police as their first TICs had the highest odds of receiving custodial sentences in the model. The odds increased from 0.02864 for those without any TICs, to 336734.1628 in respect of offences involving possession of drugs and to 178.40372 in respect of those with offences against the police as their first TICs, although that increase was

121

not significant (t-values = 0.367 and 0.235 respectively).

The influence of the total number of offences that were dealt with at the same hearing on custodial sentences shows a negative and significant estimate associated with two offences that were dealt with at the same hearing (t-value = -3.060). This meant that there was a significant decrease in the odds of custodial sentences for those young persons who appeared before the courts with a total of two offences that were dealt with at same hearing, from 0.02864 for those who appeared before the courts charged with only one offence to 0.00332. The model also predicted a negative but insignificant estimate associated with three offences that were dealt with at the same hearings (t-value = -0.366), meaning that the decrease in the odds of receiving custodial sentences in respect of those young persons who appeared before the courts with a total of three offences that were dealt with at the same hearings, from 0.02864 to 0.02155, was not significant.

When compared to the result that was obtained from the analysis of the influence of the type of the first TICs on the response, the above result indicates that the total number of offences that were dealt with at the same hearing was not important in determining custodial sentences, but that it was the type of the TICs that was more important in influencing those outcomes.

Lastly, the model predicted positive and highly significant and significant results for all young persons who were arrested or who appeared before the courts for the fifth, seventh through the ninth or more time(s) and for the second, fourth and sixth time (t-values = 4.210, 4.235, 4.573, 5.227, 1.978, 3.254 and 2.932 respectively). This suggests that the strongest highly significant increase in the odds of receiving custodial sentences as against the odds of receiving police diversionary measures, from 0.02864 for those young persons who were arrested only once to 1.17592, was found amongst those young persons who were arrested or who appeared before the courts for the ninth or more time(s). It should be noted that the increase in the odds of receiving custodial sentences, from 0.02864 to 0.08804 in respect of those young persons who were arrested or who appeared before the courts for the third time, was insignificant (t-value = 1.894).

The association in relation to race described on pages 120-1 is shown in Figure 8.1. The plotted result clearly shows that all the young persons in the model had a higher probability of receiving a police diversionary measure rather than the probability of receiving a custodial sentence when the independent variables of interest had been controlled for, as it would be expected, although the probability of such an outcome was found to have been higher for white, compared to the probabilities of Asian and black young persons. However, the result also indicates that the highest probability (only 3%) of receiving custodial sentences was found to have been amongst black young persons, whilst the probabilities of receiving custodial sentences for similar Asian and white young persons were even lower, that is, probabilities of only 2% and 1% respectively. It should be noted that, although the margin of the difference in the probabilities of receiving custodial sentences between black and similar Asian and white young persons was only 1%

and 2% respectively, the overall difference between the probabilities of receiving custodial sentences between black and white young persons was significant, as stated on pages 120-1.

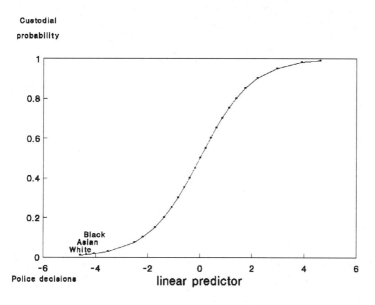

Figure 8.1   Probability of custodial sentences: Over 14s by race

The relationship in relation to the type of the primary offences described on page 121 is shown in Figure 8.2. The plotted result suggests that all the young persons in the model had a higher probability of receiving police diversionary measures and a lower probability of receiving custodial sentences, regardless of the type of the primary offences with which they were arrested or appeared before the courts. However, when compared to young persons who were arrested for having allegedly committed primary offences of theft or of handling stolen goods, those young persons who were arrested for having allegedly committed primary offences involving violence (assaults occasioning actual or bodily harm, or malicious wounding, or aggravated assaults, or robbery and aggravated robbery, or carrying offensive weapons) had the highest probability (14%) of having received custodial sentences in the courts as against the probability of receiving police diversionary measures. Those who were arrested for having allegedly committed primary offences which were police defined (going equipped for theft or possession of articles for housebreaking et cetera, and criminal attempt) had the lowest probability (only 0.00001 or 0.01E- 03) of receiving custodial sentences.

123

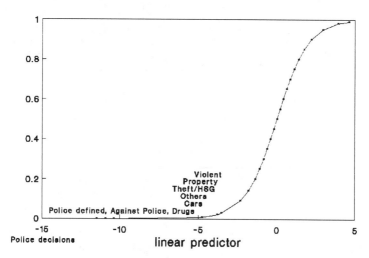

Figure 8.2 Probability of custodial sentences: Over 14s by type of primary offence

The margin of the differences in the probabilities of receiving custodial sentences between primary offences involving violence and those relating to property (burglary and aggravated burglary, destroying or damaging property of another) was only 5%. However, that gap between the probabilities between primary offences involving violence and theft or handling stolen goods increased to 11% and to 12% when compared to other summary and indictable offences, to 13% in respect of motor vehicles, to 14% in respect of possession of drugs, to 14% in respect of offences against the police and to 14% when compared to police defined offences.

Thus, there was a smaller margin of difference between the probabilities of receiving custodial sentences as against the probability of receiving police diversionary measures between those young persons who were arrested for having allegedly committed primary offences involving violence and those who were arrested for having allegedly committed primary offences relating to property. On the other hand, that margin of the difference in the probabilities of receiving custodial sentences became wider when the probabilities of custodial sentences for those who were charged with offences involving violence were compared to the probabilities of custodial sentences associated with the rest of the other types of primary offences in the model. The custodial outcomes in relation to violent and

124

property related offences reflect the seriousness with which these offences are viewed by both the police and the courts.

The association in relation to the type of the first TICs described on pages 121-2 is shown in Figure 8.3.

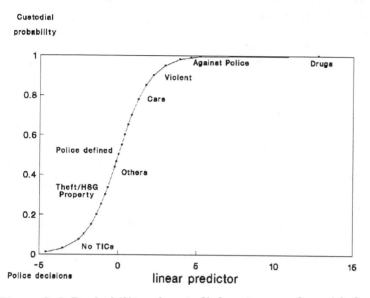

Figure 8.3 Probability of custodial sentences: Over 14s by type of first TIC

The plotted result suggests that those young persons who had offences of possession of drugs, offences against the police (assaulting or obstructing police in the execution of their duty, or of using threatening, abusive or insulting words or behaviour), offences involving violence and those involving motor vehicles taken into consideration at the same hearings as the primary offences as their first TICs, were more likely to have received custodial sentences in the courts and less likely to have had no further action taken against them by the police or to have been cautioned. Again, this implies that the police and the courts were likely to treat defendants charged with offences against the police, involving violence and motor vehicles more punitively compared other types of offences.

However, when compared to those young persons who appeared before the courts without any TICs, those who had offences of possession of drugs as their first TICs had the highest probability (nearly 100%) of having received custodial sentences as against the probability of receiving police diversionary measures.

125

On the other hand, those young persons who appeared before the courts without any TICs had the lowest probability (only 3%) of receiving custodial sentences, but were more likely to have received police diversionary measures.

The margin of the differences between the probabilities of custodial sentences between those young persons who had offences of possession of drugs as their first TICs and those who had offences against the police was under 1%. That gap between the probabilities between offences of possession of drugs as first TICs was increased to 10% when compared to offences involving violence, to 22% in respect of motor vehicles, to 54% in respect of police defined offences, to 56% in respect of other summary and indictable offences, to 67% in respect of offences of theft or of handling stolen goods, to 70% when compared to property related offences as their first TICs, and to 97% when compared to those who appeared before the courts without any TICs. Thus, there was a very small margin of difference between the probabilities of receiving custodial sentences as against the probability of receiving police diversionary measures between those young persons who had offences of possession of drugs as their first TICs and those who had offences against the police as their first TICs. This suggests that offences involving possession of drugs were treated equally seriously as offences against the police by the police and the courts.

However, the widest margins of difference in the probabilities of custodial sentences, which ranged from 54% to 97%, were found between those young persons who had possession of drugs as their first TICs and those who had police defined offences, other summary and indictable offences, theft or handling stolen goods and property related offences as their first TICs, as well as between those young persons who had no TICs.

The association in respect of the number of arrests or court appearances described on page 122 is shown in Figure 8.4. The plotted result suggests that those young persons who were arrested or who appeared before the courts for the ninth or more time(s) and for the eighth time were more likely to have received custodial sentences in the courts and less likely to have received a no further action or caution from the police. Alternatively, those who were arrested or who appeared before the courts for the seventh, fifth, sixth, fourth, third, second and for the first time were less likely to have received custodial sentences in the courts and more likely to have received police diversionary measures.

However, when compared to those young persons who were arrested or who appeared before the courts for the first time, those young persons who were arrested or who appeared before the courts more than once were found to have had higher probabilities of receiving custodial sentences in the courts as against the probability of having received police diversionary measures. In fact the probabilities of receiving custodial sentences increased as the frequency of arrests increased, that is from a probability of 3% of receiving a custodial sentence in the courts in respect of those young persons who were arrested or who appeared before the courts for the first time to a probability of 54% of receiving a similar outcome in respect of those who were arrested or who appeared before the courts for the ninth or more time(s).

The margin of the differences between the probabilities of custodial sentences between those young persons who were arrested or who appeared before the courts for the ninth or more time(s) and those who were arrested or who appeared before the courts for the eighth time was only 2%. That gap between the probabilities between the ninth or more arrest(s) or court appearance(s) increased to 14% when compared to the seventh arrest or court appearance, to 26% in respect of the fifth arrest or court appearance, to 30% in respect of the sixth arrest or court, to 38% in respect of the fourth arrest or court appearance, to 46% in respect of the third arrest or court appearance, to 46% in respect of the second arrest or court appearance and to 51% when compared to the first arrest or court appearance.

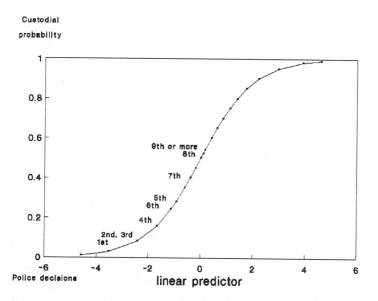

Figure 8.4   Probability of custodial sentences: Over 14s by number of arrests or court appearances

Thus, there was a very small difference in the probabilities of receiving custodial sentences as against the probability of receiving police diversionary measures between those young persons who were arrested or who appeared before the courts for the ninth or more time(s) and those who were arrested or who appeared before the courts for the eighth time. On the other hand, the widest margin of difference in the probabilities of having received custodial sentences, that is a difference of 51%, was amongst those young persons who were arrested or who appeared before the courts for the ninth or more time(s) and those who were arrested or who appeared before the courts for the first time, as it would be expected.

Table A3.13 in Appendix 3 (pp. 178-9) compares the probabilities of receiving custodial sentences as against the probability of receiving police diversionary measures by race and the various logical combinations of the control variables for all young persons in the model. However, the only control variables included in the calculations were all the constant variables, all the primary offences which had positive and significant effects on the response, first offences which were taken into consideration at the same hearings as the primary offences which had positive and highly significant effects on the response, up to a total of two offences dealt with at the same hearings and all arrests or court appearances which had both positive and significant effects on the response. These variables were primary offences of theft or of handling stolen goods, as well as primary offences relating to property and those involving violence, young persons who had no TICs, offences involving motor vehicles, as well as those involving violence as first TICs, up to a total of two offences which were dealt with at the same hearing and the first, second, fourth through the ninth or more arrest(s) or court appearance(s) (see the keys in Tables A3.13 and A3.14 in Appendix 3, pages 178-9 and 180-1 respectively).

It can thus be seen from Table A3.13 that the probabilities of custodial sentences increased as the frequency of arrests or court appearances increased, irrespective of the type of primary offences included in the calculations, as well as when a total of two offences were dealt with at the same hearings. Furthermore, black young persons were more likely to have received custodial sentences compared to their Asian and white counterparts, regardless of the combination of the control variables in the model.

Table A3.14 in Appendix 3 shows the margins of the difference between the probabilities of receiving custodial sentences as against the probability of receiving police diversionary measures between the three groups of young persons in the model, which were calculated from the probabilities of the various combinations of the control variables of interest shown in Table A3.13. Clearly, the widest margin of the difference in the probabilities of receiving custodial sentences was between black and white young persons, in favour of black young persons, followed by the margin of the difference between the probabilities between black and Asian young persons, again in favour of black young persons. The gap between the probabilities of receiving custodial sentences between Asian and white young persons was narrower, but in favour of Asian young persons.

Thus, the widest margins of the difference between the probabilities of receiving custodial sentences as opposed to the probability of receiving police diversionary measures (margins of 20%, 13% and 7% between black and white, black and Asian, and Asian and white young persons, respectively) were amongst the following young persons:

a)   those who appeared before the courts for the ninth or more time(s) charged with primary offences of theft or of handling stolen goods, but without any TICs,

b)   those who appeared before the courts for the fifth time charged with primary offences relating to property, also without any TICs,

c)   those who appeared before the courts for the sixth time charged with primary offences involving violence, also without any TICs,

d)   those who appeared before the courts for the second time with a total of two offences which were dealt with at the same hearing, that is with primary offences of theft or of handling stolen goods, as well as with offences involving motor vehicles, as their first TICs, and

e)   between those young persons who appeared before the courts for the first time with a total of two offences which were dealt with at the same hearing, that is with primary offences relating to property as well as with offences involving motor vehicles as their first TICs.

It was also found that there was almost no difference between the probabilities of receiving custodial sentences amongst the following young persons:

a)   those who were arrested or who appeared before the courts for the first time without any TICs charged with primary offences involving theft or handling stolen goods,

b)   those who were arrested or who appeared before the courts for the seventh through the ninth or more time(s) with a total of two offences that were dealt with at the same hearings, that is with primary offences involving violence, as well as with other offences also involving violence which were taken into consideration, and

c)   between those who were arrested or who appeared before the courts for the ninth or more time(s) with a total of two offences that were dealt with at the same hearings, that is with primary offences relating to property, as well as with offences involving violence which were taken into consideration.

Again, this result reflects the sentencers' propensity to treat those defendants who are arrested frequently, especially those charged with more serious offences, more strictly compared to less frequent offenders who are charged with minor offences, as expected.

Summary

The result obtained from an analysis of the relationship between the odds of all young persons receiving custodial sentences in the courts as against the odds of receiving police diversionary measures and race, type of the primary offences, type of the first TICs, the total number of offences dealt with at the same hearing and the number of arrests or court appearances suggests that white young persons in the model were significantly less likely than black young persons to have received custodial sentences in the courts and more likely to have received police diversionary measures, notwithstanding the influence of the control variables mentioned above (t-value = -2.289). On the other hand, the difference between the probabilities of receiving custodial sentences between black and Asian young persons, in favour of black young persons, was insignificant (t-value = -0.781).

The model also predicted that all young persons had a decreased probability of receiving custodial sentences in the courts and an increased probability of receiving police diversionary measures, regardless of the influence of the type of primary offences with which they were charged, as it would be expected. However, those young persons who were arrested or who appeared before the courts charged with primary offences involving violence and relating to property were significantly more likely to have received custodial sentences in the courts and less likely to have received police diversionary measures when compared to those young persons who were arrested or who appeared before the courts charged with primary offences of theft or of handling stolen goods (t-values = 3.277 and 2.644).

It was also predicted in the model that when compared to young persons who appeared before the courts without any TICs, those who had offences involving motor vehicles and violence taken into consideration at the same hearing as the primary offences as their first TICs were very significantly more likely to have received custodial sentences in the courts and less likely to have received police diversionary measures (t-values = 5.065 and 4.271 respectively). Likewise, those who had offences of theft or of handling stolen goods, relating to property, police defined offences and other summary and indictable offences as their first TICs were also significantly more likely to have received custodial sentences and less likely to have received police diversionary measures (t-values = 3.789, 3.747, 3.100 and 2.771 respectively).

A negative but significant result was found in respect of young persons who appeared before the courts with a total of two offences that were dealt with at the same hearing (t-value = -3.060). When compared with the result that was found from the analysis of the influence of the first TICs on the response, this result indicated that the total number of offences that were dealt with at the same hearing was less important in influencing custodial sentences, but that it was the type of the first offences which were taken into consideration at the same hearing as the primary offences which were important in determining those outcomes.

The model also predicted that, when compared to those young persons who were

130

arrested or who appeared before the courts for the first time, those who were arrested or who appeared before the courts for the ninth or more time(s) and the eighth, seventh and fifth time, as well as for the fourth, sixth and second time were found to have been highly significantly and significantly more likely to have received custodial sentences as opposed to receiving police diversionary measures (t-values = 5.227, 4.573, 4.235, 4.210, 3.254, 2.932 and 1.978 respectively).

Lastly, it was also found that the gap between the probabilities of receiving custodial sentences in the courts as against the probability of receiving police diversionary measures between the three groups of young persons, and in favour of black young persons, was wider when appearing before the courts charged with only one offence compared to the gap between them when appearing before the courts charged with a total of two offences that were dealt with at the same hearings. On the whole, the margins of the difference between the probabilities of receiving custodial sentences were much wider and more significant between black and white young persons than between black and Asian young persons, whilst the gap between the probabilities of receiving custodial sentences between Asian and white young persons was narrower. However, it should be noted that black and Asian defendants as ethnic minority groups were found to have been more likely to have received a custodial sentence, while their white counterparts were more likely to have been cautioned by the police.

9 Conclusions

The research reported in this book was concerned with delineating factors which impact on outcomes in the institutional processing of young offenders on a cross cultural basis. The primary aim was to test a differential outcome hypothesis between all black, Asian and white youth living in Brent, a London Metropolitan Police District comprising the largest numbers of ethnic minorities in the UK (1981 and 1991 Census data) who were arrested by the police between 1982 and 1986. The assertion was that ethnic minorities, black people in particular, have over a considerable number of years continued to receive harsher treatment compared to their white and, as shown by some recent studies (e.g., Berry 1984; Martin 1985; Hood 1992), also their Asian counterparts within the UK criminal justice system. In an attempt to test this assertion, this study carried out a multivariate analysis of the data and the process involved assessing the probability for Asian, black and white defendants of being prosecuted by the police and of receiving a court disposal, such as an acquittal or a non-custodial sentence, a social work and probation sentence and a custodial sentence as against the probability of being diverted from the courts, in line with local policy, while controlling for the influence of a number of legal and non-legal independent variables.

The data presented in the preceding chapters confirms race-specific outcomes, notwithstanding the influence of significant explanatory factors, such as the type of the primary offences allegedly committed, the type of offences which were taken into consideration at the same hearings as the primary offences, the total number of offences that were dealt with at the same hearings and the number of arrests or court appearances when considered in combination with each other. In this respect, the data make a contribution to the differential treatment debate on the basis of race. Moreover, this result was still found, irrespective of the age of the defendants in the sample and against the background of local and judicial policies designed to redress imbalances in sentencing policy; that is, between non-custodial and custodial sentences and diversion from the courts as encouraged by the Criminal Justice Act 1982. Furthermore, the data revealed that significant interactions at the 0.05 level between race and each of the above explanatory variables did not exist in predicting court disposals as against police diversionary measures. Accordingly, it was not possible, for example, to extrapolate from the data that the strong likelihood of custodial sentences in respect of black young persons was due to a statistically significant interaction between them and serious offences when compared to their Asian and white counterparts. The differences manifest cannot be attributed to a differential propensity to commit offences, or to commit offences of a particular type. This finding is almost similar to Hood's (1992) in that he found that:

> although more black offenders had appeared at the Crown Court charged with offences which could only be tried on indictment at such a court, there were no significant differences in the proportions of blacks and whites convicted of the most serious crimes of personal violence. (p. 196).

Earlier, Voakes and Fowler (1989) had discovered that, with respect to gravity of offence, differences between whites and blacks were not significant, and only marginally so between whites and Asians. On the other hand, Brown and Hullin (1992) found that differences in offending patterns were present, but that that finding was not conclusive.

However, the results presented in this study demonstrate that there were significant differences between black and white young persons in their propensity to be acquitted in the courts because of insufficient evidence from the police, in favour of black young persons. Alternatively, white young persons were found to be significantly more likely to have received police diversionary measures. The higher acquittal rate for blacks found in this study confirms the findings of other studies. For example, Walker (1988) studying 'The court disposal of young males by race in London in 1983' and with Jefferson and Seneviratne (1989) *Ethnic Minorities, Young People and the Criminal Justice System*, in Leeds, concluded that there was a significantly higher proportion of blacks than whites acquitted both in the magistrates' courts, as well as the crown courts. When asked to comment on the acquittal rate for blacks found in this study, a long-serving white magistrate on the bench of one of the principal courts examined was not surprised by the result. He informed the researcher that:

> In cases involving black defendants, oftentimes we have wondered during our deliberations whether the police would have brought them before us for trial had they been white.

The comment implies that the local magistrates view the police as treating black people unfairly and differently or perhaps more punitively than they do treat white people, as well as being eager to prosecute them (black defendants), in spite of weak or insufficient evidence with which to do so.

Similarly, significant differences were found between the propensity to receive custodial sentences between black and white young persons, again in favour of black young persons, while white young offenders were significantly more likely to have been diverted from a court appearance. This result is also supported by the findings of other studies mentioned in chapter one, such as Home Office (1986, 1989 and 1991), Walker (1986 and 1988) and with Jefferson and Seneviratne (1989), Voakes and Fowler (1989), Broad (1991), Brown and Hullin (1992), Hood (1992) and Maden et al. (1992). The most recent study confirming race differences in custodial sentencing is Hood's (1992) study of Crown Court Centres which serve the region covered by the West Midlands Police: at Birmingham, Dudley (now Wolverhampton), Coventry, Warwick and Stafford Crown Courts. He concludes:

Differences in the proportions of each ethnic category - white, black or Asian - given a custodial sentence were marked. Taking the sample as a whole, the proportion of blacks sentenced to custody was ... over 8 percentage points higher than for whites (56.6% v 48.4%). Asians, on the other hand, were sentenced to custody less often than whites or blacks (39.6%). [However], variations between the proportions of ethnic minorities sentenced to custody at the different Crown Court Centres were even larger. The black:white 'custody ratio' was particularly high for those sentenced by the Dudley courts, amounting to a difference of 17 percentage points (65% v 48%). There was a similar high black:white ratio at Warwick and Stafford, although the numbers dealt with there were much smaller. Only at Coventry were more whites and Asians sentenced to custody than blacks.   (Hood 1992: 194-5).

The significant differences between the propensities of acquittals and of custodial sentences between black and white young persons were found in this study, regardless of the control variables included in the calculations, as by Hood (1992) in the case of custodial sentences.

The differences in the propensities of receiving court non-custodial, as well as of receiving court social work and probation sentences, between the three groups of defendants were found to be insignificant. However, Asian children were found to have had slightly higher probabilities of having received court non-custodial sentences as against the probability of receiving police diversionary measures when compared to their white and black counterparts, whilst black children were slightly more likely than white children to have received court non-custodial sentences. On the other hand, black young persons were more likely than Asian and white young persons to have received court non-custodial sentences when compared to their Asian and white counterparts, whilst there was almost no difference between the propensities of receiving court non-custodial sentences between white and Asian young persons.

Likewise, both Asian children and young persons were found to have been more likely to have received social work and probation sentences compared to their white and black counterparts, who were more likely to have received police diversionary measures rather than social work and probation sentences. However, there was no difference between the probabilities of having received social work sentences between white and black children, whilst the gap between the probabilities of having received court social work and probation sentences between Asian and black young persons was found to have been very small. On the other hand, black young persons were found to have been more likely to have received court social work and probation sentences and less likely to have received police diversionary measures when compared to their white counterparts. This result confirms Martin's (1985) finding, discussed in chapter one, that African-Caribbean people were over represented in probation caseloads relative to their numbers in the Croydon population. Broad's (1991) study on *Punishment under Pressure: The Probation Service in the Inner City*, found that 41% of persons on probation supervision were black. Contrary to this, however, Hood (1992) found the opposite result; that is, that more blacks were subject to other forms of alternatives to custody, such as a suspended sentence of imprisonment or a CSO rather than a probation order.

The study reveals that, on the whole, black defendants had higher propensities of being prosecuted by the police and of being dealt with by the courts when compared to their white counterparts against whom the police were more likely to have taken no further action or to have cautioned, irrespective of age, and of the influence of the control variables of interest on the response, as shown in the example in Table 9.1 oveleaf.

Overall, police decisions accounted for 31.6% of all outcomes in the local juvenile criminal justice system, while court outcomes amounted to 68.4%. This rate of local police diversionary measures is much lower than the average rate for the MPD of 39% in 1982. Thus, the underuse of cautions locally was found to be much more pronounced against black defendants (see also Landau 1981; Tipler 1986). As stated in chapter two, this implies that the sentencers' approach to black defendants, in particular, was a legalistic one. White defendants, on the other hand, enjoyed treatment based on welfare considerations. This assertion is now based on the overwhelming evidence suggesting links between black people (black youth in particular) with more *intensive surveillance* of them by the police (Gilroy 1982; Bridges 1983; Gutzmore 1983; Norris et al 1992), higher rates of *stops* by the police (Smith 1983; Jones et al 1986; Walker, Jefferson and Seneviratne 1989; Norris, Kemp and Fielding, N. and J., 1992), *arrests* (Stephens and Willis 1979; Home Office 1983; Landau and Nathan 1983; Walker 1989; Skogan 1990), *prosecutions* (McConville, Sanders and Leng 1991), *acquittals* (Walker 1988 and with others, 1989) and *custodial sentences* (e.g., Home Office 1986, 1989, 1991 and 1992; Walker 1986, 1988 and with Jefferson and Seneviratne, 1989; Voakes and Fowler 1988; Brown and Hullin 1992; Hood 1992; Maden et al 1992).

Table 9.1

Estimated probabilities of court outcomes as opposed to police diversionary measures by race for the constant variables (theft and handling stolen goods, those without TICs, one offence dealt with at the hearing and the first arrest or court appearance) for the under and over 14s

	Black	White	Asian
Police Decisions vs Cases Dismissed			
<14s	0.043	0.029	0.000
>14s	0.184	0.120	0.101
Police Decisions vs Non-custodial Sentences			
<14s	0.170	0.154	0.201
>14s	0.461	0.386	0.376
Police Decisions vs Social Work/Probation			
<14s	0.038	0.038	0.109
>14s	0.112	0.087	0.122
Police Decisions vs Custodial Sentences			
>14s	0.028	0.013	0.017

Moreover, there was an over-representation of black young defendants (43%) dealt with by the local youth criminal justice system compared to their total numbers in Brent's youth population, of approximately 23%, while there was an under-representation of Asian young defendants (4%) compared to their total numbers of approximately 23% in the population. The representation of white young defendants (50%) was slightly below their percentage in Brent's youth population, that is of approximately 55%. Again, this over-representation of blacks and an under-representation of Asians and whites in the criminal justice system relative to their numbers in the population has been supported by PROP (1983), Martin (1985), Hood (1992) and Norris et al (1992). For instance, Hood (1992) suggests that ethnic minority defendants accounted for 28% of the males sentenced at the West Midlands Crown Courts in 1989, and that this was two and a half times greater than their proportion in the population at large, of about 11%. As he states:

> This was because Afro-Caribbeans were generally over-represented, making up 21% of those found guilty at Birmingham and 15% at the Dudley Courts..., although they accounted for less than 4% of the general male population in the age range of 16-64. (p. 194).

On the other hand, Norris et al (1992), in a recent study into the influence of race on being stopped by the police carried out in inner city London and Surrey, concluded from their data that, in relation to their actual presence in the population, the police stop white, black and Asian persons in varying ratios to the expected frequency and that, once stopped, black persons are more likely to be subject to formal police action. Smith (1983) and Jones et al (1986) also came to the same conclusion in their respective studies.

In chapter one, it was mentioned that evidence of racial bias in court dispositions from research studies is contradictory. The conflicting evidence appears in part to be due to the varied methodological sophistication and theoretical approaches employed by each of the studies (Box 1986). For example, previous studies on race and the criminal justice system have utilised small sample sizes for blacks when compared to those for whites, as shown in Table 9.2.

Table 9.2
Sample sizes of white, black and Asian defendants used by some recent studies on race and the criminal justice system, in percentages

	White	Black	Asian
Brown and Hullin (1992) (magistrates' court)	91	6	3
Crow and Cove (1984) (juvenile courts)	80	13	4
Hood (1992) (crown courts)	77	13	8
Mhlanga (1993) (magistrates' and crown)	50	43	4
Moxon (1988) (crown courts)	88	8	5
Tipler (1986) (magistrates' courts)	43	38	4
Voakes and Fowler (1989) (West Yorkshire Probation)	80	5	11
Walker (1988) (magistrates' and crown)	68	24	3
Walker et al (1989) (magistrates' and crown)	90	7	3
Walker (1989) custody study (magistrates' courts)	71	24	2
Waters (1990) (Leicester Prob)	0	21	71

Note: Some row totals do not add up to 100% due to rounding and missing data.

It is clear from Table 9.2 that the majority of studies of race and the criminal justice system have utilised smaller numbers of blacks and Asians. By and large, the areas of divergence between this study and previous ones are described below.

Areas of divergence between this and previous studies

a)   The sample size for this study was 100%, drawn from a London borough with the highest proportion of ethnic minorities in UK (1981 Census data), and whose political economy exhibits the many disadvantage indices, thought of in sociological and criminological research as likely contributors to crime.

b)   The difference between the sample sizes of combined ethnic minorities and whites in this study is very small at 3%, and 7% between blacks and whites. Tipler's (1986) 38% sample for blacks in his study of juveniles in the London borough of Hackney is a little bit below the sample size for blacks in this study. However, the gap in sample sizes between whites and blacks found in other studies is much wider, that is, much larger proportions of whites than blacks. One of the main reasons for this anomaly is the fact that there are more black people residing in some London boroughs like Brent and Hackney than in other parts of the United Kingdom. Hood's (1992) sample of 77% whites, 13% blacks and 8% Asians consisted of:

> all the identified male black and Asian defendants who were found guilty and sentenced by [the] five Crown Courts in 1989 and a random sample of male white defendants at each court.   (pp. 33-4).

However, the sample of white defendants was weighted according to the relative proportions of ethnic minorities appearing at each of the five courts studied. By way of a caveat, Hood suggests that:

> such a procedure obviously under-represents white defendants in the sample of cases as a whole in relation to blacks and Asians. In comparing the sentences imposed on the three racial groups at each court individually, the different sampling fractions taken posed no difficulties as long, of course, as the sample of whites was representative of whites dealt with at that court.   (p. 34).

In essence, Hood contends here that the problem of representativeness (the risk of incorrectly estimating the true population value from the sample value) was overcome by the method of weighting white cases that was employed in that study.

c)   The period of this study was longer (5 years), which gave the researcher ample time to follow cases through, from arrest to their first appearance in the magistrates' courts and to their final outcome in both the magistrates' courts, as well as the crown courts. The data in other studies was for 18 months (Tipler 1986), 12 months (Hood 1992), 9 months (Brown and Hullin 1992), 6 months (Walker, Jefferson and Seneviratne 1989) to mention a few.

d)   The analysis was comprehensive and a multivariate one, contrary to some previous studies which have provided primarily bivariate analyses of their data. Hood's (1992) study of race and sentencing in the West Midlands is the other recent research that employed a multivariate analysis of the data, using logistic regression models, in order to determine the relationship between race and custodial sentences, while controlling for the influence of the legal and non-legal independent variables. However, the analytic procedures that Hood and his colleagues used to analyse and to interpret their data were different from the ones employed in this study. Hood's method involved designing final multivariate regression models utilising significant variables selected from earlier separate bivariate analyses of the relationship between the independent and the dependent variables, as well as from the initial multivariate analyses that followed the bivariate analyses. The independent variables had also been subjected to tests for the presence of multicollinearity, before inclusion or exclusion in the final models. Although Hood and his colleagues found that the presence of multicollinearity in the models was low, the failure to include a relevent variable in a regression model can lead to biased and inconsistent estimators, while the inclusion of inappropriate variables leads to a loss of efficiency (Norusis 1988; Pindyck and Rubinfeld 1991). With regard to this, Hood and colleagues state that:

> there was no instability in the coefficients for variables when other variables were added or dropped from the models, nor when a random sub-sample was selected.   (Hood 1992: 256).

However, what this study did do in contrast to Hood's method was that the independent variables which were included in the final logit models were the significant variables derived from a general or parsimonious logit model, which included all the parameters with possible association effects with the paired dependent variables, either of themselves or interactively. Furthermore, it was possible to create the dichotomous dependent variables (police decisions versus each of the categories of court outcomes) which are better handled by logit, so that the bivariate probability of acquittals or any of the other court sentences as against police diversionary measures could be estimated. Consequently, this procedure satisfied the aim of this study which was designed to discover the probability for defendants of being prosecuted and of being dealt with by the courts as opposed to their probability of being diverted from a court appearance altogether by the police. In other words, the idea was to examine the effect of the 'gatekeeping' function of the police on Asian, black and white defendants with respect to court sentences.

e) The researcher was a participant observer of the system throughout the whole period of the study, as a youth justice practitioner and a 'responsible adult' for purposes of s.57 and 66 of the Police and Criminal Evidence Act 1984, pertaining to the rights of young people and the Police Code of Practice. This enabled the researcher to obtain some qualitative data, so as to understand the quantitative data.

Substantially, the above mentioned five points (particularly the enhanced sample size for black defendants) were important for the study in that they became the objective basis on which to draw some generalisable conclusions about the problem under investigation.

Areas of convergence between the studies

In spite of areas of divergence between some studies discussed above, convergence also occurs:

a) Black defendants were found to be over-represented in the criminal justice system relative to their numbers in the general population, while both whites and Asians were under-represented.

b) Black defendants were much more punitively treated than their white and Asian counterparts, since a significant proportion of them were found to have received custodial sentences.

c) A significant proportion of black defendants were found to have been acquitted in the courts because of insufficient evidence, prompting the suggestion that the police tend to prosecute black defendants when evidence is weak, while diverting white defendants from court appearances.

d) All in all black people have been found to be over-represented in stops by the police, in arrests, prosecutions, acquittals and in custodial sentences.

This clearly reinforces the view that both the police and the courts stringently apply the principles of the justice model to crime and punishment much more so to black people than to Asian and white people. The problem seems to be compounded by prevailing police perceptions about black people and crime discussed in chapter two, such as the perception that black citizens pose special problems of law enforcement and that they (black citizens) exhibit negative traits (Fielding and Fielding 1991). In connection with judges, Hood (1992) suggests that they have to reassess their attitudes and judicial responses towards black defendants, since:

> It may be that some [judges] are not yet sufficiently sensitive to the way in which racial views and beliefs may influence their judgement.
> (pp. 190-1).

It seems plausible that Hood's comment could equally apply to magistrates, given the levels of disparities in sentencing by race in the magistrates' courts. Furthermore, he suggests that the criminal justice process may contribute to indirect discrimination against black people (p. 191).

However, the differences in outcomes in the local youth criminal justice system by the racial origin of the defendant as demonstrated in this study, as well as evidence of more police surveillance, stops, arrests, prosecutions, acquittals and custodial sentences for blacks found in other studies, raise a number of questions. For example, are the differences attributable to discriminatory practices on the part of the police and the courts, or due to 'differential involvement' in criminal activity? (see Langan 1985). Opinion on this has been divided. For instance, Langan (1985) argues that 'differential involvement' can be demonstrated if more than 23% of the young offenders described by crime victims and witnesses are black; that is, more than their representation in the borough of Brent's black, Asian and white youth population. This would imply that the over-representation of black young defendants in arrests and court appearances by 20% relative to their percentage in the youth population in Brent was attributed to their more frequent offending behaviour (see Stevens and Willis 1979; Lea and Young 1984). Although this may sound persuasive, the data in this study does show that black youth in fact had a significantly higher probability of being acquitted in the courts because of insufficient evidence compared to their white and Asian counterparts. That significant proportion of black young offenders who were acquitted should not have been arrested and prosecuted by the police in the first place without the evidence. Furthermore, there was also no statistically significant interaction between race and type of offences (serious offences included) in predicting custodial sentences. Other studies which have also disputed the differential involvement in criminality

141

hypothesis on the basis of both race and class in Britain and America have been discussed in chapter two.

Hudson (1989) has argued that research seems to have been impeded by problems arising from what discrimination is or is not; and from the lack of a theoretical frame of reference within which to interpret any findings. What is beyond dispute, however, is the realisation in criminological research that a different 'mental-set' may be operating amongst sentencers, when it comes to black defendants (Hood 1993). Some American studies (Hirschi 1969; Hindelang 1978) have perceived discrimination in the administration of justice in terms of 'selection bias' on the part of the officials. In Britain, Norris et al (1992) have argued that the over representation of black persons stopped, in their sample, was the result of 'police differentiation' and categorically challenged the assertion that differential treatment of black and white persons was due to transmitted discrimination; that is the tendency of victims and witnesses to call the police more often in incidents involving black offenders. However, in his review of the literature on black offending and police prejudice, Reiner (1985) has stated that:

> it seems clear that the disproportionate black arrest rate is the product of black deprivation, police stereotyping and the process by which each of these factors amplifies each other.   (p. 132).

Brogden et al (1988) also suggest that the key sociological determinants of policing derive from age, race, sex and class and, as Holdaway (1983) has demonstrated in the context of urban Britain, these variables are directly related to shared assumptions contained within the police occupational culture as to the moral worth of people. With regard to race, there is overwhelming evidence of hostile and prejudiced attitudes towards black persons on the part of the street level officers (Smith and Gray 1983; Norris 1987), although the link between prejudice and practice which can be found in, for example, the translation of negative attitudes into discriminatory action is not necessarily straightforward (Norris et al 1992).

However, Hudson (1989) and Fitzgerald (1991) have also argued that the finding of differential treatment, if based on statistical interrogation of data alone, obscures the nuances of sentencing behaviour and at best offers only an explanandum (something to be explained) rather than an explanans (something which is, of itself, an explanation). This suggests that, ideally, to explain any differences, studies or statistical series which make inter-ethnic comparisons should provide relevant background, for example, socio-demographic characteristics, type of offences allegedly committed, offending history, as well as other relevant information, such as observational data. Recent methodological debates deriving from disparate theoretical positions (Fielding and Fielding 1986; Abell 1988; Dale et al 1988 and Burrows 1989) have all come to broadly the same conclusion, that the demonstration of relatively enduring correlations within the empirical domain should be the beginning of research rather than an end in itself. In this regard, the demonstration of significantly different propensities of acquittals and custodial sentences in favour of black defendants as against the propensity of receiving police diversionary measures, regardless of the influence of significant control variables mentioned above, now requires further explication in more qualitative or narrative terms. These 'findings' become 'social facts' in the Durkhiemian sense, and the social, psychological and economic mechanisms which generate them clearly require further specification. Hence, the quantitative analysis of the sort presented in the preceding chapters alert us to possible relationships which then demand to be investigated using more intensive methods of research. This would assist in the generation and use of theory to advance our understanding of the processes by which discriminatory outcomes are produced.

What is now beyond dispute, however, is that black people are treated differently by the police, firstly through being stopped proportionately more than their white and Asian counterparts, and secondly are subject to more arrests and thirdly to more prosecutions, but are acquitted in the courts significantly more so than whites and Asians because of weak or insufficient evidence. Given the higher acquittal rate for blacks in the courts than whites, it can be concluded that blacks were unjustifiably stopped, arrested and prosecuted in the first place without the evidence of their wrong-doing. The fact that over half of the £500,000 that the MET paid out as compensation to citizens who had been wrongly arrested in 1989 went to black people (The Voice, 6th March 1990) and that, combined with the recent verdicts in the Court of Appeal of 'unsafe and unsatisfactory' convictions on black defendants, such as the Tottenham 3, the Cardiff 3 and the Hackney and Stoke Newington 4, seems to reinforce the above view. Furthermore, as it has already been shown, for those black defendants who get convicted, a significantly greater proportion of them receive custodial sentences than their white and Asian counterparts, thus reflecting the courts sentencing practices towards blacks. Looked at in this light, it means that black persons continue to receive punitive and 'justice oriented' treatment from both the police, as well as the courts.

In order to sound the police's view about this, the researcher asked some police officers during the period of the research to comment on media reports about police prejudice and black young people, in particular. Their view was that:

> There is always one bad apple in every barrel, but the Force take a very serious view of racial prejudice amongst officers and every effort is taken by the police themselves to deal with those few bad apples [through internal disciplinary measures].

This response implies that the police perceive remnants of police prejudice as containable, that such cases were/are few and far in between and in that regard, did not form part of a contrived police culture to discriminate against ethnic minorities. However, officers who advocated for 'more coloured constables who know the lifestyle and customs of people they are dealing with', saw the breakdown in trust between the police and young black people as compounded by:

> The attitude of some of the West Indian youth who reject the system. Some of them are against authority and just want to hang out, and perhaps find themselves getting into trouble. Their attitude is totally different from that of their parents or the older generation of West Indians.

In this respect, some black youths were thought of by those officers and by some court officers as being particularly susceptible to trouble with the law, difficult and uncooperative (see also Fielding and Fielding 1991).

Although it could be argued that increasing black representation at all levels of the police force and in political offices may help to improve the position of black people vis-a-vis the criminal justice system, as well as improving police/black community perceptions and relations, it could equally be argued that what people mostly needed was 'substantive' rather than mere 'descriptive representation' (Pitkin 1967). Pitkin argues that people are descriptively represented when certain of their demographic characteristics - race or ethnicity, gender, social class - coincide with those of their representative. Substantive representation occurs when a representative actually advances the interests of his or her constituents. However, Swain (1993) suggests that:

> Descriptive representation may or may not coincide with substantive representation. Black faces in political offices [and in decision-making positions within the criminal justice system], in and of themselves, do not quarantee that black interests will be served. (p. 221).

In this context, black officers are first and foremost police officers. Hence, they may find it difficult to function outside the prevailing police occupational culture of their force(s) which, as suggested by Fielding and Fielding (1991), might regard personal attributes as irrelevant and that all offenders are equal when it comes to guilt. Moreover, black officers might also have positive perceptions about the black community, which may not necessarily be shared by their white colleagues. In this regard, black officers might be faced with a dilemma if expected to advance police 'tactics' to combat community resistance, such as:

> - saturation policing, dawn raids, going in 'mob-handed' - all of which are, in turn, justified by singling out the black community for special treatment. In other words, it is not that black criminality justifies the use of such tactics; rather, such tactics are justified by the prior stigmatization of the [black] community as criminogenic. Practicability (the ability to do the job) is, therefore, used in this context not to abandon 'normal' policing but to impose coercive policing upon the black community.
>
> (McConville, Sanders and Leng 1991: 186).

Given this dilemma, it is not clear whether the failure to join the police force by black people, or for those who joined but subsequently resigned, can be attributed mostly to allegations of racism within the force itself or whether it is due to their perceived inability to substantively represent disadvantaged and discriminated against black people.

However, the results presented in this study may partly be due to the influences of the characteristics of the locale - its demographical profile, political economy and the nature and scope of the local criminal justice system. For example, 70% of all cases originated from Brent South and Brent East Parliamentary Constituencies, both of which are deprived and pro-Labour and are the areas with a higher concentration of ethnic minorities in the borough. 30% of all the cases (the remainder) came from Brent North Parliamentary Constituency, which is affluent and pro-Tory and has very few black people residing there compared to Asians. According to Sim (1982) it is highly probable that the police would concentrate both manpower and resources in areas such as Brent South and Brent East, where black young people in particular may be thought of as spending their time on the streets and therefore are more likely to come into greater contact with the police, as discussed in chapter two.

Secondly, the situation of a 'hung' Council and the resultant political instability which had prevailed for much of the period of this research was not conducive to sound policy-making. For example, in the areas of child care and youth justice, the Intermediate Treatment (IT) Budget, and the local Police and Community Consultative Committee were both phased out in August 1988, consequently affecting services to vulnerable children and young persons and police/community relations initiatives in the area.

Thirdly, the modus operandi for the local criminal justice was to identify labelled youngsters, usually black young persons, in order to a) prevent their entry into the criminal justice system and b) to influence diversion from courts for those coming into contact with the police. This policy, however, appears not to have been effective, as intermediate treatment social workers (whose function it was to identify labelled youngsters and to offer 'social work packages' designed to divert them from the court system) felt 'powerless' to influence police decision-making at both the arrest and the multi-agency panel levels, as the police retain the discretion to either caution or to prosecute defendants. The realisation that some young people 'at risk' of a court appearance were being prosecuted, when they might have benefited from involvement in a diversionary scheme, led some IT social workers to comment that:

The multi-agency panel is just another police public relations exercise... The police also appear to adopt a 'colour blind' approach in their handling of cases involving black people.

This 'colour blind' approach to processing black young offenders is thought of in

145

some quarters as failure by the authorities to recognise aspects that are disadvantaging ethnic minority young people which may/may not predispose them to offending (Tipler 1986). Again, this approach may also reflect the police's view that all offenders are equal when it comes to guilt (Fielding and Fielding 1991).

In the main, the relevant areas for further research identified in this study would be as follows:

- Self-reported offending rates obtained through intensive interviews, in the light of the purported ethnic differences in patterns of offending.
- Attitudes towards crime, punishment and the criminal justice system, such as Walker (1987a, and with others 1989) and the NACRO (1991) studies.
- Structural factors, including relevant aspects of differences in lifestyles generally, which may predispose towards criminal activity and affect decisions within the criminal justice system.
- The impact of police strategies leading to arrest (other than or as well as 'stops'), such as the Norris et al. (1992) study.
- Racial identification by victims and/or witnesses.
- The differences in official crime statistics between black and Asian communities.
- Whether black people's experience of the criminal justice system may be criminalising or may result in higher re-offending rates (the 'deviancy amplification' hypothesis).
- An analysis of female official referrals and self-reported offending, in order to compare their experiences of the criminal justice system with that of their male counterparts.
- The organisational characteristics and the decision-making process of Multi-Agency Panels.
- Charges brought on arrest and the role of the Crown Prosecution Service in relation to intended prosecutions of ethnic minorities.

At a practical level, research will require the co-operation and trust between the agencies of the criminal justice system to collect information on ethnic origin, as recommended by the House of Lords amendment to the Criminal Justice Bill 1990. The clause, which is now section 95(1)(b) of the Criminal Justice Act 1991, reads:

(1) The Secretary of State shall in each year publish such information as he considers expedient for the purpose of -...
    (b) facilitating the performance by such persons [those engaged in the administration of criminal justice] of their duty to avoid discriminating against any persons on the grounds of race or sex or any other improper ground.

In this respect, it is to be hoped that the present levels of official concern about the treatment of black people in the criminal justice system will be sustained. Other examples of this level of concern are the Home Office (Home Office Circular 38/1991, *Magistrates' Courts Service: Race*) requesting a service-wide survey of the ethnic background of all magistrates' courts committee members and staff on 30 June, to be followed by regular recording of such information for new staff, and also the Lord Chancellor approving a paper entitled, *An Introduction to Ethnic Awareness Training*, which was issued by the Magisterial Committee of the Judicial Studies Board during early 1991, to those who train lay magistrates. Furthermore, The Judicial Studies Board in its Report for 1987-1991 states that:

> It is axiomatic that no court should treat a defendant differently from any other simply because of his [her] race or ethnic origin. Any court that exhibited prejudice against a defendant from an ethnic minority would be failing in its basic duty to treat all defendants before it equally. (p. 18).

However, this study has thus far attempted to make a contribution to the debate surrounding racial factors and the institutional processing of young offenders by employing a multi-factorial analysis of data, which included a number of variables which need to be taken into account in isolating a race effect on police action and court sentencing. As stated in chapters one and four, a multi-factorial approach to analysing data had, hitherto, been lacking (Walker 1987a; Hudson 1989; Hood 1992). A final practical consideration is that no single study will yield the answers to the questions raised in this research, but rather information which already exists needs systematically to be brought together for a coherent picture to emerge. Accomplishing this would mean that our understanding of the characteristics, origins and treatment modalities of delinquency in any of its constituent parts would be further enhanced and hopefully be of use to policy-makers in their development of effective and equitable services for the population as a whole.

APPENDIX 1

Facility:	Programme:	Staffing:	Client:	Disposal:
High intensity day care (some weekend work).	Correctional curriculum Vocational training. Remedial education. Leisure activities.	Intermediate treatment centre social workers. Remedial teachers. Trade instructors. Volunteers.	High risk persistent offender. Unable to attend school or work.	To evening care or weekly group.
High intensity evening care and weekend work.	Correctional curriculum. Vocational training and remedial education if necessary. Leisure activities.	Intermediate treatment centre social workers. Remedial teachers and trade instructors. Volunteers.	High risk persistent offender from custody. Attending school or working.	To weekly group or youth club.
Medium intensity weekly group and weekend work.	Modified correctional curriculum. Leisure activities.	Area intermediate treatment social workers. Other social workers or youth workers. Volunteers.	Persistent petty offender, at risk of further offending.	To youth club or other positive leisure activity.
Low intensity youth club or other structured leisure activity.	Leisure activities.	Youth workers. Volunteers.	Occasional offender.	Continuing attendance without official direction.

Figure A1.1   The organisation of community support for young offenders in Brent

Source: *Report Number 40/82 to Brent's Social Services Committee* (8 September 1982)

150

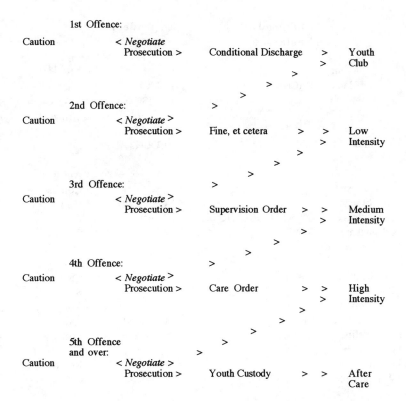

1st Offence:

Caution   < *Negotiate*
                        Prosecution >   Conditional Discharge   >   Youth
                                                                      >   Club
                                                            >
                                                    >
                                            >
        2nd Offence: >

Caution   < *Negotiate* >
                        Prosecution >   Fine, et cetera   >   >   Low
                                                                      >   Intensity
                                                            >
                                                    >
        3rd Offence: >

Caution   < *Negotiate* >
                        Prosecution >   Supervision Order   >   >   Medium
                                                                         >   Intensity
                                                            >
                                                    >
        4th Offence: >

Caution   < *Negotiate* >
                        Prosecution >   Care Order   >   >   High
                                                                  >   Intensity
                                                            >
                                                    >
        5th Offence   >
        and over: >
Caution   < *Negotiate* >
                        Prosecution >   Youth Custody   >   >   After
                                                                            Care

**Figure A 1. 2 A diagrammatic representation of a negotiating strategy
for a community support outcome at both the Multi-
Agency Panel (MAP) and court levels by recidivism**

Source: *Draft report of the local youth justice system working party -
Brent Social Services Department* (October 1985)

151

	Independent Variables		Dependent Variables	
Asian				NFA
Black	RACE		POLICE	Caution
White			DECISIONS	MAP Ctn
				Strings Ctn
Under 14	AGE		ACQUITTALS	
Over 14				
				Absdis
Employed				Condis
(bysegs)			NON-CUST	Botkp
Unemployed	SOCIO-ECONOMIC		(Court)	Fine
Residential area	STATUS			Comp
Housing type				ACO
Theft & Handling				CSO
Conveyances				SO
Property				SOIT
Violent	OFFENCES		NON-CUST	SAR
Police defined	(primary		(S/W+Pron)	Prob
Against Police	& tics)			Remcar
Possessing drugs				Resco
Other sum & Indictable				CO
Noh	RECIDIVISM			Remcus
Noca/arrests			CUSTODIAL	DC
				YC
Magistrates'	COURTS			
Crown				
Siragency				
Type of SIRR	SOCIAL INQUIRY			
Nospec	REPORTS			
Nosir				
Yes				
Successful	APPEALS			
Unsuccessful				
Local	POLICIES			
Judicial				

Figure A1.3   Hypothesis model of outcomes in a local youth criminal   justice system

The independent variables

term	*description*
Constant	GM (Grand Mean) for the first level of each variable
RRAC(1)	Black
RRAC(2)	White
RRAC(3)	Asian
TYP1(1)	Primary offences of theft or of handling stolen goods (HSG)
TYP1(2)	" " involving conveyances
TYP1(3)	" " relating to property
TYP1(4)	" " involving violence
TYP1(5)	" " which are police defined
TYP1(6)	" " against the police
TYP1(7)	" " involving possession of illicit drugs
TYP1(8)	Other summary and indictable primary offences
RTY2(1)	Defendants without offences taken into consideration (TICs)
RTY2(2)	Offences of theft or of HSG as the first TICs
RTY2(3)	" involving conveyances as the first TICs
RTY2(4)	" relating to property " "
RTY2(5)	" involving violence " "
RTY2(6)	" which are police defined "
RTY2(7)	" against the police "
RTY2(8)	" of possession of drugs "
RTY2(9)	Other summary and indictable offences "
NOH(1)	One offence(s) dealt with at the hearing
NOH(2)	Two " " "
NOH(3)	Three " " "
NOH(4)	Four " " "
NOCA(1)	First arrest or court appearance
NOCA(2)	Second " "
NOCA(3)	Third " "
NOCA(4)	Fourth " "
NOCA(5)	Fifth " "
NOCA(6)	Sixth " "
NOCA(7)	Seventh " "
NOCA(8)	Eighth " "
NOCA(9)	Nineth or more arrest(s) or court appearance(s)

The paired dependent variables

1.	Police Decisions vs Cases Dismissed in Court
2.	" " vs Court Non-custodial Sentences
3.	" " vs Court Social Work and Probation Sentences
4.	" " vs Custodial Sentences

Figure A1.4 Description of the independent and dependent variables for the final logit models fitted to the data

153

APPENDIX 2

term	description	estimate	s.e.	odds*	t-value
Constant		-3.112	0.6367	0.04451	-4.888**
RRAC(1)	Black	-	-	-	-
RRAC(2)	White	-0.3877	0.7280	0.67862	-0.533
RRAC(3)	Asian	-8.268	67.86	0.00026	-0.122
TYP1(1)	Theft & HSG	-	-	-	-
TYP1(2)	Conveyances	0.4459	1.332	1.56189	0.335
TYP1(3)	Property	0.6067	0.9100	1.83437	0.667
TYP1(4)	Violent	0.04026	1.298	1.04108	0.031
TYP1(5)	Police Defined	-9.136	58.45	0.00011	-0.156
TYP1(6)	Against Police	0.000	aliased	0.00000	0.000
TYP1(7)	Possessing Drugs	0.000	aliased	0.00000	0.000
TYP1(8)	Other Sum & Indict	0.04165	1.261	1.04253	0.033
RTY2(1)	Absence of TICs	-	-	-	-
RTY2(2)	Theft & HSG	0.2577	136.4	1.29395	0.002
RTY2(3)	Conveyances	0.7334	180.2	2.08215	0.004
RTY2(4)	Property	8.380	127.5	4359.00893	0.066
RTY2(5)	Violent	-7.236	127.5	0.00072	-0.057
RTY2(6)	Police Defined	1.753	149.8	5.77189	0.012
RTY2(7)	Against Police	-0.1220	234.6	0.88515	-0.001
RTY2(8)	Possessing Drugs	0.000	aliased	0.00000	0.000
RTY2(9)	Other Sum & Indict	0.3059	234.6	1.35785	0.001
NOH(1)	One Offence(s)	-	-	-	-
NOH(2)	Two "	-8.372	127.5	2.31E-04	-0.066
NOH(3)	Three "	-8.606	165.7	1.83E-04	-0.052
NOH(4)	Four "	-15.94	147.8	1.19E-07	-0.108
NOCA(1)	1st Arrest/Ct App	-	-	-	-
NOCA(2)	2nd " "	0.7884	0.9180	2.19987	0.859
NOCA(3)	3rd " "	-8.101	59.59	0.00030	-0.136
NOCA(4)	4th " "	2.023	1.403	7.56097	1.442
NOCA(5)	5th " "	2.679	0.9448	14.57051	2.836**
NOCA(6)	6th " "	-8.399	138.2	0.00022	-0.061
NOCA(7)	7th " "	1.070	205.5	2.91538	0.005
NOCA(8)	8th " "	13.30	100.8	597195.61380	0.132
NOCA(9)	9th + " "	13.12	100.8	498819.70660	0.130

Note:

1. The parameter for the first level of each variable is set to 1
2. * = Odds expressed in multiplicative form or as the parameter estimates anti log
3. ** = Significant t-values
4. 'Aliased' cells have missing data
5. Scaled deviance = 68.556 at cycle 10
   d.f. = 182   from 208 observations

Figure A2.1 Parameter estimates for the odds of cases dismissed in court as opposed to police diversionary measures for the under 14 age group

term	description	estimate	s.e.	odds*	t-value
Constant		-1.491	0.3221	0.22515	-4.629**
RRAC(1)	Black	-	-	-	-
RRAC(2)	White	-0.5051	0.2429	0.60345	-2.079**
RRAC(3)	Asian	-0.6914	0.6148	0.50087	-1.125
TYP1(1)	Theft & HSG	-	-	-	-
TYP1(2)	Conveyances	-0.1406	0.3760	0.86884	-0.374
TYP1(3)	Property	0.02460	0.3371	1.02491	0.073
TYP1(4)	Violent	1.134	0.3705	3.10806	3.061**
TYP1(5)	Police Defined	0.2824	0.4817	1.32631	0.586
TYP1(6)	Against Police	-0.7043	0.7231	0.49445	-0.974
TYP1(7)	Possessing Drugs	-0.7649	1.120	0.46538	-0.683
TYP1(8)	Other Sum & Indict	-0.2203	0.4511	0.80228	-0.488
RTY2(1)	Absence of TICs	-	-	-	-
RTY2(2)	Theft & HSG	-0.9331	1.177	0.39333	-0.793
RTY2(3)	Conveyances	-0.9392	1.232	0.39094	-0.762
RTY2(4)	Property	-3.221	1.589	0.03992	-2.027**
RTY2(5)	Violent	1.705	1.597	5.50139	1.068
RTY2(6)	Police Defined	-0.6793	1.291	0.50697	-0.526
RTY2(7)	Against Police	0.000	aliased	0.00000	0.000
RTY2(8)	Possessing Drugs	5.734	8.395	309.20361	0.683
RTY2(9)	Other Sum & Indict	-2.518	1.823	0.08062	-1.381
NOH(1)	One Offence(s)	-	-	-	-
NOH(2)	Two "	0.8855	1.185	2.42420	0.747
NOH(3)	Three "	1.969	1.331	7.16351	1.479
NOH(4)	Four "	0.000	aliased	0.00000	0.000
NOCA(1)	1st Arrest/Ct App	-	-	-	-
NOCA(2)	2nd " "	0.4804	0.3613	1.61672	1.330
NOCA(3)	3rd " "	1.156	0.3597	3.17720	3.214**
NOCA(4)	4th " "	0.5714	0.4122	1.77074	1.386
NOCA(5)	5th " "	1.525	0.4518	4.59514	3.375**
NOCA(6)	6th " "	1.135	0.5703	3.11117	1.990**
NOCA(7)	7th " "	1.822	0.6545	6.18421	2.784**
NOCA(8)	8th " "	1.822	0.6531	6.18421	2.790**
NOCA(9)	9th + " "	2.505	0.5072	12.24356	4.939**

Note:

1. The parameter for the first level of each variable is set to 1
2. * = Odds expressed in multiplicative form or as the parameter estimates anti log
3. ** = Significant t-values
4. 'Aliased' cells have missing data
5. Scaled deviance = 482.81 at cycle 5
   d.f. = 434   from 461 observations

Figure A2.2 Parameter estimates for the odds of cases dismissed in court as opposed to police diversionary measures for the over 14 age group

term	description	estimate	s.e.	odds*	t-value
Constant		-1.587	0.2902	0.20454	-5.469**
RRAC(1)	Black	-	-	-	-
RRAC(2)	White	-0.1159	0.2755	0.89056	-0.421
RRAC(3)	Asian	0.2059	0.7691	1.22863	0.268
TYP1(1)	Theft & HSG	-	-	-	-
TYP1(2)	Conveyances	-1.077	0.7808	0.34062	-1.379
TYP1(3)	Property	0.4319	0.3458	1.54018	1.249
TYP1(4)	Violent	-0.05067	0.5612	0.95059	-0.090
TYP1(5)	Police Defined	-2.506	1.204	0.08159	-2.081**
TYP1(6)	Against Police	6.437	22.51	624.53040	0.286
TYP1(7)	Possessing Drugs	0.000	aliased	0.00000	0.000
TYP1(8)	Other Sum & Indict	-0.3827	0.5061	0.68202	-0.756
RTY2(1)	Absence of TICs	-	-	-	-
RTY2(2)	Theft & HSG	1.311	1.606	3.70988	0.816
RTY2(3)	Conveyances	2.917	1.930	18.48575	1.511
RTY2(4)	Property	0.8710	1.607	2.38930	0.542
RTY2(5)	Violent	1.623	1.588	5.06827	1.022
RTY2(6)	Police Defined	-7.132	16.29	0.00080	-0.438
RTY2(7)	Against Police	-6.086	43.99	0.00228	-0.138
RTY2(8)	Possessing Drugs	0.000	aliased	0.00000	0.000
RTY2(9)	Other Sum & Indict	2.639	2.029	13.99920	1.301
NOH(1)	One Offence(s)	-	-	-	-
NOH(2)	Two "	-0.8419	1.540	0.43089	-0.547
NOH(3)	Three "	-1.056	1.715	0.34784	-0.616
NOH(4)	Four "	0.4841	1.699	1.62271	0.285
NOCA(1)	1st Arrest/Ct App	-	-	-	-
NOCA(2)	2nd " "	2.298	0.3279	9.95425	7.008**
NOCA(3)	3rd " "	2.491	0.4598	12.07334	5.418**
NOCA(4)	4th " "	3.090	0.6708	21.97708	4.606**
NOCA(5)	5th " "	1.877	0.6637	6.53387	2.828**
NOCA(6)	6th " "	2.483	0.8808	11.97714	2.819**
NOCA(7)	7th " "	3.418	1.557	30.50834	2.195**
NOCA(8)	8th " "	8.497	22.51	4900.04663	0.378
NOCA(9)	9th + " "	7.931	22.54	2782.20762	0.352

Note:

1. The parameter for the first level of each variable is set to 1
2. * = Odds expressed in multiplicative form or as the parameter estimates anti log
3. ** = Significant t-values
4. 'Aliased' cells have missing data
5. Scaled deviance = 349.91 at cycle 7
   d.f. = 320   from 347 observations

Figure A2.3   Parameter estimates for the odds of court non-custodial sentences as opposed to police diversionary measures for the under 14 age group

term	description	estimate	s.e.	odds*	t-value
Constant		-0.1564	0.2079	0.85522	-0.752
RRAC(1)	Black	-	-	-	-
RRAC(2)	White	-0.3080	0.1643	0.73492	-1.875
RRAC(3)	Asian	-0.3514	0.3634	0.70370	-0.967
TYP1(1)	Theft & HSG	-	-	-	-
TYP1(2)	Conveyances	0.08331	0.2323	1.08688	0.359
TYP1(3)	Property	-0.3515	0.2310	0.70363	-1.522
TYP1(4)	Violent	0.01675	0.3055	1.01689	0.055
TYP1(5)	Police Defined	-0.4666	0.3833	0.62713	-1.217
TYP1(6)	Against Police	0.3459	0.3872	1.41326	0.893
TYP1(7)	Possessing Drugs	0.1333	0.5197	1.14259	0.257
TYP1(8)	Other Sum & Indict	-0.7421	0.3174	0.47611	-2.338**
RTY2(1)	Absence of TICs	-	-	-	-
RTY2(2)	Theft & HSG	0.3509	0.4992	1.42035	0.703
RTY2(3)	Conveyances	1.108	0.5629	3.02830	1.968**
RTY2(4)	Property	0.3230	0.5669	1.38127	0.570
RTY2(5)	Violent	2.741	1.134	15.50248	2.417**
RTY2(6)	Police Defined	-0.01335	0.6659	0.98674	-0.020
RTY2(7)	Against Police	5.899	4.558	364.67261	1.294
RTY2(8)	Possessing Drugs	5.660	7.864	287.14864	0.720
RTY2(9)	Other Sum & Indict	0.9759	0.7036	2.65355	1.387
NOH(1)	One Offence(s)	-	-	-	-
NOH(2)	Two "	-0.1502	0.4897	0.86054	-0.307
NOH(3)	Three "	0.2940	0.6182	1.34178	0.476
NOH(4)	Four "	0.000	aliased	0.00000	0.000
NOCA(1)	1st Arrest/Ct App	-	-	-	-
NOCA(2)	2nd " "	0.8188	0.2215	2.26778	3.697**
NOCA(3)	3rd " "	0.9181	0.2427	2.50453	3.783**
NOCA(4)	4th " "	0.6634	0.2587	1.94138	2.564**
NOCA(5)	5th " "	0.9237	0.3309	2.51859	2.792**
NOCA(6)	6th " "	1.169	0.3740	3.21877	3.126**
NOCA(7)	7th " "	1.368	0.4782	3.92749	2.861**
NOCA(8)	8th " "	0.7075	0.5383	2.02891	1.314
NOCA(9)	9th + " "	1.072	0.4231	2.92122	2.534**

Note:

1. The parameter for the first level of each variable is set to 1
2. * = Odds expressed in multiplicative form or as the parameter estimates anti log
3. ** = Significant t-values
4. The 'aliased' cell has missing data
5. Scaled deviance = 981.5 at cycle 6
   d.f. = 766 from 794 observations

Figure A2.4 Parameter estimates for the odds of court non-custodial sentences as opposed to police diversionary measures for the over 14 age group

term	description	estimate	s.e.	odds*	t-value
Constant		-3.240	0.5011	0.03916	-6.466**
RRAC(1)	Black	-	-	-	-
RRAC(2)	White	0.004023	0.4534	1.00403	0.009
RRAC(3)	Asian	1.141	0.9865	3.12990	1.157
TYP1(1)	Theft & HSG	-	-	-	-
TYP1(2)	Conveyances	-0.6335	1.263	0.53073	-0.502
TYP1(3)	Property	0.8150	0.5205	2.25918	1.566
TYP1(4)	Violent	0.1693	0.7726	1.18448	0.219
TYP1(5)	Police Defined	-0.2603	0.9947	0.77082	-0.262
TYP1(6)	Against Police	7.734	22.54	2284.72284	0.343
TYP1(7)	Possessing Drugs	0.000	aliased	0.00000	0.000
TYP1(8)	Other Sum & Indict	-0.4201	0.8826	0.65698	-0.476
RTY2(1)	Absence of TICs	-	-	-	-
RTY2(2)	Theft & HSG	0.3592	1.955	1.43218	0.184
RTY2(3)	Conveyances	0.03159	2.636	1.03209	0.012
RTY2(4)	Property	0.8048	1.990	2.23625	0.404
RTY2(5)	Violent	1.950	1.807	7.02869	1.079
RTY2(6)	Police Defined	-7.107	17.05	0.00082	-0.417
RTY2(7)	Against Police	1.417	2.811	4.12473	0.504
RTY2(8)	Possessing Drugs	0.000	aliased	0.00000	0.000
RTY2(9)	Other Sum & Indict	-5.226	44.00	0.00538	-0.119
NOH(1)	One Offence(s)	-	-	-	-
NOH(2)	Two "	-0.1041	1.863	0.90114	-0.056
NOH(3)	Three "	1.315	2.154	3.72475	0.611
NOH(4)	Four "	1.477	2.110	4.37979	0.700
NOCA(1)	1st Arrest/Ct App	-	-	-	-
NOCA(2)	2nd " "	2.228	0.4982	9.28129	4.472**
NOCA(3)	3rd " "	2.846	0.6111	17.21877	4.657**
NOCA(4)	4th " "	2.866	0.9194	17.56661	3.117**
NOCA(5)	5th " "	0.8993	1.209	2.45788	0.744
NOCA(6)	6th " "	2.728	1.253	15.30225	2.177**
NOCA(7)	7th " "	3.723	1.377	41.38837	2.704**
NOCA(8)	8th " "	0.000	aliased	0.00000	0.000
NOCA(9)	9th + " "	11.10	22.55	66171.16017	0.492

Note:

1.   The parameter for the first level of each variable is set to 1
2.   * = Odds expressed in multiplicative form or as the parameter estimates anti log
3.   ** = Significant t-values
4.   'Aliased' cells have missing data
5.   Scaled deviance = 170.55 at cycle 7
     d.f. = 221   from 247 observations

Figure A2.5 Parameter estimates for the odds of court social work sentences as opposed to police diversionary measures for the under 14 age group

term	description	estimate	s.e.	odds*	t-value
Constant		-2.070	0.3528	0.12619	-5.867**
RRAC(1)	Black	-	-	-	-
RRAC(2)	White	-0.2774	0.2427	0.75775	-1.143
RRAC(3)	Asian	0.09350	0.4839	1.09801	0.193
TYP1(1)	Theft & HSG	-	-	-	-
TYP1(2)	Conveyances	-0.7054	0.3873	0.49391	-1.821
TYP1(3)	Property	0.08842	0.3179	1.09245	0.278
TYP1(4)	Violent	-0.04492	0.4587	0.95607	-0.098
TYP1(5)	Police Defined	-0.2560	0.5080	0.77414	-0.504
TYP1(6)	Against Police	-0.6644	0.7271	0.51458	-0.914
TYP1(7)	Possessing Drugs	-1.450	1.274	0.23457	-1.138
TYP1(8)	Other Sum & Indict	-0.5809	0.4793	0.55940	-1.212
RTY2(1)	Absence of TICs	-	-	-	-
RTY2(2)	Theft & HSG	1.963	0.5624	7.12066	3.490**
RTY2(3)	Conveyances	3.028	0.6847	20.65588	4.422**
RTY2(4)	Property	2.174	0.5732	8.79339	3.793**
RTY2(5)	Violent	4.488	1.241	88.94338	3.616**
RTY2(6)	Police Defined	1.649	0.8029	5.20178	2.054**
RTY2(7)	Against Police	8.474	13.70	4788.63174	0.619
RTY2(8)	Possessing Drugs	10.38	8.893	32208.96149	1.167
RTY2(9)	Other Sum & Indict	2.591	0.8430	13.34311	3.074**
NOH(1)	One Offence(s)	-	-	-	-
NOH(2)	Two "	-1.152	0.5371	0.31600	-2.145**
NOH(3)	Three "	-0.1661	0.6469	0.84696	-0.257
NOH(4)	Four "	0.000	aliased	0.00000	0.000
NOCA(1)	1st Arrest/Ct App	-	-	-	-
NOCA(2)	2nd " "	0.9003	0.3777	2.46034	2.384**
NOCA(3)	3rd " "	1.497	0.3783	4.46826	3.957**
NOCA(4)	4th " "	1.510	0.4052	4.52673	3.727**
NOCA(5)	5th " "	1.636	0.4824	5.13459	3.391**
NOCA(6)	6th " "	2.028	0.5154	7.59887	3.935**
NOCA(7)	7th " "	2.211	0.6019	9.12484	3.673**
NOCA(8)	8th " "	1.482	0.6987	4.40174	2.121**
NOCA(9)	9th + " "	2.453	0.5438	11.62316	4.511**

Note:

1. The parameter for the first level of each variable is set to 1
2. * = Odds expressed in multiplicative form or as the parameter estimates anti log
3. ** = Significant t-values
4. The 'aliased' cell has missing data
5. Scaled deviance = 494.68 at cycle 6
   d.f. = 463   from 491 observations

Figure A2.6 Parameter estimates for the odds of court social work and probation sentences as opposed to police diversionary measures for the over 14 age group

term	description	estimate	s.e.	odds*	t-value
Constant		-3.553	0.5799	0.02864	-6.127**
RRAC(1)	Black	-	-	-	-
RRAC(2)	White	-0.8051	0.3517	0.44704	-2.289**
RRAC(3)	Asian	-0.5190	0.6644	0.59512	-0.781
TYP1(1)	Theft & HSG	-	-	-	-
TYP1(2)	Conveyances	-1.235	0.6920	0.29084	-1.785
TYP1(3)	Property	1.228	0.4644	3.41439	2.644**
TYP1(4)	Violent	1.738	0.5304	5.68596	3.277**
TYP1(5)	Police Defined	-7.966	14.59	0.00035	-0.546
TYP1(6)	Against Police	-7.374	18.57	0.00063	-0.397
TYP1(7)	Possessing Drugs	-6.836	24.20	0.00107	-0.283
TYP1(8)	Other Sum & Indict	-0.2593	0.7272	0.77159	-0.357
RTY2(1)	Absence of TICs	-	-	-	-
RTY2(2)	Theft & HSG	2.862	0.7554	17.49649	3.789**
RTY2(3)	Conveyances	4.807	0.9491	122.36397	5.065**
RTY2(4)	Property	2.703	0.7213	14.92444	3.747**
RTY2(5)	Violent	5.761	1.349	317.66584	4.271**
RTY2(6)	Police Defined	3.401	1.097	29.99408	3.100**
RTY2(7)	Against Police	8.737	37.11	6229.18011	0.235
RTY2(8)	Possessing Drugs	16.28	44.31	11757477.75000	0.367
RTY2(9)	Other Sum & Indict	3.298	1.190	27.05847	2.771**
NOH(1)	One Offence(s)	-	-	-	-
NOH(2)	Two "	-2.156	0.7045	0.11579	-3.060**
NOH(3)	Three "	-0.2843	0.7768	0.75254	-0.366
NOH(4)	Four "	0.000	aliased	0.00000	0.000
NOCA(1)	1st Arrest/Ct App	-	-	-	-
NOCA(2)	2nd " "	1.122	0.5673	3.07099	1.978**
NOCA(3)	3rd " "	1.123	0.5930	3.07406	1.894
NOCA(4)	4th " "	1.881	0.5781	6.56006	3.254**
NOCA(5)	5th " "	2.620	0.6223	13.73572	4.210**
NOCA(6)	6th " "	2.410	0.8221	11.13396	2.932**
NOCA(7)	7th " "	3.152	0.7443	23.38278	4.235**
NOCA(8)	8th " "	3.643	0.7966	38.20628	4.573**
NOCA(9)	9th + " "	3.715	0.7108	41.05859	5.227**

Note:

1. The parameter for the first level of each variable is set to 1
2. * = Odds expressed in multiplicative form or as the parameter estimates anti log
3. ** = Significant t-values
4. The 'aliased' cell has missing data
5. Scaled deviance = 275.33 at cycle 8
   d.f. = 408 from 436 observations

Figure A2.7 Parameter estimates for the odds of custodial sentences as opposed to police diversionary measures for the over 14 age group

APPENDIX 3

Table A3.1

Probabilities of acquittal by race and the controlling factors: Under 14s

Estimated probabilities of cases dismissed in court as opposed to police diversionary measures by race and type of primary offence, type of first TIC, the total number of offences dealt with at the same hearing and the number of arrests or court appearances for the under 14 age group

| | Race | | |
Parameters	Black	Asian	White
TYP1(1),RTY2(1),NOH(1),NOCA(1)	0.043	0.01E-03	0.029
TYP1(2),RTY2(1),NOH(1),NOCA(1)	0.065	0.02E-03	0.045
TYP1(3),RTY2(1),NOH(1),NOCA(1)	0.076	0.02E-03	0.052
TYP1(4),RTY2(1),NOH(1),NOCA(1)	0.044	0.01E-03	0.031
TYP1(8),RTY2(1),NOH(1),NOCA(1)	0.044	0.01E-03	0.031
TYP1(1),RTY2(1),NOH(1),NOCA(5)	0.393	0.02E-02	0.306
TYP1(2),RTY2(1),NOH(1),NOCA(5)	0.503	0.03E-02	0.407
TYP1(3),RTY2(1),NOH(1),NOCA(5)	0.543	0.03E-02	0.447
TYP1(4),RTY2(1),NOH(1),NOCA(5)	0.403	0.02E-02	0.314
TYP1(8),RTY2(1),NOH(1),NOCA(5)	0.403	0.02E-02	0.315

Key

TYP1(1) = Primary offences of theft or of handling stolen goods
TYP1(2) =   "   "   involving motor vehicles
TYP1(3) =   "   "   relating to property
TYP1(4) =   "   "   involving violence
TYP1(8) = Other summary and indictable primary offences
RTY2(1) = Defendants without any TICs
NOH(1) = Only one offence that was dealt with at the hearing
NOCA(1) and (5) = First and fifth arrest or court appearance

Table A3.2
Margins of the difference between the probabilities of acquittal between racial groups: Under 14s

Margins of the difference between the probabilities of cases dismissed in court as opposed to police diversionary measures between the three racial groups of the under 14s by type of primary offence, type of first TIC, the total number of offences dealt with at the same hearing and the number of arrests or court appearances in percentages

	Race		
Parameters	Black v Asian	White v Asian	Black v White
TYP1(3),RTY2(1),NOH(1),NOCA(5)	54	45	10
TYP1(2),RTY2(1),NOH(1),NOCA(5)	50	41	10
TYP1(4),RTY2(1),NOH(1),NOCA(5)	40	31	9
TYP1(8),RTY2(1),NOH(1),NOCA(5)	40	31	9
TYP1(1),RTY2(1),NOH(1),NOCA(5)	39	31	9
TYP1(3),RTY2(1),NOH(1),NOCA(1)	8	5	2
TYP1(2),RTY2(1),NOH(1),NOCA(1)	6	4	2
TYP1(4),RTY2(1),NOH(1),NOCA(1)	4	3	1
TYP1(8),RTY2(1),NOH(1),NOCA(1)	4	3	1
TYP1(1),RTY2(1),NOH(1),NOCA(1)	4	3	1

Key

TYP1(1) = Primary offences of theft or of handling stolen goods
TYP1(2) =   "   "   involving motor vehicles
TYP1(3) =   "   "   relating to property
TYP1(4) =   "   "   involving violence
TYP1(8) = Other summary and indictable primary offences
RTY2(1) = Defendants without any TICs
NOH(1) = Only one offence that was dealt with at the hearing
NOCA(1) and (5) = First and fifth arrest or court appearance

Note: The control variables are listed in order of the combination with the widest margin of difference between the probabilities of receiving an acquittal in the courts between the three groups of the under 14 year old defendants.

Table A3.3
Probabilities of acquittal by race and the controlling factors: Over 14s

Estimated probabilities of cases dismissed in court as opposed to police diversionary measures by race and type of primary offence, type of first TIC, the total number of offences dealt with at the same hearing and the number of arrests or court appearances for the over 14 age group

| | | Race | |
Parameters	Black	Asian	White
TYP1(1),RTY2(1),NOH(1),NOCA(1)	0.184	0.101	0.120
TYP1(3),RTY2(1),NOH(1),NOCA(1)	0.188	0.104	0.122
TYP1(4),RTY2(1),NOH(1),NOCA(1)	0.412	0.260	0.297
TYP1(5),RTY2(1),NOH(1),NOCA(1)	0.230	0.130	0.153
TYP1(1),RTY2(1),NOH(1),NOCA(3)	0.417	0.264	0.302
TYP1(3),RTY2(1),NOH(1),NOCA(3)	0.423	0.269	0.307
TYP1(4),RTY2(1),NOH(1),NOCA(3)	0.690	0.527	0.573
TYP1(5),RTY2(1),NOH(1),NOCA(3)	0.487	0.341	0.384
TYP1(3),RTY2(1),NOH(1),NOCA(5)	0.515	0.347	0.390
TYP1(4),RTY2(1),NOH(1),NOCA(5)	0.763	0.617	0.660
TYP1(5),RTY2(1),NOH(1),NOCA(5)	0.579	0.407	0.453
TYP1(1),RTY2(1),NOH(1),NOCA(6)	0.412	0.259	0.297
TYP1(3),RTY2(1),NOH(1),NOCA(6)	0.418	0.265	0.302
TYP1(4),RTY2(1),NOH(1),NOCA(6)	0.685	0.522	0.568
TYP1(5),RTY2(1),NOH(1),NOCA(6)	0.482	0.318	0.359
TYP1(1),RTY2(1),NOH(1),NOCA(7)	0.582	0.411	0.457
TYP1(3),RTY2(1),NOH(1),NOCA(7)	0.588	0.417	0.463
TYP1(4),RTY2(1),NOH(1),NOCA(7)	0.812	0.684	0.723
TYP1(5),RTY2(1),NOH(1),NOCA(7)	0.649	0.481	0.527
TYP1(1),RTY2(1),NOH(1),NOCA(8)	0.582	0.411	0.457
TYP1(3),RTY2(1),NOH(1),NOCA(8)	0.588	0.417	0.463
TYP1(4),RTY2(1),NOH(1),NOCA(8)	0.812	0.684	0.723
TYP1(5),RTY2(1),NOH(1),NOCA(8)	0.649	0.481	0.527
TYP1(1),RTY2(1),NOH(1),NOCA(9)	0.734	0.580	0.625
TYP1(3),RTY2(1),NOH(1),NOCA(9)	0.739	0.586	0.630
TYP1(4),RTY2(1),NOH(1),NOCA(9)	0.895	0.811	0.838
TYP1(5),RTY2(1),NOH(1),NOCA(9)	0.785	0.647	0.688

Key

TYP1(1) = Primary offences of theft or of handling stolen goods
TYP1(3) =   "   "   involving motor vehicles
TYP1(4) =   "   "   involving violence
TYP1(5) =   "   "   which are police defined
RTY2(1) = Defendants without TICs
NOH(1) = One offence dealt with at the hearing
NOCA(1),(3),(5) thru (9) = First, third, fifth and up to the ninth or more arrest(s) or court appearance(s)

Table A3.4
Margins of the difference between the probabilities of acquittal between racial groups: Over 14s

Margins of the difference between the probabilities of cases dismissed in court as opposed to police diversionary measures between the three racial groups of the over 14s by type of primary offence, type of first TIC, the total number of offences dealt with at the same hearing and the number of arrests or court apearances in percentages

| | Race | | |
Parameters	Black v Asian	Black v White	White v Asian
TYP1(5),RTY2(1),NOH(1),NOCA(5)	17	13	5
TYP1(1),RTY2(1),NOH(1),NOCA(7)	17	13	5
TYP1(3),RTY2(1),NOH(1),NOCA(7)	17	13	5
TYP1(1),RTY2(1),NOH(1),NOCA(8)	17	13	5
TYP1(3),RTY2(1),NOH(1),NOCA(8)	17	13	5
TYP1(3),RTY2(1),NOH(1),NOCA(5)	17	13	4
TYP1(5),RTY2(1),NOH(1),NOCA(7)	17	12	5
TYP1(5),RTY2(1),NOH(1),NOCA(8)	17	12	5
TYP1(1),RTY2(1),NOH(1),NOCA(5)	17	12	4
TYP1(4),RTY2(1),NOH(1),NOCA(3)	16	12	5
TYP1(4),RTY2(1),NOH(1),NOCA(6)	16	12	5
TYP1(5),RTY2(1),NOH(1),NOCA(3)	16	12	4
TYP1(5),RTY2(1),NOH(1),NOCA(6)	16	12	4
TYP1(4),RTY2(1),NOH(1),NOCA(1)	15	12	4
TYP1(1),RTY2(1),NOH(1),NOCA(3)	15	12	4
TYP1(3),RTY2(1),NOH(1),NOCA(3)	15	12	4
TYP1(1),RTY2(1),NOH(1),NOCA(6)	15	12	4
TYP1(3),RTY2(1),NOH(1),NOCA(6)	15	12	4
TYP1(1),RTY2(1),NOH(1),NOCA(9)	15	11	4
TYP1(3),RTY2(1),NOH(1),NOCA(9)	15	11	4
TYP1(4),RTY2(1),NOH(1),NOCA(5)	15	10	4
TYP1(5),RTY2(1),NOH(1),NOCA(9)	14	10	4
TYP1(4),RTY2(1),NOH(1),NOCA(7)	13	9	4
TYP1(4),RTY2(1),NOH(1),NOCA(8)	13	9	4
TYP1(5),RTY2(1),NOH(1),NOCA(1)	10	8	2
TYP1(3),RTY2(1),NOH(1),NOCA(1)	8	7	2
TYP1(4),RTY2(1),NOH(1),NOCA(9)	8	6	3
TYP1(1),RTY2(1),NOH(1),NOCA(1)	8	6	2

Key

TYP1(1) = Primary offences of theft or of handling stolen goods
TYP1(3) = " " relating to property
TYP1(4) = " " involving violence
TYP1(5) = " " which are police defined
RTY2(1) = Defendants without any TICs
NOH(1) = Only one offence that was dealt with at the hearing
NOCA(1),(3),(5) thru (9) = first, third, fifth and up to the ninth or more arrest(s) or court appearance(s)

Note: The control variables are listed in order of the combination with the widest margin of difference between the probabilities of receiving an acquittal in the courts between the three groups of the over 14 year old defendants.

Table A3.5
Probabilities of court non-custodial sentences by race and the controlling factors: Under 14s

Estimated probabilities of court non-custodial sentences as opposed to police diversionary measures by race and type of primary offence, type of first TIC, the total number of offences dealt with at the same hearing and the number of arrests or court appearances for the under 14 age group

| | Race | | |
Parameters	Black	Asian	White
TYP1(1),RTY2(1),NOH(1),NOCA(1)	0.170	0.201	0.154
TYP1(3),RTY2(1),NOH(1),NOCA(1)	0.240	0.279	0.219
TYP1(6),RTY2(1),NOH(1),NOCA(1)	0.992	0.994	0.991
TYP1(1),RTY2(1),NOH(1),NOCA(2)	0.671	0.714	0.645
TYP1(3),RTY2(1),NOH(1),NOCA(2)	0.758	0.794	0.736
TYP1(6),RTY2(1),NOH(1),NOCA(2)	0.999	0.999	0.999
TYP1(1),RTY2(1),NOH(1),NOCA(3)	0.712	0.752	0.687
TYP1(3),RTY2(1),NOH(1),NOCA(3)	0.792	0.824	0.772
TYP1(6),RTY2(1),NOH(1),NOCA(3)	0.999	0.999	0.999
TYP1(1),RTY2(1),NOH(1),NOCA(4)	0.818	0.847	0.800
TYP1(3),RTY2(1),NOH(1),NOCA(4)	0.874	0.895	0.861
TYP1(6),RTY2(1),NOH(1),NOCA(4)	0.999	0.999	0.999
TYP1(1),RTY2(1),NOH(1),NOCA(5)	0.572	0.622	0.543
TYP1(3),RTY2(1),NOH(1),NOCA(5)	0.673	0.717	0.647
TYP1(6),RTY2(1),NOH(1),NOCA(5)	0.999	0.999	0.999
TYP1(1),RTY2(1),NOH(1),NOCA(6)	0.710	0.751	0.686
TYP1(3),RTY2(1),NOH(1),NOCA(6)	0.791	0.823	0.771
TYP1(6),RTY2(1),NOH(1),NOCA(6)	0.999	0.999	0.999
TYP1(1),RTY2(1),NOH(1),NOCA(7)	0.862	0.885	0.848
TYP1(3),RTY2(1),NOH(1),NOCA(7)	0.906	0.922	0.895
TYP1(6),RTY2(1),NOH(1),NOCA(7)	0.999	0.999	0.999

Key

TYP1(1) = Primary offences of theft or of handling stolen goods
TYP1(3) =   "   "   relating to property
TYP1(6) =   "   "   against the police
RTY2(1) = Defendants without TICs
NOH(1) = One offence dealt with at the hearing
NOCA(1) thru (7) = First and up to the seventh arrest or court appearance

Table A3.6
Margins of the difference between the probabilities of court non-custodial sentences between racial groups: Under 14s

Margins of the difference between the probabilities of court non-custodial sentences as opposed to police diversionary measures between the three racial groups of the under 14s by type of the primary offences, type of the first TICs, the total number of offences dealt with at the same hearing and the number of arrests or court appearances in percentages.

	Race		
Parameters	Asian v White	Asian v Black	Black v White
TYP1(1),RTY2(1),NOH(1),NOCA(5)	8	5	3
TYP1(1),RTY2(1),NOH(1),NOCA(2)	7	4	3
TYP1(1),RTY2(1),NOH(1),NOCA(3)	7	4	3
TYP1(3),RTY2(1),NOH(1),NOCA(5)	7	4	3
TYP1(1),RTY2(1),NOH(1),NOCA(6)	7	4	2
TYP1(3),RTY2(1),NOH(1),NOCA(1)	6	4	2
TYP1(3),RTY2(1),NOH(1),NOCA(2)	6	4	2
TYP1(1),RTY2(1),NOH(1),NOCA(1)	5	3	2
TYP1(3),RTY2(1),NOH(1),NOCA(3)	5	3	2
TYP1(1),RTY2(1),NOH(1),NOCA(4)	5	3	2
TYP1(3),RTY2(1),NOH(1),NOCA(6)	5	3	2
TYP1(1),RTY2(1),NOH(1),NOCA(7)	4	2	1
TYP1(3),RTY2(1),NOH(1),NOCA(4)	3	2	1
TYP1(3),RTY2(1),NOH(1),NOCA(7)	3	2	1
TYP1(6),RTY2(1),NOH(1),NOCA(1)	0.003	0.002	0.001
TYP1(6),RTY2(1),NOH(1),NOCA(5)	0.0004	0.0002	0.0001
TYP1(6),RTY2(1),NOH(1),NOCA(2)	0.0002	0.0002	0.0001
TYP1(6),RTY2(1),NOH(1),NOCA(3)	0.0002	0.0001	0.0001
TYP1(6),RTY2(1),NOH(1),NOCA(6)	0.0002	0.0001	0.0001
TYP1(6),RTY2(1),NOH(1),NOCA(4)	0.0001	0.0001	0.00004
TYP1(6),RTY2(1),NOH(1),NOCA(7)	0.0001	0.0001	0.00003

Key

TYP1(1) = Primary offences of theft or of handling stolen goods
TYP1(3) =   "   "   relating to property
TYP1(6) =   "   "   against the police
RTY2(1) = Defendants without any TICs
NOH(1) = Only one offence that was dealt with at the hearing
NOCA(1) thru (7) = First and up to the seventh arrest or court appearance

Note: The control variables are listed in order of the combination with the widest margin of difference between the probabilities of receiving court non-custodial sentences between the three groups of the under 14 year old defendants.

Table A3.7
Probabilities of court non-custodial sentences by race and the controlling factors: Over 14s

Estimated probabilities of court non-custodial sentences as opposed to police diversionary measures by race and type of primary offence, type of first TIC, the total number of offences dealt with at the same hearing and the number of arrests or court appearances for the over 14 age group

Parameters	Race		
	Black	Asian	White
TYPI(1),RTY2(1),NOH(1),NOCA(1)	0.461	0.376	0.386
TYPI(2),RTY2(1),NOH(1),NOCA(1)	0.482	0.395	0.406
TYPI(4),RTY2(1),NOH(1),NOCA(1)	0.465	0.380	0.390
TYPI(6),RTY2(1),NOH(1),NOCA(1)	0.547	0.460	0.470
TYPI(7),RTY2(1),NOH(1),NOCA(1)	0.494	0.408	0.418
TYPI(1),RTY2(1),NOH(1),NOCA(2)	0.660	0.577	0.588
TYPI(2),RTY2(1),NOH(1),NOCA(2)	0.678	0.597	0.608
TYPI(4),RTY2(1),NOH(1),NOCA(2)	0.664	0.581	0.592
TYPI(6),RTY2(1),NOH(1),NOCA(2)	0.733	0.659	0.668
TYPI(7),RTY2(1),NOH(1),NOCA(2)	0.689	0.609	0.620
TYPI(1),RTY2(1),NOH(1),NOCA(3)	0.682	0.601	0.612
TYPI(2),RTY2(1),NOH(1),NOCA(3)	0.700	0.621	0.631
TYPI(4),RTY2(1),NOH(1),NOCA(3)	0.685	0.605	0.616
TYPI(6),RTY2(1),NOH(1),NOCA(3)	0.752	0.681	0.690
TYPI(7),RTY2(1),NOH(1),NOCA(3)	0.710	0.633	0.643
TYPI(1),RTY2(1),NOH(1),NOCA(4)	0.624	0.539	0.550
TYPI(2),RTY2(1),NOH(1),NOCA(4)	0.643	0.559	0.570
TYPI(4),RTY2(1),NOH(1),NOCA(4)	0.628	0.543	0.554
TYPI(6),RTY2(1),NOH(1),NOCA(4)	0.701	0.623	0.633
TYPI(7),RTY2(1),NOH(1),NOCA(4)	0.655	0.572	0.582
TYPI(1),RTY2(1),NOH(1),NOCA(5)	0.683	0.603	0.613
TYPI(2),RTY2(1),NOH(1),NOCA(5)	0.701	0.622	0.632
TYPI(4),RTY2(1),NOH(1),NOCA(5)	0.687	0.607	0.617
TYPI(6),RTY2(1),NOH(1),NOCA(5)	0.753	0.682	0.691
TYPI(7),RTY2(1),NOH(1),NOCA(5)	0.711	0.634	0.644
TYPI(1),RTY2(1),NOH(1),NOCA(6)	0.734	0.660	0.669
TYPI(2),RTY2(1),NOH(1),NOCA(6)	0.750	0.678	0.687
TYPI(4),RTY2(1),NOH(1),NOCA(6)	0.737	0.663	0.673
TYPI(6),RTY2(1),NOH(1),NOCA(6)	0.796	0.733	0.741
TYPI(7),RTY2(1),NOH(1),NOCA(6)	0.759	0.689	0.698
TYPI(1),RTY2(1),NOH(1),NOCA(7)	0.771	0.703	0.712
TYPI(2),RTY2(1),NOH(1),NOCA(7)	0.785	0.720	0.729
TYPI(4),RTY2(1),NOH(1),NOCA(7)	0.774	0.706	0.715
TYPI(6),RTY2(1),NOH(1),NOCA(7)	0.826	0.770	0.777
TYPI(7),RTY2(1),NOH(1),NOCA(7)	0.793	0.730	0.738
TYPI(1),RTY2(1),NOH(1),NOCA(9)	0.714	0.637	0.647
TYPI(2),RTY2(1),NOH(1),NOCA(9)	0.731	0.657	0.666
TYPI(4),RTY2(1),NOH(1),NOCA(9)	0.718	0.641	0.651
TYPI(6),RTY2(1),NOH(1),NOCA(9)	0.779	0.713	0.722
TYPI(7),RTY2(1),NOH(1),NOCA(9)	0.741	0.668	0.677
TYPI(1),RTY2(3),NOH(2),NOCA(1)	0.690	0.610	0.621
TYPI(6),RTY2(3),NOH(2),NOCA(1)	0.759	0.689	0.698
TYPI(1),RTY2(5),NOH(2),NOCA(1)	0.919	0.889	0.893
TYPI(6),RTY2(5),NOH(2),NOCA(1)	0.942	0.919	0.922
TYPI(1),RTY2(3),NOH(2),NOCA(2)	0.835	0.781	0.788
TYPI(6),RTY2(3),NOH(2),NOCA(2)	0.877	0.834	0.840
TYPI(1),RTY2(5),NOH(2),NOCA(2)	0.963	0.948	0.950
TYPI(6),RTY2(5),NOH(2),NOCA(2)	0.973	0.963	0.964
TYPI(1),RTY2(3),NOH(2),NOCA(3)	0.848	0.797	0.804

Parameters	Black	Asian	White
TYP1(6),RTY2(3),NOH(2),NOCA(3)	0.888	0.847	0.853
TYP1(1),RTY2(5),NOH(2),NOCA(3)	0.966	0.953	0.955
TYP1(6),RTY2(5),NOH(2),NOCA(3)	0.976	0.966	0.967
TYP1(1),RTY2(3),NOH(2),NOCA(4)	0.812	0.753	0.761
TYP1(6),RTY2(3),NOH(2),NOCA(4)	0.860	0.811	0.818
TYP1(1),RTY2(5),NOH(2),NOCA(4)	0.957	0.940	0.942
TYP1(6),RTY2(5),NOH(2),NOCA(4)	0.969	0.957	0.958
TYP1(1),RTY2(3),NOH(2),NOCA(5)	0.849	0.798	0.805
TYP1(6),RTY2(3),NOH(2),NOCA(5)	0.888	0.848	0.854
TYP1(1),RTY2(5),NOH(2),NOCA(5)	0.966	0.953	0.955
TYP1(6),RTY2(5),NOH(2),NOCA(5)	0.976	0.966	0.968
TYP1(1),RTY2(3),NOH(2),NOCA(6)	0.878	0.835	0.841
TYP1(6),RTY2(3),NOH(2),NOCA(6)	0.910	0.877	0.882
TYP1(1),RTY2(5),NOH(2),NOCA(6)	0.974	0.963	0.964
TYP1(6),RTY2(5),NOH(2),NOCA(6)	0.981	0.973	0.975
TYP1(1),RTY2(3),NOH(2),NOCA(7)	0.898	0.860	0.866
TYP1(6),RTY2(3),NOH(2),NOCA(7)	0.925	0.897	0.901
TYP1(1),RTY2(5),NOH(2),NOCA(7)	0.978	0.969	0.971
TYP1(6),RTY2(5),NOH(2),NOCA(7)	0.985	0.978	0.979
TYP1(1),RTY2(3),NOH(2),NOCA(9)	0.867	0.821	0.827
TYP1(6),RTY2(3),NOH(2),NOCA(9)	0.902	0.866	0.871
TYP1(1),RTY2(5),NOH(2),NOCA(9)	0.971	0.959	0.961
TYP1(6),RTY2(5),NOH(2),NOCA(9)	0.979	0.971	0.972

Key

TYP1(1) = Primary offences of theft or of handling stolen goods
TYP1(2) =   "   "   involving motor vehicles
TYP1(4) =   "   "   involving violence
TYP1(6) =   "   "   against the police
TYP1(7) =   "   "   involving possession of illicit drugs
RTY2(1) = Defendants without TICs
RTY2(3) = Offences involving motor vehicles, as the first TICs
RTY2(5) =   "   "   violence, as the first TICs
NOH(1) = One offence dealt with at the hearing
NOH(2) = Two offences dealt with at the same hearing
NOCA(1) up to (7) and (9) = First and up to the seventh and ninth or more arrest(s) or court appearance(s)

Table A3.8

Margins of the difference between the probabilities of court non-custodial sentences between racial groups: Over 14s

Margins of the difference between the probabilities of court non custodial sentences as opposed to police diversionary measures between the three racial groups of the over 14s by type of primary offence, type of first TIC, the total number of offences dealt with at the same hearing and the number of arrests or court appearances in percentages

Parameters	Race Black v Asian	Black v White	White v Asian
TYP1(1),RTY2(1),NOH(1),NOCA(1)	9	8	1
TYP1(2),RTY2(1),NOH(1),NOCA(1)	9	8	1
TYP1(4),RTY2(1),NOH(1),NOCA(1)	9	8	1
TYP1(6),RTY2(1),NOH(1),NOCA(1)	9	8	1
TYP1(7),RTY2(1),NOH(1),NOCA(1)	9	8	1
TYP1(1),RTY2(1),NOH(1),NOCA(2)	8	7	1
TYP1(2),RTY2(1),NOH(1),NOCA(2)	8	7	1
TYP1(4),RTY2(1),NOH(1),NOCA(2)	8	7	1
TYP1(7),RTY2(1),NOH(1),NOCA(2)	8	7	1
TYP1(1),RTY2(1),NOH(1),NOCA(3)	8	7	1
TYP1(2),RTY2(1),NOH(1),NOCA(3)	8	7	1
TYP1(4),RTY2(1),NOH(1),NOCA(3)	8	7	1
TYP1(7),RTY2(1),NOH(1),NOCA(3)	8	7	1
TYP1(1),RTY2(1),NOH(1),NOCA(4)	8	7	1
TYP1(2),RTY2(1),NOH(1),NOCA(4)	8	7	1
TYP1(4),RTY2(1),NOH(1),NOCA(4)	8	7	1
TYP1(6),RTY2(1),NOH(1),NOCA(4)	8	7	1
TYP1(7),RTY2(1),NOH(1),NOCA(4)	8	7	1
TYP1(1),RTY2(1),NOH(1),NOCA(5)	8	7	1
TYP1(2),RTY2(1),NOH(1),NOCA(5)	8	7	1
TYP1(4),RTY2(1),NOH(1),NOCA(5)	8	7	1
TYP1(7),RTY2(1),NOH(1),NOCA(5)	8	7	1
TYP1(1),RTY2(1),NOH(1),NOCA(9)	8	7	1
TYP1(4),RTY2(1),NOH(1),NOCA(9)	8	7	1
TYP1(1),RTY2(3),NOH(2),NOCA(1)	8	7	1
TYP1(6),RTY2(1),NOH(1),NOCA(2)	7	7	1
TYP1(1),RTY2(1),NOH(1),NOCA(6)	7	7	1
TYP1(2),RTY2(1),NOH(1),NOCA(9)	7	7	1
TYP1(6),RTY2(1),NOH(1),NOCA(3)	7	6	1
TYP1(6),RTY2(1),NOH(1),NOCA(5)	7	6	1
TYP1(2),RTY2(1),NOH(1),NOCA(6)	7	6	1
TYP1(4),RTY2(1),NOH(1),NOCA(6)	7	6	1
TYP1(7),RTY2(1),NOH(1),NOCA(6)	7	6	1
TYP1(1),RTY2(1),NOH(1),NOCA(7)	7	6	1
TYP1(2),RTY2(1),NOH(1),NOCA(7)	7	6	1
TYP1(4),RTY2(1),NOH(1),NOCA(7)	7	6	1
TYP1(6),RTY2(1),NOH(1),NOCA(9)	7	6	1
TYP1(7),RTY2(1),NOH(1),NOCA(9)	7	6	1
TYP1(6),RTY2(3),NOH(2),NOCA(1)	7	6	1
TYP1(6),RTY2(1),NOH(1),NOCA(6)	6	6	1
TYP1(7),RTY2(1),NOH(1),NOCA(7)	6	6	1
TYP1(6),RTY2(1),NOH(1),NOCA(7)	6	5	1
TYP1(1),RTY2(3),NOH(2),NOCA(4)	6	5	1
TYP1(1),RTY2(3),NOH(2),NOCA(2)	5	5	1
TYP1(1),RTY2(3),NOH(2),NOCA(3)	5	4	1
TYP1(6),RTY2(3),NOH(2),NOCA(4)	5	4	1
TYP1(1),RTY2(3),NOH(2),NOCA(5)	5	4	1

172

Parameters	Black v Asian	Black v White	White v Asian
TYP1(1),RTY2(3),NOH(2),NOCA(9)	5	4	1
TYP1(6),RTY2(3),NOH(2),NOCA(2)	4	4	1
TYP1(6),RTY2(3),NOH(2),NOCA(3)	4	4	1
TYP1(1),RTY2(3),NOH(2),NOCA(6)	4	4	1
TYP1(6),RTY2(3),NOH(2),NOCA(5)	4	3	1
TYP1(1),RTY2(3),NOH(2),NOCA(7)	4	3	1
TYP1(6),RTY2(3),NOH(2),NOCA(9)	4	3	1
TYP1(6),RTY2(3),NOH(2),NOCA(6)	3	3	1
TYP1(1),RTY2(5),NOH(2),NOCA(1)	3	3	0.004
TYP1(6),RTY2(3),NOH(2),NOCA(7)	3	2	0.004
TYP1(6),RTY2(5),NOH(2),NOCA(1)	2	2	0.003
TYP1(1),RTY2(5),NOH(2),NOCA(4)	2	2	0.002
TYP1(1),RTY2(5),NOH(2),NOCA(2)	2	1	0.002
TYP1(1),RTY2(5),NOH(2),NOCA(3)	1	1	0.002
TYP1(1),RTY2(5),NOH(2),NOCA(5)	1	1	0.002
TYP1(6),RTY2(5),NOH(2),NOCA(5)	1	1	0.002
TYP1(6),RTY2(5),NOH(2),NOCA(6)	1	1	0.002
TYP1(1),RTY2(5),NOH(2),NOCA(7)	1	1	0.002
TYP1(1),RTY2(5),NOH(2),NOCA(9)	1	1	0.002
TYP1(6),RTY2(5),NOH(2),NOCA(2)	1	1	0.001
TYP1(6),RTY2(5),NOH(2),NOCA(3)	1	1	0.001
TYP1(6),RTY2(5),NOH(2),NOCA(4)	1	1	0.001
TYP1(1),RTY2(5),NOH(2),NOCA(6)	1	1	0.001
TYP1(6),RTY2(5),NOH(2),NOCA(7)	1	1	0.001
TYP1(6),RTY2(5),NOH(2),NOCA(9)	1	1	0.001

Key

TYP1(1) = Primary offences of theft or of handling stolen goods
TYP1(2) =   "   "   involving motor vehicles
TYP1(4) =   "   "   involving violence
TYP1(6) =   "   "   against the police
TYP1(7) =   "   "   involving possession of illicit drugs
RTY2(1) = Defendants without any TICs
RTY2(3) = Offences involving motor vehicles, as the first TICs
RTY2(5) =   "   " violence, as the first TICs
NOH(1) = Only one offence dealt with at the hearing
NOH(2) = Two offences dealt with at the same hearing
NOCA(1) up to (7) and (9) = First and up to the seventh and the ninth or more arrest(s) or court appearance(s)

Note: The control variables are listed in order of the combination with the widest margin of difference between the probabilities of receiving court non-custodial sentences between the three groups of the over 14 year old defendants.

Table A3.9
Probabilities of court social work sentences by race and the controlling factors: Under 14s

Estimated probabilities of court social work sentences as opposed to police diversionary measures by race and type of primary offence, type of first TIC, the total number of offences dealt with at the same hearing and the number of arrests or court appearances for the under 14 age group

Parameters	Race		
	Black	Asian	White
TYP1(1),RTY2(1),NOH(1),NOCA(1)	0.038	0.109	0.038
TYP1(3),RTY2(1),NOH(1),NOCA(1)	0.081	0.217	0.082
TYP1(4),RTY2(1),NOH(1),NOCA(1)	0.044	0.127	0.045
TYP1(6),RTY2(1),NOH(1),NOCA(1)	0.989	0.996	0.989
TYP1(1),RTY2(1),NOH(1),NOCA(2)	0.267	0.532	0.267
TYP1(3),RTY2(1),NOH(1),NOCA(2)	0.451	0.720	0.452
TYP1(4),RTY2(1),NOH(1),NOCA(2)	0.301	0.574	0.302
TYP1(6),RTY2(1),NOH(1),NOCA(2)	0.999	0.999	0.999
TYP1(1),RTY2(1),NOH(1),NOCA(3)	0.403	0.679	0.404
TYP1(3),RTY2(1),NOH(1),NOCA(3)	0.604	0.827	0.605
TYP1(4),RTY2(1),NOH(1),NOCA(3)	0.444	0.714	0.445
TYP1(6),RTY2(1),NOH(1),NOCA(3)	0.999	0.999	0.999
TYP1(1),RTY2(1),NOH(1),NOCA(4)	0.408	0.683	0.409
TYP1(3),RTY2(1),NOH(1),NOCA(4)	0.609	0.830	0.609
TYP1(4),RTY2(1),NOH(1),NOCA(4)	0.449	0.718	0.450
TYP1(6),RTY2(1),NOH(1),NOCA(4)	0.999	0.999	0.999
TYP1(1),RTY2(1),NOH(1),NOCA(6)	0.375	0.652	0.376
TYP1(3),RTY2(1),NOH(1),NOCA(6)	0.575	0.809	0.576
TYP1(4),RTY2(1),NOH(1),NOCA(6)	0.415	0.690	0.416
TYP1(6),RTY2(1),NOH(1),NOCA(6)	0.999	0.999	0.999
TYP1(1),RTY2(1),NOH(1),NOCA(7)	0.618	0.835	0.619
TYP1(3),RTY2(1),NOH(1),NOCA(7)	0.786	0.920	0.786
TYP1(4),RTY2(1),NOH(1),NOCA(7)	0.658	0.857	0.658
TYP1(6),RTY2(1),NOH(1),NOCA(7)	0.999	0.999	0.999

Key

TYP1(1) = Primary offences of theft or of handling stolen goods
TYP1(3) =   "   "   relating to property
TYP1(4) =   "   "   involving violence
TYP1(6) =   "   "   against the police
RTY2(1) = Defendants without any TICs
NOH(1) = One offence dealt with at the hearing
NOCA(1) up to (4),(6) and (7) = First and up to the fourth, sixth and seventh arrest or court appearance

Table A3.10

Margins of the difference between the probabilities of court social work sentences between racial groups: Under 14s

Margins of the difference between the probabilities of court social work sentences as opposed to police diversionary measures between the three racial groups of the under 14s by type of primary offence, type of first TIC, the total number of offences dealt with at the same hearing and the number of arrests or court appearances in percentages

	Race		
Parameters	Asian v White	Asian v Black	White v Black
TYP1(1),RTY2(1),NOH(1),NOCA(3)	28	28	0.001
TYP1(1),RTY2(1),NOH(1),NOCA(6)	28	28	0.001
TYP1(1),RTY2(1),NOH(1),NOCA(2)	27	27	0.001
TYP1(3),RTY2(1),NOH(1),NOCA(2)	27	27	0.001
TYP1(4),RTY2(1),NOH(1),NOCA(2)	27	27	0.001
TYP1(4),RTY2(1),NOH(1),NOCA(3)	27	27	0.001
TYP1(1),RTY2(1),NOH(1),NOCA(4)	27	27	0.001
TYP1(4),RTY2(1),NOH(1),NOCA(4)	27	27	0.001
TYP1(4),RTY2(1),NOH(1),NOCA(6)	27	27	0.001
TYP1(3),RTY2(1),NOH(1),NOCA(6)	23	23	0.001
TYP1(3),RTY2(1),NOH(1),NOCA(3)	22	22	0.001
TYP1(3),RTY2(1),NOH(1),NOCA(4)	22	22	0.001
TYP1(1),RTY2(1),NOH(1),NOCA(7)	22	22	0.001
TYP1(4),RTY2(1),NOH(1),NOCA(7)	20	20	0.001
TYP1(3),RTY2(1),NOH(1),NOCA(1)	14	14	0.001
TYP1(3),RTY2(1),NOH(1),NOCA(7)	13	13	0.001
TYP1(4),RTY2(1),NOH(1),NOCA(1)	8	8	0.001
TYP1(1),RTY2(1),NOH(1),NOCA(1)	7	7	0.0002
TYP1(6),RTY2(1),NOH(1),NOCA(1)	1	1	0.00004
TYP1(6),RTY2(1),NOH(1),NOCA(2)	0.001	0.001	0.00002
TYP1(6),RTY2(1),NOH(1),NOCA(6)	0.001	0.001	0.000003
TYP1(6),RTY2(1),NOH(1),NOCA(4)	0.0004	0.0004	0.00001
TYP1(6),RTY2(1),NOH(1),NOCA(3)	0.0004	0.0004	0.000003
TYP1(6),RTY2(1),NOH(1),NOCA(7)	0.0002	0.0002	0.000001

Key

TYP1(1) = Primary offences of theft or of handling stolen goods
TYP1(3) =   "   "   relating to property
TYP1(4) =   "   "   involving violence
TYP1(6) =   "   "   against the police
RTY2(1) = Defendants without any TICs
NOH(1) = One offence dealt with at the hearing
NOCA(1) up to (4),(6) and (7) = First and up to the fourth, sixth and seventh arrest or court appearance

Note: The control variables are listed in order of the combination with the widest margin of difference between the probabilities of receiving court social work sentences between the three groups of the under 14 year old defendants.

Table A3.11
Probabilities of court social work and probation sentences by race and the controlling factors: Over 14s

Estimated probabilities of court social work and probation sentences as opposed to police diversionary measures by race and type of primary offence, type of first TIC, the total number of offences dealt with at the same hearing and the number of arrests or court appearances for the over 14 age group

	Race		
Parameters	Black	Asian	White
TYP1(1),RTY2(1),NOH(1),NOCA(1)	0.112	0.122	0.087
TYP1(3),RTY2(1),NOH(1),NOCA(1)	0.121	0.132	0.095
TYP1(1),RTY2(1),NOH(1),NOCA(2)	0.237	0.254	0.191
TYP1(3),RTY2(1),NOH(1),NOCA(2)	0.253	0.271	0.205
TYP1(1),RTY2(1),NOH(1),NOCA(3)	0.361	0.382	0.299
TYP1(3),RTY2(1),NOH(1),NOCA(3)	0.381	0.404	0.318
TYP1(1),RTY2(1),NOH(1),NOCA(4)	0.363	0.386	0.302
TYP1(3),RTY2(1),NOH(1),NOCA(4)	0.384	0.407	0.321
TYP1(1),RTY2(1),NOH(1),NOCA(5)	0.393	0.416	0.329
TYP1(3),RTY2(1),NOH(1),NOCA(5)	0.415	0.437	0.349
TYP1(1),RTY2(1),NOH(1),NOCA(6)	0.490	0.513	0.421
TYP1(3),RTY2(1),NOH(1),NOCA(6)	0.512	0.535	0.443
TYP1(1),RTY2(1),NOH(1),NOCA(7)	0.535	0.558	0.466
TYP1(3),RTY2(1),NOH(1),NOCA(7)	0.557	0.580	0.488
TYP1(1),RTY2(1),NOH(1),NOCA(8)	0.357	0.379	0.296
TYP1(3),RTY2(1),NOH(1),NOCA(8)	0.378	0.400	0.315
TYP1(1),RTY2(1),NOH(1),NOCA(9)	0.595	0.617	0.526
TYP1(3),RTY2(1),NOH(1),NOCA(9)	0.616	0.638	0.548
TYP1(1),RTY2(3),NOH(2),NOCA(1)	0.452	0.475	0.384
TYP1(3),RTY2(3),NOH(2),NOCA(1)	0.474	0.497	0.405
TYP1(1),RTY2(3),NOH(2),NOCA(2)	0.670	0.690	0.606
TYP1(3),RTY2(3),NOH(2),NOCA(2)	0.689	0.709	0.627
TYP1(1),RTY2(3),NOH(2),NOCA(3)	0.786	0.802	0.736
TYP1(3),RTY2(3),NOH(2),NOCA(3)	0.801	0.815	0.753
TYP1(1),RTY2(3),NOH(2),NOCA(4)	0.789	0.804	0.739
TYP1(3),RTY2(3),NOH(2),NOCA(4)	0.803	0.817	0.755
TYP1(1),RTY2(3),NOH(2),NOCA(5)	0.809	0.823	0.762
TYP1(3),RTY2(3),NOH(2),NOCA(5)	0.822	0.835	0.778
TYP1(1),RTY2(3),NOH(2),NOCA(6)	0.862	0.873	0.826
TYP1(3),RTY2(3),NOH(2),NOCA(6)	0.872	0.883	0.838
TYP1(1),RTY2(3),NOH(2),NOCA(7)	0.883	0.892	0.851
TYP1(3),RTY2(3),NOH(2),NOCA(7)	0.891	0.900	0.862
TYP1(1),RTY2(3),NOH(2),NOCA(8)	0.784	0.799	0.733
TYP1(3),RTY2(3),NOH(2),NOCA(8)	0.798	0.813	0.750
TYP1(1),RTY2(3),NOH(2),NOCA(9)	0.905	0.913	0.879
TYP1(3),RTY2(3),NOH(2),NOCA(9)	0.913	0.920	0.888

Key

TYP1(1) = Primary offences of theft or of handling stolen goods
TYP1(3) =   "   "   relating to property
RTY2(1) = Defendants without any TICs
RTY2(3) = Offences involving motor vehicles as the first TICs
NOH(1) = One offence dealt with at the hearing
NOH(2) = Two offences dealt with at the same hearing
NOCA(1) up to (9) = First and up to the ninth or more arrest(s) or court appearance(s)

Table A3.12
Margins of the difference between the probabilities of court social work and probation sentences between racial groups: Over 14s

Margins of the difference between the probabilities of court social work and probation sentences as opposed to police diversionary measures between the three racial groups of the over 14s by type of primary offence, type of first TIC, the total number of offences dealt with at the same hearing and the number of arrests or court appearances in percentages

	Race		
Parameters	Asian v White	Black v White	Asian v Black
TYP1(1),RTY2(3),NOH(2),NOCA(1)	9	7	2
TYP1(3),RTY2(3),NOH(2),NOCA(1)	9	7	2
TYP1(3),RTY2(1),NOH(1),NOCA(5)	9	7	2
TYP1(1),RTY2(1),NOH(1),NOCA(6)	9	7	2
TYP1(3),RTY2(1),NOH(1),NOCA(6)	9	7	2
TYP1(1),RTY2(1),NOH(1),NOCA(7)	9	7	2
TYP1(3),RTY2(1),NOH(1),NOCA(7)	9	7	2
TYP1(1),RTY2(1),NOH(1),NOCA(9)	9	7	2
TYP1(3),RTY2(1),NOH(1),NOCA(9)	9	7	2
TYP1(3),RTY2(1),NOH(1),NOCA(3)	9	6	2
TYP1(3),RTY2(1),NOH(1),NOCA(4)	9	6	2
TYP1(1),RTY2(1),NOH(1),NOCA(5)	9	6	2
TYP1(1),RTY2(3),NOH(2),NOCA(2)	8	6	2
TYP1(3),RTY2(3),NOH(2),NOCA(2)	8	6	2
TYP1(1),RTY2(1),NOH(1),NOCA(3)	8	6	2
TYP1(1),RTY2(1),NOH(1),NOCA(4)	8	6	2
TYP1(1),RTY2(1),NOH(1),NOCA(8)	8	6	2
TYP1(3),RTY2(1),NOH(1),NOCA(8)	8	6	2
TYP1(3),RTY2(1),NOH(1),NOCA(2)	7	5	2
TYP1(1),RTY2(3),NOH(2),NOCA(3)	7	5	2
TYP1(1),RTY2(3),NOH(2),NOCA(4)	7	5	2
TYP1(1),RTY2(3),NOH(2),NOCA(8)	7	5	2
TYP1(1),RTY2(1),NOH(1),NOCA(2)	6	5	2
TYP1(3),RTY2(3),NOH(2),NOCA(8)	6	5	2
TYP1(3),RTY2(3),NOH(2),NOCA(3)	6	5	1
TYP1(3),RTY2(3),NOH(2),NOCA(4)	6	5	1
TYP1(1),RTY2(3),NOH(2),NOCA(5)	6	5	1
TYP1(3),RTY2(3),NOH(2),NOCA(5)	6	4	1
TYP1(1),RTY2(3),NOH(2),NOCA(6)	5	4	1
TYP1(3),RTY2(3),NOH(2),NOCA(6)	5	3	1
TYP1(1),RTY2(1),NOH(1),NOCA(1)	4	3	1
TYP1(3),RTY2(1),NOH(1),NOCA(1)	4	3	1
TYP1(1),RTY2(3),NOH(2),NOCA(7)	4	3	1
TYP1(3),RTY2(3),NOH(2),NOCA(7)	4	3	1
TYP1(1),RTY2(3),NOH(2),NOCA(9)	3	3	1
TYP1(3),RTY2(3),NOH(2),NOCA(9)	3	3	1

Key

TYP1(1) = Primary offences of theft or of handling stolen goods
TYP1(3) =   "   "   relating to property
RTY2(1) = Defendants without any TICs
RTY2(3) = Offences involving motor vehicles as the first TICs
NOH(1) = One offence dealt with at the hearing
NOH(2) = Two offences dealt with at the same hearing
NOCA(1) up to (9) = First and up to the ninth or more arrest(s) or court appearance(s)

Table A3.13
Probabilities of custodial sentences by race and the controlling factors: Over 14s

Estimated probabilities of custodial sentences as opposed to police diversionary measures by race and type of primary offence, type of first TIC, the total number of offences dealt with at the same hearing and the number of arrests or court appearances for the over age group

	Race		
Parameters	Black	Asian	White
TYP1(1),RTY2(1),NOH(1),NOCA(1)	0.028	0.017	0.013
TYP1(3),RTY2(1),NOH(1),NOCA(1)	0.089	0.055	0.042
TYP1(4),RTY2(1),NOH(1),NOCA(1)	0.140	0.088	0.068
TYP1(1),RTY2(1),NOH(1),NOCA(2)	0.081	0.050	0.038
TYP1(3),RTY2(1),NOH(1),NOCA(2)	0.231	0.152	0.118
TYP1(4),RTY2(1),NOH(1),NOCA(2)	0.333	0.229	0.183
TYP1(1),RTY2(1),NOH(1),NOCA(4)	0.158	0.101	0.223
TYP1(4),RTY2(1),NOH(1),NOCA(4)	0.517	0.389	0.323
TYP1(1),RTY2(1),NOH(1),NOCA(5)	0.282	0.190	0.150
TYP1(3),RTY2(1),NOH(1),NOCA(5)	0.573	0.444	0.375
TYP1(4),RTY2(1),NOH(1),NOCA(5)	0.691	0.571	0.500
TYP1(1),RTY2(1),NOH(1),NOCA(6)	0.242	0.160	0.125
TYP1(3),RTY2(1),NOH(1),NOCA(6)	0.521	0.393	0.327
TYP1(4),RTY2(1),NOH(1),NOCA(6)	0.645	0.519	0.448
TYP1(1),RTY2(1),NOH(1),NOCA(7)	0.401	0.285	0.230
TYP1(3),RTY2(1),NOH(1),NOCA(7)	0.696	0.576	0.506
TYP1(4),RTY2(1),NOH(1),NOCA(7)	0.792	0.694	0.630
TYP1(1),RTY2(1),NOH(1),NOCA(8)	0.523	0.394	0.329
TYP1(3),RTY2(1),NOH(1),NOCA(8)	0.789	0.690	0.626
TYP1(4),RTY2(1),NOH(1),NOCA(8)	0.862	0.787	0.736
TYP1(1),RTY2(1),NOH(1),NOCA(9)	0.540	0.412	0.345
TYP1(3),RTY2(1),NOH(1),NOCA(9)	0.801	0.705	0.642
TYP1(4),RTY2(1),NOH(1),NOCA(9)	0.870	0.799	0.749
TYP1(1),RTY2(3),NOH(2),NOCA(1)	0.289	0.195	0.154
TYP1(3),RTY2(3),NOH(2),NOCA(1)	0.581	0.452	0.383
TYP1(4),RTY2(3),NOH(2),NOCA(1)	0.698	0.579	0.508
TYP1(1),RTY2(3),NOH(2),NOCA(2)	0.555	0.426	0.358
TYP1(3),RTY2(3),NOH(2),NOCA(2)	0.810	0.717	0.655
TYP1(4),RTY2(3),NOH(2),NOCA(2)	0.876	0.808	0.760
TYP1(1),RTY2(3),NOH(2),NOCA(4)	0.727	0.613	0.543
TYP1(3),RTY2(3),NOH(2),NOCA(4)	0.901	0.844	0.803
TYP1(4),RTY2(3),NOH(2),NOCA(4)	0.938	0.900	0.871
TYP1(1),RTY2(3),NOH(2),NOCA(5)	0.848	0.768	0.714
TYP1(3),RTY2(3),NOH(2),NOCA(5)	0.951	0.919	0.895
TYP1(4),RTY2(3),NOH(2),NOCA(5)	0.969	0.950	0.934
TYP1(1),RTY2(3),NOH(2),NOCA(6)	0.819	0.729	0.669
TYP1(3),RTY2(3),NOH(2),NOCA(6)	0.939	0.902	0.873
TYP1(4),RTY2(3),NOH(2),NOCA(6)	0.963	0.939	0.920
TYP1(1),RTY2(3),NOH(2),NOCA(7)	0.905	0.850	0.809
TYP1(3),RTY2(3),NOH(2),NOCA(7)	0.970	0.951	0.935
TYP1(4),RTY2(3),NOH(2),NOCA(7)	0.982	0.970	0.960
TYP1(1),RTY2(3),NOH(2),NOCA(8)	0.939	0.902	0.874
TYP1(3),RTY2(3),NOH(2),NOCA(8)	0.982	0.969	0.960
TYP1(4),RTY2(3),NOH(2),NOCA(8)	0.989	0.981	0.975
TYP1(1),RTY2(3),NOH(2),NOCA(9)	0.943	0.908	0.882
TYP1(3),RTY2(3),NOH(2),NOCA(9)	0.983	0.971	0.962
TYP1(4),RTY2(3),NOH(2),NOCA(9)	0.990	0.983	0.977
TYP1(1),RTY2(5),NOH(2),NOCA(1)	0.513	0.385	0.320
TYP1(3),RTY2(5),NOH(2),NOCA(1)	0.783	0.682	0.617

Parameters	Black	Asian	White
TYP1(4),RTY2(5),NOH(2),NOCA(1)	0.857	0.781	0.728
TYP1(1),RTY2(5),NOH(2),NOCA(2)	0.764	0.658	0.591
TYP1(3),RTY2(5),NOH(2),NOCA(2)	0.917	0.868	0.832
TYP1(4),RTY2(5),NOH(2),NOCA(2)	0.948	0.916	0.892
TYP1(1),RTY2(5),NOH(2),NOCA(4)	0.874	0.804	0.756
TYP1(3),RTY2(5),NOH(2),NOCA(4)	0.959	0.934	0.913
TYP1(4),RTY2(5),NOH(2),NOCA(4)	0.975	0.959	0.946
TYP1(1),RTY2(5),NOH(2),NOCA(5)	0.935	0.896	0.866
TYP1(3),RTY2(5),NOH(2),NOCA(5)	0.980	0.967	0.957
TYP1(4),RTY2(5),NOH(2),NOCA(5)	0.988	0.980	0.974
TYP1(1),RTY2(5),NOH(2),NOCA(6)	0.921	0.875	0.840
TYP1(3),RTY2(5),NOH(2),NOCA(6)	0.976	0.960	0.947
TYP1(4),RTY2(5),NOH(2),NOCA(6)	0.985	0.975	0.968
TYP1(1),RTY2(5),NOH(2),NOCA(7)	0.961	0.936	0.917
TYP1(3),RTY2(5),NOH(2),NOCA(7)	0.988	0.980	0.974
TYP1(4),RTY2(5),NOH(2),NOCA(7)	0.993	0.988	0.984
TYP1(1),RTY2(5),NOH(2),NOCA(8)	0.976	0.960	0.947
TYP1(3),RTY2(5),NOH(2),NOCA(8)	0.993	0.988	0.984
TYP1(4),RTY2(5),NOH(2),NOCA(8)	0.996	0.993	0.990
TYP1(1),RTY2(5),NOH(2),NOCA(9)	0.977	0.963	0.951
TYP1(3),RTY2(5),NOH(2),NOCA(9)	0.993	0.989	0.985
TYP1(4),RTY2(5),NOH(2),NOCA(9)	0.996	0.993	0.991

Key

TYP1(1) = Primary offences of theft or of handling stolen goods
TYP1(3) =   "   "   relating to property
TYP1(4) =   "   "   involving violence
RTY2(1) = Defendants without any TICs
RTY2(3) = Offences involving motor vehicles as first TICs
RTY2(5) =   "   "   violence as first TICs
NOH(1) = One offence dealt with at the hearing
NOH(2) = Two offences dealt with at the same hearing
NOCA(1),(2),(4) up to (9) = First, second, fourth and up to the ninth or more arrests or
court appearances

Table A3.14

Margins of the difference between the probabilities of custodial sentences between racial groups: Over 14s

Margins of the difference between the probabilities of custodial sentences as opposed to police diversionary measures between the three racial groups of the over 14s by type of primary offence, type of first TIC, the total number of offences dealt with at the same hearing and the number of arrests or court appearances in percentages

Parameters	Race		
	Black v White	Black v Asian	Asian v White
TYP1(1),RTY2(1),NOH(1),NOCA(9)	20	13	7
TYP1(3),RTY2(1),NOH(1),NOCA(5)	20	13	7
TYP1(4),RTY2(1),NOH(1),NOCA(6)	20	13	7
TYP1(1),RTY2(3),NOH(2),NOCA(2)	20	13	7
TYP1(3),RTY2(3),NOH(2),NOCA(1)	20	13	7
TYP1(1),RTY2(1),NOH(1),NOCA(8)	19	13	7
TYP1(3),RTY2(1),NOH(1),NOCA(6)	19	13	7
TYP1(4),RTY2(1),NOH(1),NOCA(4)	19	13	7
TYP1(1),RTY2(5),NOH(2),NOCA(1)	19	13	7
TYP1(3),RTY2(1),NOH(1),NOCA(7)	19	12	7
TYP1(4),RTY2(1),NOH(1),NOCA(5)	19	12	7
TYP1(4),RTY2(3),NOH(2),NOCA(1)	19	12	7
TYP1(1),RTY2(3),NOH(2),NOCA(4)	18	12	7
TYP1(1),RTY2(1),NOH(1),NOCA(7)	17	12	6
TYP1(3),RTY2(1),NOH(1),NOCA(4)	17	12	5
TYP1(1),RTY2(5),NOH(2),NOCA(2)	17	11	7
TYP1(3),RTY2(5),NOH(2),NOCA(1)	17	10	7
TYP1(3),RTY2(1),NOH(1),NOCA(8)	16	10	6
TYP1(3),RTY2(1),NOH(1),NOCA(9)	16	10	6
TYP1(4),RTY2(1),NOH(1),NOCA(7)	16	10	6
TYP1(4),RTY2(1),NOH(1),NOCA(2)	15	10	5
TYP1(3),RTY2(3),NOH(2),NOCA(2)	15	9	6
TYP1(1),RTY2(3),NOH(2),NOCA(6)	15	9	6
TYP1(1),RTY2(3),NOH(2),NOCA(1)	14	9	4
TYP1(1),RTY2(1),NOH(1),NOCA(5)	13	9	4
TYP1(4),RTY2(1),NOH(1),NOCA(8)	13	8	5
TYP1(1),RTY2(3),NOH(2),NOCA(5)	13	8	5
TYP1(4),RTY2(5),NOH(2),NOCA(1)	13	8	5
TYP1(1),RTY2(1),NOH(1),NOCA(6)	12	8	4
TYP1(4),RTY2(1),NOH(1),NOCA(9)	12	7	5
TYP1(4),RTY2(3),NOH(2),NOCA(2)	12	7	5
TYP1(1),RTY2(5),NOH(2),NOCA(4)	12	7	5
TYP1(3),RTY2(1),NOH(1),NOCA(2)	11	8	3
TYP1(1),RTY2(3),NOH(2),NOCA(7)	10	6	4
TYP1(3),RTY2(3),NOH(2),NOCA(4)	10	6	4
TYP1(3),RTY2(5),NOH(2),NOCA(2)	9	5	4
TYP1(1),RTY2(1),NOH(1),NOCA(4)	8	6	2
TYP1(1),RTY2(5),NOH(2),NOCA(6)	8	5	4
TYP1(4),RTY2(1),NOH(1),NOCA(1)	7	5	2
TYP1(1),RTY2(3),NOH(2),NOCA(8)	7	4	3
TYP1(1),RTY2(5),NOH(2),NOCA(5)	7	4	3
TYP1(3),RTY2(3),NOH(2),NOCA(6)	7	4	3
TYP1(4),RTY2(3),NOH(2),NOCA(4)	7	4	3
TYP1(1),RTY2(3),NOH(2),NOCA(9)	6	4	3
TYP1(3),RTY2(3),NOH(2),NOCA(5)	6	3	2
TYP1(4),RTY2(5),NOH(2),NOCA(2)	6	3	2
TYP1(3),RTY2(1),NOH(1),NOCA(1)	5	3	1

Parameters	Black v White	Black v Asian	Asian v White
TYP1(3),RTY2(5),NOH(2),NOCA(4)	5	3	2
TYP1(1),RTY2(1),NOH(1),NOCA(2)	4	3	1
TYP1(3),RTY2(3),NOH(2),NOCA(7)	4	2	2
TYP1(4),RTY2(3),NOH(2),NOCA(5)	4	2	2
TYP1(4),RTY2(3),NOH(2),NOCA(6)	4	2	2
TYP1(1),RTY2(5),NOH(2),NOCA(7)	4	2	2
TYP1(1),RTY2(5),NOH(2),NOCA(8)	3	2	1
TYP1(1),RTY2(5),NOH(2),NOCA(9)	3	1	1
TYP1(3),RTY2(5),NOH(2),NOCA(6)	3	2	1
TYP1(4),RTY2(5),NOH(2),NOCA(4)	3	2	1
TYP1(3),RTY2(3),NOH(2),NOCA(8)	2	1	1
TYP1(3),RTY2(3),NOH(2),NOCA(9)	2	1	1
TYP1(4),RTY2(3),NOH(2),NOCA(7)	2	1	1
TYP1(3),RTY2(5),NOH(2),NOCA(5)	2	1	1
TYP1(4),RTY2(5),HOH(2),NOCA(6)	2	1	1
TYP1(4),RTY2(3),NOH(2),NOCA(8)	1	1	1
TYP1(3),RTY2(5),NOH(2),NOCA(7)	1	1	1
TYP1(4),RTY2(5),NOH(2),NOCA(5)	1	1	1
TYP1(4),RTY2(3),NOH(2),NOCA(9)	1	1	1
TYP1(1),RTY2(1),NOH(1),NOCA(1)	1	1	0.004
TYP1(3),RTY2(5),NOH(2),NOCA(8)	1	1	0.004
TYP1(4),RTY2(5),NOH(2),NOCA(7)	1	1	0.004
TYP1(3),RTY2(5),NOH(2),NOCA(9)	1	0.004	0.004
TYP1(4),RTY2(5),NOH(2),NOCA(8)	1	0.003	0.003
TYP1(4),RTY2(5),NOH(2),NOCA(9)	1	0.003	0.002

Key

TYP1(1) = Primary offences of theft or of handling stolen goods
TYP1(3) =   "   "   relating to property
TYP1(4) =   "   "   involving violence
RTY2(1) = Defendants without any TICs
RTY2(3) = Offences involving motor vehicles as first TICs
RTY2(5) =   "   "   violence as first TICs
NOH(1) = Only one offence dealt with at the hearing
NOH(2) = Two offences dealt with at the same hearing
NOCA(1),(2),(4) up to (9) = First, second, fourth and up to the nineth or more arrest(s) or court appearance(s)

Note: The control variables are listed in order of the combination with the widest margin of difference between the probabilities of receiving custodial sentences between the three groups of the over 14 year old defendants.

Bibliography

Abell, P. (1988) *The Syntax of Social Life*, Oxford: Oxford University Press.

Adams, R. (1981) *A Measure of Diversion?: Case Studies in Intermediate Treatment*, National Youth Bureau.

Ageton, S. and Elliott, D. (1974) 'The effects of legal processing on delinquent orientations', *Social Problems*, 22, 87-100.

Akers, R. (1964) 'Socio-economic status and delinquent behaviour: A retest', *Journal of Research in Crime and Delinquency*, 1, (January), 38-46.

Akers, R. (1973) *Deviant Behaviour: A Social Learning Approach*, Belmont, California: Wadsworth.

Arnold, W. (1965) 'Continuities in research: Scaling delinquent behaviour', *Social Problems*, 13, 59-66.

Ashworth, A. (1986) speaking on 'Disentangling disparity in criminal sentencing', ESRC Law and Psychology Conference, Oxford, (14-16 April).

Bachman, J., et al. (1978) *Youth in Transition*, Vol. 6, Ann Arbor, Mich: Institute for Social Research, University of Michigan.

Bahr, S. (1979) 'Family determinants and effects of deviance', in W. Burr et al., eds., *Contemporary Theories about the Family: Research-Based Theories*, 1, New York:Free Press; London:Collier-Macmillan

Barber, A. (1985) 'Ethnic origin and economic status', *Employmentì Gazette*, 93, 467-77.

Barrow, Derbyshire and Jordan, (1983) *Some Aspects of Juvenile Cautioning in Lancashire*, Lancashire Social Services Department.

Batta, I., et al. (1975) 'A study of juvenile delinquency among Asians and half Asians', *British Journal of Criminology*, 15, 32-42.

Bazak, Y. (1981) *Punishment Principles and Applications*, Jerusalem: Dvir Co., Ltd.

Bean, P. (1976) *Rehabilitation and deviance*, Routledge & Kegan Paul.

Becker, H. (1963) *Outsiders*, New York: Free Press.

Belson, W. (1968) 'The extent of stealing by London boys', *Advancement of Science*, 25, 171-84.

Bennett, T. (1979) 'The social distribution of criminal labels: police "proaction" or "reaction"?', *British Journal of Criminology*, 19, 134-45.

Berger, A. and Simon, W. (1974) 'Black families and the Moynihan report: a research evaluation', *Social Problems*, 22, 145-161.

Berry, S. (1984) *Ethnic Minorities and the Juvenile Court*, Research and Information Unit, Nottinghamshire Social Services Department. Unpublished.

Black, D. and Reiss, A. (1970) 'Police control of juveniles', *American Review*, 35, 63-77.

Black Report (1979) *Report of the Children and Young Persons Review Group*, Chairman, Sir Harold Black, Belfast: HMSO, 32-4.

Blackmore, J. (1984) 'Delinquency theory and practice - a link through IT', *Youth and Policy*, 9, (Summer), 45-9.

Box, S. (1986) *Deviance, Reality and Society*, 2nd ed., Cassell.

Brake, M. (1980) *The Sociology of Youth Cultures and Youth Subcultures*, London: Routledge and Kegan Paul.

Braithwaite, J. (1979) *Inequality, Crime and Public Policy*, London: Routledge.

Braithwaite, J. (1981) 'The myth of social class and criminality reconsidered', *American Sociological Review*, 46(1), (February).

Brent (The London Borough of), (1985) *A Child in Trust*, Report of an Inquiry into the case of Jasmine Beckford.

Brent Cross Council Review (1984).

Brent Cross Council Review (1985).

Brent Employment Bulletin (1983), (Winter).

Brent Employment Bulletin (1984), (Spring).

Briar, S. and Piliavin, I. (1965) 'Delinquency, situational inducements and commitment to conformity', *Social Problems*, 13, (Summer), 35-45.

Bridges, L. (1983) 'Policing the Urban Wasteland', *Race and Class*, XXV(2): 31-4.

Broad, B. (1991) *Punishment under Pressure: The Probation Service in the Inner City*, Kingsley Publishers.

Brogden, M., et al. (1988) *Introducing Police Work*, Unwin.

Brown, I. and Hullin, R. (1992) 'A study of sentencing in the Leeds magistrates' courts: the treatment of ethnic minority and white offenders', *British Journal of Criminology*, 32(1), 41-53.

Burney, E. (1985) 'All things to all men: justifying custody under the 1982 Act', *Criminal Law Review*, (May), 284-93.

Burrows, R. (1989) 'Some notes towards a realistic realism: the practical implications of realist philosophies of science for social research methods', *International Journal of Sociology and Social Policy*, 9(4).

Cain, M. (1973) *Society and the Policeman's Role*, London: Routledge and Kegan Paul.

Cashmore, E. and McLaughlin, E. (1990) *Out of Order: The Policing of Black People*, London: Routledge.

Cernkonvich, S. (1978b) 'Value orientations and delinquency involvement', *Criminology*, 15, 443-57.

Chambliss, W. (1969) *Crime and the Legal Order*, New York: McGrow-Hill.

Chambliss, W. and Nagasawa, R. (1969) 'On the validity of official statistics - a comparison of White, Black and Japanese High School boys', *Journal of Research in Crime and Delinquency*, 6, 71-7.

Christie, N., et al. (1965) 'A study of self-reported crime', *Scandinavian Studies in Criminology*, 1, 86-117.

Cicourel, A. (1976) *The Social Organisation of Juvenile Justice*, London: Heinemann.

Cloward, R. and Ohlin, L. (1960) *Delinquency and Opportunity*, New York: Free Press.

Cohen, A. (1956) *Delinquent Boys: The Culture of the Gang*, London: Routledge and Kegan Paul.

Cohen, S. (1979) 'Community control: a new utopia', *New Society*, (March, 15), 47(858), 609-11.

Collison, M. (1981) 'Questions of juvenile justice', in P. Carlen and M. Collison (eds.), *Radical Issues in Criminology*, Macmillan, 153-212.

Commission for Racial Equality (1978) *Looking for Work - Black and White School Leavers in Lewisham*, CRE.

Commission for Racial Equality (1981) *Youth in Multi-Racial Society: The Urgent Need for New Policies*, CRE.

Commission for Racial Equality and West Midlands Probation and After-Care Service (1981) *Probation and After-Care in a Multi-Racial Society*, London: CRE.

Commission for Racial Equality (1984) *Racial Equality and the Youth Training Scheme*, CRE.

Committee Report 40/82, Brent Social Services.

Community Relations Commission (1977) *Housing Choice and Ethnic Concentration: An Attitude Study*.

Community Relations Commission (1977) *Urban Deprivation, Racial Inequality and Social Policy: A Report*, London: HMSO.

Community Relations Commissions and the Commission for Racial Equality, (1978) *Aspirations versus Opportunities - Asian and White School Leavers in the Midlands*, (Walsall and Leicester).

Cressey, D. (1964) *Delinquency, Crime and Differential Association*, The Hague: Martinus Nijhoff.

Crow, I. (1987) 'Black people and criminal justice in the UK', *Howard Journal of Criminal Justice*, (Special Issue on Ethnic Minorities), 26(4), 303-13.

Crow, I. and Cove, J. (1984) 'Ethnic minorities and the courts', *Criminal Law Review*, (July), 413-17.

184

Cullington, (1969) *Council Housing Purposes, Procedures and Policies*, London: HMSO.

Dale, A., et al. (1988) *Doing Secondary Analysis*, London: Unwin.

Denman, G. (1982) *Intensive Intermediate Treatment with Juvenile Offenders: A Handbook on Assessment and Groupwork Practice*, Lancaster: University of Lancaster.

Department of Employment, (1984) 'Unemployment and ethnic minorities', *Employment Gazette*, 92, 260-4.

D.H.S.S. (1980) *Getting on with Intermediate Treatment*, London:HMSO.

Ditchfield, J. (1976) *Police Cautioning in England and Wales*, London: HMSO.

Dodd, D. (1978) 'Police and thieves on the streets of Brixton', *New Society*, (16 March).

Downes, D. (1966) *The Delinquent Solution: A Study of Sub-cultural Theory*, London: Routledge and Kegan Paul.

Downes, D. (1978) 'Sociological theories of social problems', Prepared for Open University courses.

Durkin, T. (1985) *Evidence to the West London Inquiry*, Brent Trades Council.

Elliott, D. and Voss, H. (1974) *Delinquency and Dropout*, Toronto and London: Lexington Books.

Elliott, D. and Ageton, S. (1980) 'Reconciling race and class differences in self-reported and official estimates of delinquency', *American Sociological Review*, 45, 95-110.

Farrington, D. (1979) 'Longitudinal research on crime and delinquency', in, N. Morris and M. Tonry (eds.), *Criminal Justice: An annual review of research*, 1.

Farrington, D. and Bennett, T. (1981) 'Police Cautioning of Juveniles in London', *British Journal of Criminology*, 21, 123-35.

Faulkner, D. (1988) 'Magistrates' Courts and Race Issues', *The Magistrate*, (February 1988).

Field, S. (1990) *Crime and Consumption*, Home Office Research and Statistics Department, Research Bulletin Number 29.

Fielding, N. (1986) 'Social control and the community', *Howard Journal of Criminal Justice*, 25(3), 172-89.

Fielding, N. (1987) 'Being used by the Police', *British Journal of Criminology*, 27(1), 64-9.

Fielding, N. and Fielding, J. (1986) *Linking Data*, London: Sage.

Fielding, N. and Fielding, J. (1991) 'Police attitudes to crime and punishment: certainties and dilemmas', *British Journal of Criminology*, 31(1), 39-53.

FitzGerald, M. (1991) 'Ethnic minorities and the criminal justice system in the U.K.: Research issues'. Paper presented to British Criminology Conference, 1991 (July).

Fitzgerald, M. (1975) 'Developments in Massachussetts', *New Era*, (15 March), 56(6), 126-31.

Fludger, N. (1981) *Ethnic Minorities in Borstal*, London: Home Office.

Forslund, M. (1975) 'A self-report comparison of Indian and Anglo delinquents in Wyoming', *Criminology*, 13, 193-7.

Foster, J. et al. (1972) 'Perceptions of stigma following public intervention for delinquent behaviour', *Social Problems*, 86, 202- 9.

Freeman, J. (1983) 'Delinquency and deviant social behaviour', *British Journal of Criminology*, 21(3).

Friend, A. and Metcalf, A. (1981) *Slump City*, London: Pluto Press.

Frith, S. (1978) *Sociology of Rock*, London: Constable.

Frith, S. (1984) *The Sociology of Youth*, Causeway Books.

Geach, H. and Szwed, E. (eds.) (1983) *Providing Civil Justice for Children*, London: Edward Arnold.

Genders, E. and Player, E. (1989) *Race Relations in Prisons*, Oxford: Clarendon Press

Giggs, J. and Erickson, M. (1975) 'Major developments in the sociological study of deviance', *Annual Review of Sociology*, 1, 21-42.

Giller, H. (1986) 'Is there a role for a Juvenile Court?', *Howard Journal of Criminal Justice*, 25(3), 161-71.

Gilroy, P. (1982) 'The myth of black criminality', *Socialist Register*, London: Merlin.

Gold, M. (1966) 'Undetected delinquent behaviour', *Journal of Research in Crime and Delinquency*, 3, 27-46.

Gold, M. (1970) *Delinquent Behaviour in an American City*, California: Brooks/Cole.

Gold, M. and Reiner, D. (1974) 'Changing patterns of delinquents behaviour among Americans 13 to 16 years old - 1972', Report No. 1 of the *National Survey of Youth, 1972*, Ann Arbor, Michigan: University of Michigan Press.

Gold, M. and Williams, J. (1969) 'National study of the aftermath of apprehension', *Prospectus*, 3, 3-12.

Gould, L. (1969) 'Who defines delinquency: a comparison of self-reported delinquency for three racial groups', *Social Problems*, 16, 325-36.

Graef, R. (1989) *Talking Blues*, London: Williams Collins & Sons.

Greater London Council (1976) *Race and Council Housing*, A Preliminary Report of the GLC Lettings Survey, GLC.

Greater London Council (1979) *Greater London House Condition Survey*, GLC.

Greater London Council (1984) *The West London Report*, (May), GLC.

Greater London Council (1985) *West London Public Enquiry into Jobs and Industry*, GLC

Greater London Enterprise Board, (1984) *Black Business - Redressing the Balance*, GLC.

Griswold, D. (1983) 'The trend towards determinate sentencing: Emerging issues', unpublished paper presented to International Symposium on the *Impact of Criminal Justice Reform*, San Francisco.

Guest, C. (1984) *A Comparative Analysis of the Career Patterns of Black People and White Young Offenders*, (M. Sc. Thesis), Cranfield: Cranfield Institute of Technology.

Gutzmore, C. (1983) 'Capital, 'Black Youth' and Crime', *Race and Class*, XXV(2): 13-30.

H.M.S.O. (1969) *Children and Young Persons Act*, London: HMSO.

H.M.S.O. (1982) *Criminal Justice Act*, London: HMSO.

H.M.S.O. (1984) *Police and Criminal Evidence Act*, London: HMSO.

H.M.S.O. (1986) *The Sentence of the Court*, A Handbook for Courts on the Treatment of Offenders, London: HMSO.

H.M.S.O. (1991) *Criminal Justice Act*, London: HMSO.

H.M.S.O. (1992) *Judicial Studies Board Report for 1987-1991*, London: HMSO.

Hagan, J. (1979) 'Private and public trouble: Prosecutors and the allocation of court resources', *Social Problems*, 26, 439-51.

Hall, S., et al. (1978) *Policing London*, London: Macmillan.

Hardt, R. and Bodine, G. (1965) 'Development of self-report instruments in delinquency research', Syracuse University: Youth Development Centre. Cited by Hirschi (1969).

Hassin, Y. (1986) 'Two models for predicting recidivism, clinical versus statistical: Another view', *British Journal of Criminology*, 26(3).

Healey, M. J. R. (1988) GLIM: *An Introduction*, Oxford: Clarendon Press.

Hewitt, J. (1970) *Social Stratification and Deviant Behaviour*, New York: Random House.

Hindelang, M. (1978) 'Race and involvement in common law personal crimes', *American Sociological Review*, 43, 93-109.

Hindelang, M., et al. (1979) 'Correlates of delinquency: the illusion of discrepancy between self-report and official measures', *American Sociological Review*, 44, 995-1014.

Hine, J., McWilliams, W. and Pease, K. (1978) 'Recommendations, social information and sentencing', *Howard Journal of Criminal Justice*, 17(2), 91-100.

Hirschi, T. (1969) *Causes of Delinquency*, Berkeley and Los Angeles: University of California Press.

Hoghughi, M. (1983) *The Delinquent: Directions for Social Control*, Burnett Books.

Holdaway, S. (1983) *Inside the British Police: A Force at Work*, London: Blackwell.

Holland, T. and Johnson, N. (1979) 'Offender ethnicity and presentence decision making: A multi-variate analysis', *Criminal Justice and Behaviour*, 6, 227-38.

Home Office (1965) *The Child, the Family and the Young Offender*, Cmnd 2742, London: HMSO.

Home Office (1968) *Children in Trouble*, Cmnd 3601, London: HMSO.

Home Office (1980) *Criminal Statistics England and Wales 1979*, London: HMSO.

Home Office, et al. (1980) *Young Offenders*, Cmnd 8045.

Home Office (1983a) 'Crime statistics for the metropolitan police district analysed by ethnic group', *Statistical Bulletin*, 22/83.

Home Office (1984) *Cautioning By The Police*, London: HMSO.

Home Office (1985) *The Cautioning of Offenders*, Home Office Circular 14/1985.

Home Office (1986) 'The ethnic origin of prisoners: the prison population on January 30th 1985 and persons received, July 1984 - March 1985', *Home Office Statistical Bulletin*, 17/86.

Home Office *Statistical Branch Bulletins*, 5/89 and 6/89.

Home Office (1989) *Prison Statistics: England and Wales 1988*, London: HMSO.

Home Office (1991) *Prison Statistics 1990*, London: HMSO.

Home Office (1991) *Magistrates' Courts Service: Race,* Circular 38/1991.

Home Office (1992/1994/1995) *Race and the Criminal Justice System*, Home Office publications under section 95 of the Criminal Justice Act 1991.

Hood, R. (1992) *Race and Sentencing: A Study in the Crown Court*, A Report for the Commission for Racial Equality, Oxford: Clarendon Press.

Hood, R. (1993) 'Race and sentencing', paper given to the London branch of the British Society of Criminology, (17th March 1993).

Howard League (1987) *Justice 2000: Justice For A New Century*, The Draft Report of A Working Group, (August), Howard League Information.

Hudson, B. (1987) *Justice through Punishment*, Macmillan.

Hudson, B. (1989) 'Discrimination and disparity: Researching the influence of race on sentencing'. Paper presented at British Criminology Conference, 1989.

Institute of Race Relations (1979) *Police Against Black People*, Evidence submitted to the Ray Commission on Criminal Procedure, London: Institute of Race Relations.

Institute of Race Relations (1987) *Policing Against Black People*, Evidence compiled by the Institute of Race Relations, IRR.

Jaakkola, I. (1970) as reported in R.M. Lopez, *Crime: An Analytical Appraisal*, London: Routledge , 12-13.

Jensen, G. and Eve, R. (1976) 'Sex differences in delinquency: An examination of popular sociological explanations', *Criminology*, 13, Chicago and London: University of Chicago Press, 289-348/427-48.

Jones, T., et al. (1986) *The Islington Crime Survey*, Aldershot, Gower.

Johnson, R. (1979) *Juvenile Delinquency and Its Origins: An Integrated Theoretical Approach*, Cambridge University Press.

Johnstone, J. (1978) 'Social class, social areas and delinquency', *Sociology and Social Research*, 63, 49-72.

Kelly, M. (1982) 'The racial numbers game in our prisons', *New Society*, (30 September), 535-7.

Kinsey, R. (1985) *Survey of Merseyside Police Officers: First Report*, Liverpool: Merseyside County Council.

Kitsuse, J. and Cicourel, A. (1963) 'A note on the uses of official statistics', *Social Problems*, 131-9.

Landau, S. (1981) 'Juveniles and the police', *British Journal of Criminology*, 21, 27-46.

Landau, S. and Nathan, G. (1983) 'Selecting delinquents for cautioning in the London Metropolitan Area', *British Journal of Criminology*, 23, 128-49.

Langan, P. A. (1985) 'Racism on trial: New evidence to explain the racial composition of prisons in the United States', *The Journal of Criminal Law and Criminology*, 76(3), 666-83.

Laycock, G. and Tarling, R. (1984) 'Police force cautioning: policy and practice', *Home Office Research Bulletin*, No. 19, London: HMSO.

Lea, J. and Young, J. (1984) *What Is To Be Done About Law and Order?*, Harmondsworth: Penguin Books.

Lemert, E. (1972) *Human Deviance, Social Problems and Social Control*, 2nd ed., Englewood Cliffs, N.J.: Prentice-Hall.

Little, W. and Ntsekhe, V. (1959) 'Social class background of young offenders from London', *British Journal of Criminology*, 10, 130- 35.

McConville, M. and Baldwin, J. (1982) 'The influence of race on sentencing in England', *Criminal Law Review*, (July), 652-8.

McCOnville, M., Sanders, A. and Leng, R. (1991) *The Case for the Prosecution*, London: Routledge.

McNeely, R. and Pope, C. (1978) 'Race and involvement in common law personal crime: A response to Hindelang', *Review of Black Political Economy*, 8, 405-10.

McNeely, R. and Pope, C. (1981) 'Race, crime and criminal justice', *Perspectives in Criminal Justice*, 2, Sage.

Maden, A., et al. (1992) 'The ethnic origin of women serving a prison sentence', *British Journal of Criminology*, 32(2), 218-21.

Mair, G. (1986) 'Ethnic minorities, probation and the magistrates courts', *British Journal of Criminology*, 26(2), 147-55.

Mannheim, H., et al. (1957) 'Magisterial policy in the London juvenile courts', *British Journal of Delinquency*, 18, 13-33/119-38.

Manpower Services Commission Report (1982/83) *Ethnic Minority Unemployed in the London Boroughs*, MSC.

Martin, D. (1985), A report on probation caseloads and ethnic minorities in Croydon, prepared for the South East London Probation Service.

Matza, D. (1964) *Delinquency and Drift*, New York and London: Wiley.

May, D. (1975) *Juvenile Offenders and the Organisation of Juvenile Delinquency in Aberdeen, 1959-67*, Unpublished PhD, University of Aberdeen.

Mays, J. (1954) *Growing up in the City*, Liverpool University Press.

Mays, J. (1972) *Juvenile Delinquency: The Family and the Social Group*, A Reader, London: Longmans.

Mellish, (1984) *Juvenile Offenders: Review of Policy*, Metropolitan Police District, A7 Branch Document: Community Relations Branch.

Merton, R. (1938) 'Social structure and anomie', *American Sociological Review*,

(October), 3, 672-82.

Merton, R. (1957) *Social Theory and Social Structure*, New York: Free Press.

Meyers, M. (1979) 'Official parties and official reactions: Victims and the sentencing of criminal defendants', *Sociological Quarterly*, 20, 529-40.

Miller, J. (1985) speaking on 'Decarcerating Young Offenders: An international perspective', Association for Juvenile Justice conference, Retford, (November).

Minnesota Sentencing Guidelines Commission (1980) *Minnesota Sentencing Guidelines*, St Paul, Minnesota.

Moore, R. (1975) *Racism and Black Resistence*, London: Plato.

Morris, T. (1957) *The Criminal Area*, London: Routledge.

Morris, A. et al. (1980) *Justice for Children*, London: Manmillan.

Morris, A. and Giller, H. (eds.), (1983) *Providing Criminal Justice for Children*, London: Edward Arnold.

Moxon, D., et al. (1985) *Juvenile Sentencing: Is There a Tariff?*, London: Home Office Research and Planning Unit.

Moxon, D. (1988) *Sentencing Practice in the Crown Courts*, Home Office Research Study No. 103, London: HMSO.

Murray, C. and Cox, L. (1979) *Beyond Probation: Juvenile Corrections and the Chronic Delinquent*, 94, Sage.

N.A.C.R.O. (1986) *Black People and the Criminal Justice System*, Race Issues Advisory Committee, NACRO.

N.A.C.R.O. (1988) *Cautioning Juvenile Offenders*, NACRO Briefing Paper, Juvenile Crime Section.

N.A.C.R.O. (1991) *Black People's Experience of Criminal Justice*, NACRO.

Nellis, M. (1985) 'Intermediate treatment: Strategies for an uncertain future', *The Abolitionist*, No. 19, (1985 no. 1), 11-34.

Nie, N. H., et al. (1975) *Statistical Package for the Social Sciences*, 2nd ed., McGraw-Hill Book Co., New York.

Norris, C. A. (1987) *Policing Trouble: an observational study of Police patrol work in two police forces*, Unpublished PhD Thesis, University of Surrey.

Norris, C., Fielding, N., Kemp, C., and Fielding, J. (1992) 'Black and Blue: an analysis of the influence of race on being stopped by the police', *British Journal of Sociology*, 43(2), 207.

Norusis, M. J. (1987) *The SPSS Guide to Data Analysis for SPSS-X*, SPSS Inc.

Nye, F. (1958) *Family Relationships and Delinquent Behaviour*, New York: Wiley.

Office of Population Census and Surveys, (1981) *Census Data for Brent and London*, DOE, Inner Cities Directorate, 1983.

Ouston, J. (1983) 'Delinquency, family background and educational attainment', *British Journal of Criminology*.

Parker, Casburn and Turnbull, (1981) *Receiving Juvenile Justice*, Blackwell.

Parliamentary All-Party Penal Affairs Group, (1983) *The Prevention of Crime among Young People*, (September).

Payne, J. (1987) 'Does unemployment run in families?. Some findings from the

General Household Survey', *Sociology*, 21(2).

Piliavin, I. and Briar, S. (1974) 'Police encounters with juveniles', *American Journal of Sociology*, 70, 206-14.

Pindyck, R. and Rubinfeld, D. (1991) *Econometric Models & Economic Forecasts*, 3rd ed., McGraw-Hill.

Pitkin, H. (1967) *The Concept of Representation*, Berkeley: University of California Press.

Pitts, J. (1984) *Young Black People and the Juvenile Justice System*, in, I.T. Mailing No.17 (July), National Youth Bureau.

Platt, S. (1985) 'A Tale of Two Boroughs', in, *New Society*, (27 September), 446.

Plummer, K. (1979) 'Misunderstanding labelling perspectives', in, D. Downes and P. Rock (eds.), *Deviant Interpretations*, London: Martin Robertson.

Polk, K. and Halferty, D. (1966) 'Adolescence, commitment and delinquency', *Journal of Research in Crime and Delinquency*, (July) 4, 82-96.

Pope, C. (1978) 'Post arrest release decisions: An empirical examination of social and legal criteria', *Journal of Research in Crime and Delinquency*, (January), 35-53.

Pratt, J. (1985) 'Juvenile justice, social work and social control: the need for positive thinking', *British Journal of Social Work*, 15, 1-24.

PROP (Preservation of Rights of Prisoners) (1983).

Pryce, K. (1979) *Endless Pressure*, Harmondsworth: Penguin.

Quinney, R. (1970) *Explaining Crime*, Boston: Little Brown.

Quinney, R. (1974) 'A critical theory of criminal law', in, R. Quinney (ed.), *Criminal Justice in America*, Boston: Little Brown, 1-25.

Raynor, P. (1985) *Social Work, Justice and Control*, Oxford: Basil Blackwell.

Registrar General's Classification of Occupations, (1980), London:HMSO.

Reiner, R. (1985) *The Politics of the Police*, Brighton: Wheatsheaf.

Rex, J. and Moore, R. (1967) *Race, Community and Conflict: Study of Sparkbrook*, London: Oxford University Press for The Institute of Race Relations.

Reynolds, F. (1985) 'Magistrates' justifications for making custodial orders on juvenile offenders', *Criminal Law Review*, (May), 294-8.

Richards, P. (1979) *Crime as Play: Delinquency in a Middle-Class Suburb*, Harper and Row.

Roberts, M. (1982) *Discussion Document on I.T. in Brent*, Brent Social Services.

Rutherford, A. (1986) *Growing Out of Crime: Society and Young People in Trouble*, Penguin Books.

Rutter, M., et al. (1976) *Cycles of Disadvantage: A review of research*, London: Heinemann.

Rutter, M., et al. (1979) *Fifteen Thousand Hours: Secondary Schools and their Effects on Children*, London:Open Books; Cambridge, Mass.: Harvard University Press.

Rutter, M. and Giller, H. (1983) *Juvenile Delinquency, Trends and Perspectives*,

Penguin Books.

Samuels, A. (1986) speaking on 'Consistency: criteria, multifariousness and discretion in criminal sentencing', ESRC Law and Psychology Conference, Oxford, (14-16 April).

Scull, A. (1983) 'Community connections: panacea, progress or pretence', in, D. Garland and P. Young (eds.), *The Power to Punish, Contemporary Penality and Social Analysis*, London: Heinemann; New Jersey: Humanities Press.

Shapland, J. (1986) speaking on 'Who controls sentencing?: Influences on the sentencer', ESRC Law and Psychology Conference, Oxford, (14-16 April).

Shaw, C. and Mckay, H. (1942) *Juvenile Delinquency in Urban Areas*, Chicago: University of Chicago Press.

Sim, J. (1982) 'Scarman: The Police Counter-attack', *Socialist Register*, 57-77.

Skogan, W. (1990) *The Police and Public in England and Wales*, Home Office Research Study, No. 117, London: HMSO.

Smith, D., et al. (1975) *Public Housing and Racial Minorities*, PEP.

Smith, D. (1976) *The Facts of Racial Disadvantage: A National Survey*, PEP.

Smith, D. (1981) *Unemployment and Racial Minorities*, Policy Studies Institute, Report No. 598, London: PSI.

Smith, D. (1983) *Police and People in London*: Vol I 'A Survey of Londoners', London: PSI.

Smith, D. and Gray, J. (1983) *Police and People in London*: Vol IV 'The Police in Action', London: PSI.

Smith, J. and Hogan, B. (1988) *Criminal Law*, 6th ed., Butterworths.

Solomos, J. (1988) *Black Youth, Racism and the State*, Cambridge University Press.

Stark, R. (1979) 'Whose status counts?', *American Sociological Review*, 44(4), 668-70.

Stevens, P. and Willis, C. (1979) *Race, Crime and Arrests*, Home Office Research Study, No. 58, London: HMSO.

Sullivan, D. and Siegel, L. (1972) 'How police use information to make decisions', *Crime and Delinquency*, 18, 253-62.

Sutherland, E. and Cressey, D. (1974) *Criminology*, (9th edn.), Philadelphia: Lippincott.

Swain, C. (1993) 'Double standard, double bind: African-American leadership after the Thomas debacle', in, T. Morrison (ed.), *Race-ing Justice, En-Gendering Power*, London: Chatto & Windus.

Tarling, R., et al. (1985) 'Sentencing of adults and juveniles in magistrate's courts', in D. Moxon (ed.), *Managing Criminal Justice*, Home Office Research and Planning Unit Publications, London: HMSO.

Taylor, I., et al. (1974) *The New Criminology*, New York: Harper and Row.

Taylor, J. (1976) *The Half-Way Generation: A Study of Asian Youths in Newcastle-upon-Tyne*, Slough, N.F.E.R.

Thomas, D. (1979) *Principles of Sentencing*, London: Heinemann.

Thorpe, D., et al. (1980) *Out of Care: Community Support of Juvenile Offenders*, Allen and Unwin.

Tipler, J. (1986) *Is Juvenile Justice Colour Blind?: A study of the impact of race in the juvenile justice system in Hackney*, Hackney Social Services Research Note No. 6.

Tittle, R. and Villemez, W. (1977) 'Social class and criminality', *Social Forces*, 56, 474-502.

Tittle, R., et al. (1978) 'The myth of social class criminality: an empirical assessment of the empirical evidence', *American Sociological Review*, 43, 643-56.

Tittle, R., et al. Reply To Stark (1979) 'Whose status counts?', *American Sociological Review*, 44(4), 669-70.

Tutt, N. and Giller, H. (1984a) *Diversion*, Lancaster: Lancaster Information Systems.

Tutt, N. and Giller, H. (1984b) *Social Inquiry Reports*, Lancaster: Lancaster Information Systems.

Vennard, J. (1982) *Contested Trials in Magistrates' Courts*, Home Office Research Study No. 71, London: HMSO.

Voakes, R. and Fowler, Q. (1989) *Sentencing, Race and Social Enquiry Reports*, Wakefield: West Yorkshire Probation Service.

Wadsworth, M. (1979) *Roots of Delinquency: Infancy, Adolescence and Crime*, Oxford: Martin Robertson.

Walberg, H. et al. (1974) 'Family background, ethnicity and urban delinquency', *Journal of Research in Crime and Delinquency*, 11, 80-7.

Walker, I. (1985) *Evidence to the West London Inquiry*, Brent Local Economy Resource Unit.

Walker, M. (1986) 'The court disposal of young males, by race in London in 1983', *British Journal of Criminology*, 28(4), 441-60.

Walker, M. (1987a) 'Interpreting race and crime statistics', *Journal of the Royal Statistical Society A.*, 150(1), 39-56.

Walker, M. (1987b) 'Note: ethnic origin of prisoners', *British Journal of Criminology*, 27(2), 202-6

Walker, M. (1988) 'The court disposal of young males by race in London in 1983', *British Journal of Criminology*, 28(4), 441-60.

walker, M. (1989) 'The court disposal and remands of White, Afro-Caribbean, and Asian men (London 1983)', *British Journal of Criminology*, 29(4), 353-67.

Walker, M., Jefferson, T. and Seneviratne, M. (1989) *Ethnic Minorities, Young People and the Criminal Justice System*, Centre for Criminological and Socio-legal Studies, University of Sheffield, ESRC Project No. E06250023: Main Report.

Wellford, C. (1975) 'Labelling theory and criminology: an assessment', *Social Problems*, 22, 332-45.

West, D. and Farrington, D. (1973) *Who Becomes Delinquent?*, London:

Heinemann.

West, D. (1982) *Delinquency: Its Roots, Careers and Prospects*, London: Heinemann.

Williams, J. and Gold, M. (1972) 'From delinquent behaviour to official delinquency', *Social Problems*, 20, 209-29.

Willmott, P. (1966) *Adolescent Boys of East London*, London: Routledge and Kegan Paul.

Wilson, P. (1983) *Black Business Enterprise in Britain: A Survey of Afro Caribbean and Asian Small Businesses in Brent*, Runnymede Trust.

Wolfgang, M. et al. (1972) *Delinquency in a Birth Cohort*, Chicago: University of Chicago Press.

Wolpert, J. and Wolpert, E. (1976) 'The relocation of released mental patients into residential communities', *Policy Sciences*, 7, 31- 51.

Wootton, B. (1959) *Social Science and Social Pathology*, London: Allen and Unwin.

Young, J. et al. (1986) *Losing The Fight Against Crime*, Oxford: Blackwell.